Experiencing Accents: A Kr.
Speechwork® Guide for Acting in Accent

Experiencing Accents: A Knight-Thompson Speechwork® Guide for Acting in Accent presents a comprehensive and systematic approach to accent acquisition for actors. It lays out an accessible and effective set of tools, exercises, and theoretical frameworks grounded in current linguistic science, as well as more than two decades of teaching, actor training, and coaching developed by Knight-Thompson Speechwork®.

This book dismantles the notions that accents exist on a spectrum of good and bad or that "neutral," "general," or "standard" can serve as ideals for speech. By de-centering elitist and authoritarian worldviews, it gives actors a path to mobilize their innate language abilities to acquire any accent, relying on descriptive and experiential knowledge. The innovative approach of the Four Ps – People, Prosody, Posture, and Pronunciation – builds cultural competence that honors accents as they exist in the world, increases the physical and perceptive skills of the actor, and provides a rich variety of applications to encourage fluid and embodied accent performance. Each of the Four Ps is investigated and practiced separately and then synthesized in the art of the performer, allowing actors to address the complexity of acting in accent through a deliberate and sequential layering of skills, rendering the final expression of their technique meticulously accurate and deeply authentic.

Organized into fifteen modules to correspond with a typical semester, *Experiencing Accents* is perfect for theatre students in voice, speech, and accents courses, along with working actors interested in improving their accent work.

Philip Thompson is Professor of Drama at the University of California, Irvine. At UCI he has served as the head of the MFA program in acting, and as head of voice and speech. In 2002, he co-founded Knight-Thompson Speechwork® with his mentor Dudley Knight. KTS has more than fifty certified teachers teaching this method in training programs across the country and, increasingly, around the world.

Tyler Seiple is an actor and freelance voice and speech coach in Los Angeles, California. He is the founder of Accents in Action™, which brings Knight-Thompson Speechwork® to actors, public speakers, and other performers through individual and group coaching. Tyler is Associate Teacher of Fitzmaurice Voicework® and Master Teacher of Knight-Thompson Speechwork®, and teaches at CSU Long Beach and CSU Fullerton. Learn more at accentcoachla.com.

Andrea Caban is Head of Voice and Speech in the Theatre Arts Department at CSU Long Beach, Associate Specialist in the UCI Department of Neurology, Co-Director of Knight-Thompson Speechwork®, and one of the first Master Teachers of KTS. Her text, *Experiencing Speech: A Skills-Based, Panlingual Approach to Actor Training*, was also published by Routledge and is intended to precede this text. Learn more at andreaccaban.com.

Experiencing Accents: A Knight-Thompson Speechwork® Guide for Acting in Accent

Philip Thompson, Tyler Seiple, and Andrea Caban

Illustrations by Siobhan Doherty Buffett and Philip Thompson

Routledge
Taylor & Francis Group

NEW YORK AND LONDON

Designed cover image: Siobhan Doherty Buffett and Philip Thompson

First published 2024
by Routledge
605 Third Avenue, New York, NY 10158

and by Routledge
4 Park Square, Milton Park, Abingdon, Oxon, OX14 4RN

Routledge is an imprint of the Taylor & Francis Group, an informa business

© 2024 Philip Thompson, Tyler Seiple and Andrea Caban

Illustrations © 2024 Siobhan Doherty Buffett and Philip Thompson

Library of Congress Cataloging-in-Publication Data
Names: Thompson, Philip (Professor of Drama), author, illustrator. |
    Seiple, Tyler, author. | Caban, Andrea, author. | Doherty Buffett,
    Siobhan, illustrator.
Title: Experiencing accents: a Knight-Thompson speechwork® guide for
    acting in accent / Philip Thompson, Tyler Seiple and Andrea Caban ;
    illustrations by Siobhan Doherty Buffett and Philip Thompson.
Description: New York, NY : Routledge, 2024. | Includes bibliographical
    references and index.
Identifiers: LCCN 2023024835 (print) | LCCN 2023024836 (ebook) |
    ISBN 9781032324159 (hardback) | ISBN 9781032324142
    (paperback) | ISBN 9781003314905 (ebook)
Subjects: LCSH: Acting. | English language—Dialects. | English
    language—Pronunciation.
Classification: LCC PN2071.F6 T46 2024 (print) | LCC PN2071.F6
    (ebook) | DDC 792.02/8—dc23/eng/20230705
LC record available at https://lccn.loc.gov/2023024835
LC ebook record available at https://lccn.loc.gov/2023024836

ISBN: 978-1-032-32415-9 (hbk)
ISBN: 978-1-032-32414-2 (pbk)
ISBN: 978-1-003-31490-5 (ebk)

DOI: 10.4324/9781003314905

Typeset in Adobe Caslon Pro
by Apex CoVantage, LLC

Access the Instructor and Student Resources: https://ktspeechwork.org/

CONTENTS

ACKNOWLEDGMENTS

This book is the culmination of decades of thinking, acting, teaching, playing, writing, and collaborating within the community of Knight-Thompson Speechwork. Our pedagogical and philosophical forebear, Dudley Knight, continues to inspire us and our teaching, and we hope this book brings to fruition the principles he advanced in *Speaking with Skill*. We owe massive thanks to Erik Singer for his brilliance, diligence, and innovation in his contributions to KTS, and to Catherine Fitzmaurice for the many ways she taught all of us to be more attentive, empathetic, and embodied teachers. Thank you to Siobhan Doherty for enhancing the visual quality of this book and making us look far better than we thought possible. The KTS Council – and especially Julie Foh and Nathan Crocker – have our eternal gratitude for ensuring the constant refinement and advancement of our accentwork, including through their masterful teaching and administrative efficiency. We are indebted to our ever-growing community of KTS Certified Teachers, who consistently invigorate and improve what we do. We are always grateful to our students and clients for demanding our mutual commitment to the best versions of this work. And, finally, this book would never exist without the love, support, and patience of Amy, Eleanor, Tira, Maja, Mike, and Sophie. Thank you.

TEACHER INTRODUCTION

Welcome to *Experiencing Accents*! Thank you for adopting this text for your teaching. We hope it will be useful in constructing a meaningful and effective course in accentwork for your students. To that end, we'd like to check in with you as a teacher and offer you some insight into our approach and how it might best serve your classroom.

There's also an introduction for students, right after this one. We've chosen to address the two audiences independently to focus attention on what we think is most useful to each. We encourage you to read both! Students can benefit from understanding the teacher's framework, and teachers can benefit from revisiting the student mindset. There are no spoilers here that will interrupt the learning of either group.

Who is this text for?

Our target audience includes anyone and everyone who wants to act in accent, but we've organized this book to give instructors maximum flexibility in a classroom curriculum. Reflecting the nature of the skills we investigate, this text is laid out in a series of distinct modules imagining a 16-week progression. The amount of time spent in each module is flexible. You may find that one module can be sufficiently explored in a day, whereas your students may need more than a week to explore a different module. This book can also be adapted to serve the private coach, the conservatory setting, a combination voice/speech course, or any host of scenarios in which the reader wants to deepen their understanding of accentwork, as well as their skills.

While this text attempts to be accessible to all who want to learn, it imagines learners who are able to hear, as well as speak.

What's accentwork?

Accentwork is a made-up, portmanteau word that we hope will serve as a reminder that our topic here is not just accents but the artistic skill of *performing* in accent. Accentwork is something we do: a process, an enterprise, a suite of skills that we're striving to embody as well as understand. This is largely the work of actors. While it's certainly possible that singers, comedians, and curious autodidacts will find this work useful, accentwork as we see it is grounded in acting.

In using this word, we're following a tradition that we trace to one of our teachers and inspirations, Catherine Fitzmaurice, founder of Fitzmaurice Voicework®. And, of course, this book is written by teachers of Knight-Thompson Speechwork®. We think accentwork fits in with those designations quite nicely.

What is Knight-Thompson Speechwork?

Knight-Thompson Speechwork® (KTS) is a methodology, an organization, and a community of teachers.

As a methodology, KTS is a skills-based approach to speech and accent training for actors that places emphasis on developing the speaker's detailed awareness of – and deep engagement with – the precise physical actions that make up speech. By combining a rigorous investigation of those actions with playful, experiential exercises, this work seeks to make speech training accessible and efficient for *all* learners. The primary guiding principle is curious, attentive interrogation, focusing on *descriptive*, sociolinguistically aware skills for the actor that culminate in fluid, creative *play*. It engages in thoughtful investigation of what any text, moment, or medium might require from the actor in terms of skilled speech.

Dudley Knight (1939–2013) was a renowned actor, dialect coach, and voice teacher perhaps best known for his deep investigations into how speech methodology could most effectively be taught to actors.

Dudley spent a significant part of his career as a professor of drama at the University of California, Irvine, where he first encountered his eventual pedagogical partner, Philip Thompson, as a student during the 1980s.

Phil followed in Dudley's footsteps upon graduating – acting in and coaching plays across the country. While Head of Acting at the Ohio State University, Phil developed teaching and coaching strategies inspired by the techniques he had learned from Dudley. Phil returned to UC Irvine in 2001 to work alongside Dudley Knight as a faculty member, whereupon he discovered that the two of them had made similar inquiries in their speech training research.

Together they worked to expand, explore, and refine their nascent method. They began offering workshops to other teachers in 2002, and, in 2012, offered the first Teacher Certification course in their newly minted technique. Through multiple yearly workshops as well as annual Teacher Certifications, KTS has grown to encompass dozens of Certified Teachers and hundreds of KTS-trained educators, coaches, and performers around the world.

Is it necessary to do everything in this book exactly as written?

KTS isn't particularly keen on rules. We have principles, and arguments, and maybe a few provisional constructs, but we're not in the business of insisting on orthodoxy.

You may have had the good fortune of avoiding learning environments that are deformed around the teacher's desire to exert their authority over students simply for the sake of personal aggrandizement. If so, you'll just have to trust us that it's no fun. Nor is it an effective way to teach artists.

Instead, we prefer an approach that invites investigation, stimulates curiosity, and allows students and teachers of this work to find their most effective and authentic means of engaging. As authors, we hope you'll find our ideas compelling enough to test out for yourself.

How does this book intersect with other KTS books?

This is the third book in the KTS library. Dudley Knight's *Speaking with Skill* (2012) is an in-depth introduction to the work. It represents the culmination of a great deal of experience and knowledge, and for that reason it's a marvelous book for a graduate school acting program or conservatory training program, where students and teachers have the luxury of speech training for multiple terms in sequence. It's also a book that anyone teaching from one of the other books would be well advised to read and contemplate.

Experiencing Speech (2021) articulates a sequence of exercises that can be used in programs that do not share that same curricular real estate. The text is modeled on a 16-week term that seeks to establish a foundation of speech skills prior to the complex task of performing in accent. It leads logically to this book, creating a two-term sequence whereby students work through *Experiencing Speech* in one semester, followed by a semester working through *Experiencing Accents*.

What is the place of phonetics in this work?

Phonetics is a wonderfully detailed system for describing the gestures of speech, and as such, it is an essential tool for building awareness and grounding our work in physical and acoustic realities. Students who have learned from *Experiencing Speech* will have an excellent foundation in phonetics that will serve them well in tackling the skills in this book. While this book will ask students to step more deeply into the descriptive possibilities of the International Phonetic Alphabet (IPA), it will be only one of the tools we use to understand and appreciate accents. In this book, phonetic transcription is not a goal in and of itself.

Neither this book, nor the other KTS books, are intended to be a comprehensive course in phonetic transcription. We encourage practical experience in using the IPA as a tool for understanding and communicating articulatory information. KTS offers workshops to this end, which you can learn about on our website: ktspeechwork.org.

Do we need to start our work in accents by learning a shared standard accent?

This one's easy: no. It had been a generally accepted notion in the past that students of speech must pass through a phase of standardizing their accent to an ideal reference accent before moving on to learn others. We disagree with this assertion. Students of accentwork need a grounding in the anatomy of speech and a detailed understanding of the physical reality of the sounds of human language. They need skills in listening to and analyzing speech, and practice in producing the full range of speech sounds humans make. They need curiosity, imagination, and a connection to their own artistic impulses as performers. They do not need to all speak the same way or to have signed on to the orthodox view of how an actor "ought" to sound.

The requirement to acquire an accepted accent probably arose as a convenience for teachers. After all, if we only have to describe speech as it fits within the confines of one accent – especially if that's the teacher's accent – then our phonetic descriptions and our understanding of the performance of speech have a much reduced footprint. There is certainly a place for generalizations and conventional understandings in learning a new set of skills, but a basic understanding of any sophisticated art is not a place to linger, nor can a set of conventions have any claim to moral or aesthetic preeminence.

Even if it were necessary to have a reference accent, every reader of this book or student in your class has a reference accent that they compare with an accent they're learning: their own. It's a perfectly cromulent accent and is probably a richer source of authentic, human detail than any accent they've adopted in drama school.

Experiencing Speech was panlingual. What about this book?

The overall project of KTS is panlingual in that its principles and methods can be applied to any language. This is one of the benefits of releasing ourselves from the idea that our task is to bring our students to a single standard of speech. The goals of training are no longer tied to a single language or accent. It's up to the speakers (and listeners) of any language to determine what articulations are intelligible, or sweet, or magical, or perfectly suited to the needs of the storyteller in that language. This work is about building the awareness and skill to understand and create those articulations; that process is universal and applicable to all languages.

That said, we should point out a particularly obvious limitation of this text: it's in English! That limits the way we talk about speech and accents, as well as the way we think about the topic. Moreover, it limits our audience to those who read English, just as it will limit our discussion of accents to primarily those that occur in English. As authors, we are fluent, comfortable, and most practiced at expressing ourselves in English (and the American version at that). There's a great deal we gain from our fluency in English, and from yours, but it does mean that for this work to become panlingual in practice rather than just in aspiration, it will need to have translators. We don't just mean translators of the words of this text, but translators of the references, examples, metaphors, and tools as well.

We firmly believe that there is much material in this book that can be used in studying accents in all languages, but that will involve transformation as well as translation. We invite you to begin that process now by encouraging and including the expertise of all your students. All sounds are useful for the actor, and your students can be a resource, bringing skills for sounds you may not possess, as well as examples from languages other than English and accents different than your own. Your students' diverse linguistic experiences are an asset to the process of skill-building for the entire class. This active inclusion also serves to empower multilingual students to take ownership of their expertise.

What is the best way to use this text?

Do everything. Accent is performance, and that entails the embodiment of knowledge. This is obviously true for your students, but we strongly encourage you to put yourself into relation with this material by experiencing and re-experiencing it yourself. Not only will this deepen your empathetic response to your students' process, but you'll also get an opportunity to check our assumptions and bring your own adaptations to bear. We encourage you to do this work in front of your students. Sharing your own skills, your pleasure in those skills, and even, inevitably, your mistakes and realizations will enrich your students' experience immeasurably.

Check It Out!

We've had to discipline ourselves not to share *all* the tidbits we've gathered, so when we feel the impulse to dive down a rabbit hole, we've decided instead to step out of the flow and put a box around the idea. In these **Check It Out!** boxes we may give a short explanation of the detour we're declining to take, but our main goal is to provide the reader with enough search terms (and even resources) that they can follow the trail on their own.

Web Resources

When we need to provide material in audio or video form, or when we simply have more information we'd like to share than can be squeezed into this book, we'll refer you to a dedicated website: https://ea.ktspeechwork.org (the password is "Somenish").

The Big Accent Project

In Module Three, we'll be introducing the idea of the Big Accent Project, which we refer to as the BAP /bæp/ (see page 44). This project provides an opportunity for you, as an instructor, to assign a long-term project for your students. It could serve production design, curricular demands, or the desires of your classrooms (we especially like that last one!). Students could all explore the same accent, you could assign them accents in groups, or you could allow each student to pursue their own line of inquiry. We offer the BAP with the intention of giving you flexibility to direct collective exploration inside and outside class.

Do I need any special knowledge to teach the content in this book?

KTS offers teacher certification for those who find our approach compelling and want to engage more deeply with the pedagogical principles that undergird our work. We highly recommend learning more about the teacher certification process online, at https://ktspeechwork. org/teacher-certification-program. Our goal in offering certification is to provide a coherent philosophy for the study of accent that teachers can integrate, adapt, and innovate to meet the creative needs of their communities and careers.

However, we can summarize one set of overarching principles that guide our exploration in this book. If you keep these principles in mind, you'll be ready to reinvent any exercise we suggest and also build new ones based on these ideas.

We describe a way of grouping our knowledge and our cognitive abilities into two loose categories: *procedural* and *declarative* knowledge.

Very simply, *declarative* knowledge is our ability to name, describe, or explain things. We could also call it explicit or factual knowledge. This kind of knowledge is often the focus in academic settings. In contrast, *procedural* knowledge refers to our ability to perform skills. These may be mechanical skills, artistic skills, or abilities so far from our capacity to articulate that we might call them intuition or experience. Procedural knowledge could also be called tacit, or embodied knowledge, or know-how.

In the KTS approach to speech and accents, we work to escape the trap of thinking of one kind of knowledge as superior. In fact, we often work to access both types of knowledge simultaneously, or at least sequentially. It's in the movement back and forth between these two modes that we find the most effective and the most robust kind of training for actors. That movement is not quite a regular oscillation between distinct and separate poles, but more of a dance, flowing through different phases and helping students build a dynamic relationship between the two.

Take your students and yourself through the dance steps of this procedural-declarative process – and then go through them again and again. We've structured this book around our pedagogical principles, but we have confidence that you'll be able to bring them into your classroom in ways that engage and excite your students. We wish you the same process of curiosity, compassion, and playfulness that we continually rediscover in our own classrooms.

STUDENT INTRODUCTION

Welcome to *Experiencing Accents*!

Who is this text for?

We hope this book is of interest to anyone who's curious about how actors manage to do the magic trick of speaking in someone else's voice. That being said, we've built this book around the assumption that you'll be using this text as someone studying accents as part of an acting training program, with a teacher as your guide. We imagine it as part of a two-term sequence that starts with a course using *Experiencing Speech* in one semester, followed by a semester of accentwork structured around this text. That means we expect that you're already familiar with the work covered in *Experiencing Speech*, and with our little idiosyncrasies – like pretending you just asked us a question so we can answer it.

Who's "we"?

Good question! The word "we" in this text will sometimes refer to a universal assertion about "we humans," and at other times it will refer to "we, the authors." We'll try to avoid sweeping generalities, but when we're ambiguous, take your best guess.

When "we" *does* refer to the authors, we'd like you to know that we're on this journey with you. We're actors who love accents: learning about them, listening to them, and performing them. We're professional coaches for private clients, on stage and screen, across the world. We're teachers who draw upon the experiences of our students and fellow educators to make accentwork better, wherever we encounter it. And we're excited to share our insights and discoveries with you in this book.

What's accentwork?

Accentwork is a made-up word that we hope will serve as a reminder that our topic here is not just accents but the artistic skill of *performing* in accent. Accentwork is something we do: a process, an enterprise, a suite of skills that we're working to embody as well as understand.

This is largely the work of actors. While it's certainly possible that singers, comedians, and curious autodidacts will find this work useful, accentwork as we see it is grounded in acting.

Will this book tell me everything I need to know to perform in accent?

Probably not. This is the third book from Knight-Thompson Speechwork® (KTS). The first is Dudley Knight's *Speaking with Skill*, which lays out the core principles of the work and guides students through an exploratory approach to understanding speech. The second book is *Experiencing Speech: A Skills-Based, Panlingual Approach to Actor Training*, which gives a detailed progression of exercises to introduce students to the study of speech in performance.

In those books, you'll have noticed – wait, you have read those books, haven't you? You really should. Really, really, really. There's a lot of information there which will support what we're doing here. Still, it may be that you're reading this book on its own, outside a classroom, and with no previous experience of KTS. That's okay. We're not kicking you out of the book or anything. You might just have to do some extra work to connect the dots. So . . .

What is the best way to use this text?

Together. While it is possible to work through this text on your own, we believe you'll get more out of the experience in a classroom. Not only will you have a teacher to guide you, but you'll be practicing in public, and that's the natural context for performance work. Sharing your skills, your pleasure in those skills, and even, inevitably, your mistakes and realizations will enrich your experience, and that of your comrades.

Out loud. As a corollary to the previous point, we'll state the obvious. It's not enough to read an idea and commit it to memory. Accentwork exists in its embodiment. We can think about it and talk about it, but if we don't also take the risk of performing, and being seen and heard by others, we neglect something essential.

We like to talk about this distinction between thinking and doing by grouping our knowledge and our cognitive abilities into two loose categories: *procedural* and *declarative* knowledge.

Very simply, declarative knowledge is our ability to name, describe, or explain things. We could also call it explicit or factual knowledge. This kind of knowledge is often the focus in academic settings.

In contrast, procedural knowledge refers to our ability to perform skills. These may be mechanical skills, artistic skills, or abilities so far from our ability to articulate that we might call them intuition or experience. Procedural knowledge could also be called embodied knowledge or know-how.

In the KTS approach to speech and accents, we work to escape the trap of thinking of one kind of knowledge as superior. In fact, we often work to access both sorts of knowledge simultaneously, or at least sequentially. It's in the movement back and forth between these two modes that we find the most effective and the most robust kind of training for actors.

Is there anything else we need to know before we start?

Yes! Just a few quick things.

Notetaking

At times, our work in this book will involve generating ideas and reflecting on them. Some of this could be accomplished through classroom discussions, but we still find it valuable for students to articulate their thoughts in writing. We encourage you to have a single location for this writing – for example, a notebook or electronic document.

Check It Out!

We've had to discipline ourselves not to share *all* the tidbits we've gathered, so when we feel the impulse to dive down a rabbit hole, we've decided instead to step out of the flow and put a box around the idea. In these **Check It Out!** boxes we may give a short explanation of the detour we're declining to take, but our main goal is to provide you with enough search terms (and even resources) that you can follow the trail on your own.

Glossary

We love words. And we want to make sure you're able to track the words we use throughout the text, since we're applying them in specific ways to accentwork. To that end, we've included a **Glossary** for words in **bold typeface** at the back of this book.

Web Resources

When we need to provide material in audio or video form, or when we simply have more information we'd like to share than can be squeezed into the book, we'll refer you to a dedicated website: https://ea.ktspeechwork.org (the password is "Somenish").

This website icon will guide you to specific online resources:

 Web Resources

All right. Enough introduction. Let's get to work!

PREFACE
ARRIVING

Hi.

You know how it feels on the first day of class, when all you really know is the name of the class, and perhaps some of the people who are now beginning to gather in the room?

Let's take a moment to sit in that experience, in the way the room sounds, and its particular space, temperature, acoustic texture, or light.

Being in the space where a class is about to begin feels a certain way. It feels that way to some degree because of the physical characteristics of the space and your perception of them, but also because the space contains some expectation about the task to be undertaken, the reason you've shown up. It also feels a certain way to be you, and to be who you are in this place for these reasons.

That feeling is worth paying some attention to. It's worth it because you exist in this context, and because the work we'll be doing, the work described in these pages, will be happening *in you*. And *here* is exactly where you are.

You are at the start of a project. This book is a significant part of the framework that contains and defines that project, but you are where the project truly takes place. Your mind and your body and your breath and voice are the location, the material substance, the mechanism and even, you might say, the subject of this project. So, take a moment to experience what it feels like to be you, in this space, at this moment.

That, right now, is what it feels like to arrive at the beginning.

Also, it's never really the beginning. It can't be. You have a past. You have antecedents, beliefs, and experiences. You have stories about who you are, where you come from, and what that means. So does this work, the authors of this book, and the teacher who has chosen this textbook for the course you're beginning now. We all come from somewhere, and we're going to bring that history into the room. For our part, we've arrived in this room with a lot we'd like to say. This book is an attempt to articulate an approach to accent learning and performance that was developed over decades by Knight-Thompson Speechwork (KTS).

In KTS, we have a practice of approaching topics first through exploration before proceeding to any explanations. A key component of this practice is to begin our investigations from a position of *assumed ignorance*. Stated in the form of a question, we might ask ourselves, "What if I didn't already know the answer to this question I'm asking?"

So, in that spirit, let's start this investigation with a rather important question: what are we doing here?

PART I
FOUNDATIONS

Module One

Orienting

What are we doing here?

Well, first of all, we should probably ask, what are *you* doing here? What's in it for you?

Take some time to ponder what it is you're interested in learning about and what skills you're hoping to build. How do you see this knowledge and these skills connecting to other interests and other goals for your personal and professional development? It might be worth writing these ideas down.

When it comes to what this book is doing, we may have already revealed our answer in the title. We're interested in *experiencing accents*. We're also particularly interested in accents as part of performance. And, just as important as our interest in understanding, we're also interested in *doing* accents, with skill, finesse, and compassion. This is *accentwork*.

Let's take a first pass at the declarative, fact-based part of our knowledge . . . and get creative!

Exercise 1.1: What Is Accent?

The instructions for this exercise are simple: answer that question. Then answer it again. Write down your answers. Contradict yourself. Answer the question out loud as you wash the dishes. Dry your hands, and then write down what you remember. You may no longer agree (or never have agreed) with some of the things you say, but write them down anyway. Your goal is to fill up pages (or screens) with ideas and in that volume of response to evade the impulse to shut down or edit your thoughts.

Take a break. Walk around. Say hi to someone.

When you come back to your list, spend a little time looking it over, circling things or drawing lines between ideas. Maybe this gives you a second wave of thoughts, and if so, write those down as well.

If you need something to prompt your curiosity, try these questions:

What are accents made of?
Who has accents?
Is accent part of a larger category?
Are there different kinds of accents?
What do accents do for us?
Do animals have accents?
What are accents for?
What's cool about accents?
What's funny about accents?
What's dangerous about accents?
What senses do I use to perceive accents?

You now have a big, messy bundle of ideas. So do the other people in your class. Bring these ideas together and begin sorting them. It's useful to have a scribe to make a public collection of these impressions. Pay attention to the ideas that are widely shared, but also collect the outliers. Take note of ideas that you didn't think of, ideas that you don't like, ideas that you disagree with, or ideas that bother you in some way.

You've begun to organize the ideas you collected from yourself and your classmates. Great! You're bringing some order to a very big and convoluted topic.

The Accent Complex

When we (the authors) took a turn at Exercise 1.1, we came up with the following list. Compare our collection to what you gathered. How are they similar? How are they different? Is there anything you want to adopt? Anything you want to reject?

Accent is:

- of the speaker.
- of the hearer.
- of the culture.
- of the location.
- of the body.
- made of gesture.
- made of sound.
- a performance.
- a hidden signal of self.
- an intentional expression of self.
- all these things *at the same time.*
- IMMENSELY COMPLEX.

Out of our collected ideas, we'd like to take a closer look at the last one: "Accent is immensely complex."

When we say **complex**, we don't necessarily mean "difficult" or "confusing," though accentwork can occasionally feel that way. Instead, we're referring to a property inherent in many phenomena, in which seemingly simple elements interact to produce incredibly varied, intricate, and unpredictable results. Things are complex not only because they have multiple features, but also because those features interact with each other in a multitude of ways.

Complexity is certainly a feature of accentwork, but it's also a feature of our experience of the world. And, fortunately, we have ways of dealing with it. When handling complexity, whether in physics or phonetics, it can be helpful to identify basic elements and then notice how the interactions of those elements produce complex results. One big advantage of this approach is that it allows us to *describe* what we notice about accent, rather than trying to *prescribe* what it "should" be like. Let's name a superpower you already have when it comes to handling complexity.

Zooming In and Zooming Out

These terms describe your ability to shift your attention between fine details, the overarching whole, and everything in between. For example, when you consider what you'll do ten minutes from now, you're *zoomed in* on your current experience. When you think about what you want to do over the course of your life, you've *zoomed out* and are most likely also contemplating some profound and far-reaching questions. Your attention rests somewhere in between when you consider your actions over the next week, month, and year. We could also refer to these various degrees of zooming as different *scales* of your attention, much as we use different scales on maps to describe bigger or smaller areas.

Accents, being complex, have tiny features that accumulate into larger and larger patterns. A fluid focus, connected across scales, allows you to avoid getting mired in granularity or overwhelmed by chaos. You can use this versatile and interconnected ability to selectively focus your attention, appreciating detail without neglecting your overall sense of the whole.

We'll begin our exploration of accents by zooming out, exploring the largest useful concepts that can guide our understanding. When we zoom in on the fine details of accentwork in subsequent modules, we'll stay aware of how those details feed back into our experience as a whole.

Our initial, large-scale view of accents includes a lot of knowledge explored, expanded, and explained by others, most of it connected in some way to the rich territory of **linguistics**. Linguists seek to understand the many ways in which language varies and to uncover the principles that help us grasp how it operates. In accentwork, we frequently find ourselves sharing the zoomed-out perspective of linguists and borrowing generously from their work, for which we are exceptionally grateful.

However, our project is somewhat different from theirs. Our perspective is focused on *actors* and the unique ways they experience accents as part of their art. We need to ensure that our knowledge meets the practical needs of performance, which may require streamlining certain linguistic concepts in order to put them into practice.

So how do we begin to outline the scope of our task as performers? We may need to zoom out a little further to contextualize what we actually mean by "accent."

Varieties of Language

When we work with accents, we encounter ideas and terms that are frequently used in a wide variety of contexts, from the lecture hall to the movie set. Zoomed out, we know that *languages*, *dialects*, and *accents* are all part of a general body of knowledge, but what do these words mean? And what makes them different?

You first.

Exercise 1.2: Drawing Distinctions

How would you distinguish "accents," "dialects," and "languages"? Feel free to refer to your notes from Exercise 1.1!

Free-write, draw pictures, write a manifesto, create idea clouds, doodle . . . whatever it takes! Give yourself time to include as much detail as you care to, then see if you can condense that information down to one sentence for each word.

Once you have those three sentences, share them with your classmates. Notice where your definitions are similar and where they're different. Can you come to a class agreement on one sentence for each word?

How would you describe the *relationships* you discovered between "languages," "dialects," and "accents"? How would you arrange them? As a hierarchy? A tree? A series of overlapping circles? A tangled ball of loose threads?

If you found this exercise challenging, you're not alone! When it comes to accents, dialects, and languages, linguists are *still* debating what each of these words means. Final and unquestioned answers in linguistics, let alone sub-specialties like accents, are non-existent. And the same applies to any rigorous field of study: scholarship and science are about building *consensus* through carefully reasoned arguments. At the foundation of all human knowledge, fuzzy boundaries are far, far more common than absolutes.

In our work with actors, we (the authors) have commonly encountered some of the following observations:

- Accents and dialects are subsets of languages.
- Dialects are "less proper" or "corrupted" versions of a language.
- Dialects belong to a smaller geographic area (a state) than accents (a region).
- Accents belong to a smaller geographic area (a city) than dialects (a country).
- Accents include dialects.
- Dialects include accents.
- Accents and dialects are the same thing.

Did any of these come up in your exploration?

Obviously, there are contradictory statements in this list, and there may be some on your list(s) as well. Let's give ourselves permission to find consensus through *working descriptions* instead of incontrovertible definitions. These working descriptions will help us focus on "accents," so that other linguistic concepts don't trip us up. We'll also practice our zooming skills by remembering that, yes, accents are part of our larger experience of language and dialects, but they're distinct . . . for a reason.

Let's take your observations, our observations, and some insight from linguistics to start with a description for "language."

"Language" commonly describes two things:

A. *Language* is an <u>*ability*</u>, something human beings do. It's a process of encoding ideas into a transmissible form that is then reconstituted by a listener/receiver.
B. *A **language*** is a <u>*way of communicating*</u> shared by a group of people. In this description, it's a *specific variety* of encoding and transmission, like English, Farsi, Tagalog, Xhosa, or Te Reo Māori.

As actors, we'll leave much of the territory of Description A to linguistics. While it may be fascinating to know how language arose in the distant past or which biological developments influence language learning, that information won't be of much practical use for our needs as actors.

Description B of "languages" is where things get interesting for us, because the focus shifts from a general ability to the specific forms of communication that groups share. But wait . . . in our example, we claimed that "English" is a language. But what about "Australian English"? Or "American English"? Aren't those "specific forms of communicating," too? Couldn't Description B also apply to "accents" or "dialects"?

In a sense, yes! At the broadest level, "English speakers" are a group with a language in Description B's sense of a specific, shared form. "Dialect" and "accent" are other ways of *zooming in* to look more precisely at the nuances of that sharing.

The etymology of "dialect" (Greek *diá-* "inter, through" + *légō* "I speak" = *dialégomai* "to converse") arises from the same source as "dialogue." Both refer to the way a language passes between people in their daily conversation. Because human beings are wonderfully non-uniform, variations develop in interpersonal communication and, zooming out, among groups. Those variations include patterns around vocabulary (*lexicon*), ordering (*syntax*), usage (*pragmatics*), formation (*morphology*), and sound (*phonetics* and *phonology*). A **dialect** is *a variety of language* in which a particular set of patterns is shared by a group in the way they communicate.

Let's shift our perspective again. If dialects are varieties within a language, "languages" could also be described as *families of dialects*. We can zoom in on a language and find dialects, or we can zoom out on dialects and spot the overall contours of a language. So, when we zoom out to compare the way people in Australia communicate and the way people in the United States communicate, we might describe Australian and American varieties – or dialects – of a shared language: English.

These perspectives are reasonably accurate and widely accepted. The history of human interactions, however, is not so dispassionate. Imbalances of power among peoples also lead to imbalances of power in their dialects. The language varieties of elites often accumulate greater social advantages, which can reinforce the control of those who speak those dialects and exclude those who don't. This process typically leads to *another* description of "language":

C. The specific variety of communication associated with those who have power.

Description C is basically "Description B + Power" – the power to define the boundaries and membership of cultural groups and to convince or coerce others to accept those definitions. Description C can lead to a single dialect being granted the legitimacy and title of "language," while all other varieties are stigmatized as lesser "dialects" of that standard and legitimate form. This idea perpetuates disparities in power by encoding those differences into communication.

Instead of accepting the inequity encoded into Description C, in this book we rely on Description B: dialects are shared communication patterns among people, and languages are collections of similar dialects. No "right-or-wrong" required.

So where does "accent" fit into these working descriptions?

Accent as Performance

Accents are the aspect of language variation that's experienced in *physical embodiment*. Accents relate to the *action* or *performance* of communication; while they connect deeply to how we think about and structure our language, they only show up in the world when we actually express ourselves.

While the terms "accent" and "dialect" are often used interchangeably in popular culture, our concept of "accent" *does not* extend to the vocabulary, grammar, or formation aspects of dialects. For us, "accent" focuses on the physical embodiment of communication and how it's created, without treading into idioms, slang, or subject-verb agreement. This limited focus is doubly useful to the actor: we get to avoid confusion between the terms "dialect" and "accent," and we also get to leave questions of vocabulary or phrasing to the playwright or screenwriter.

Of course, we also need to point out that dialect and accent always coexist. Dialects typically include markers of embodied communication, and we often can't describe accents without also noticing the dialectal varieties they express.

Let's look at a quick example of a dialect and how it differs from accent: *Pop is so expensive anymore – just get a drink from the water fountain.*

In this example, we could call the language English and the dialect American Midland Midwest. As a written sentence, this example doesn't include any information about accent, which only arises in the process of physical embodiment. If someone from Columbus, Ohio, spoke this sentence out loud, we'd receive simultaneous information about that person's accent *and* dialect. If *you* spoke this sentence aloud, we'd still note the Midwest dialect, but that data would be intermingled with information about *your* accent.

An Unspoken Premise

Up to this moment, we've held off mentioning *speech* in our discussion of accents, dialects, and language. That choice might seem odd, considering how much of our previous KTS book, *Experiencing Speech*, focused on, well, speech.

There are patterns of communication we would call *accents* that include nuanced layers of information and don't require spoken language at all. Sign languages are forms of embodied communication with dialects and accents, as rich and varied as any spoken language on Earth.

As authors, our specialty lies within the realm of *spoken language*. The framework we offer for the accents of human speech is, we hope, robust enough to be taken apart, examined, challenged, improvised, and reassembled in a wide variety of contexts. While it is our ardent hope that the principles we explore in this book apply to as many accents as possible, we focus our attention hereafter on the accents of speech.

When we focus on the physical embodiment of accents in speech, we unsurprisingly gather a lot of information from what we hear. In fact, the **auditory** (Latin *audire* = "to hear") aspects of accent are most likely the most familiar part of our experience. Yet the speech sounds that reach our ears arise through the intricate movements of muscles, so a large part of our accentwork focuses on the **articulatory** realities of physical action. In the pages ahead, we'll track how speaking and hearing interact to produce the incredible diversity and complexity of speech that we call "accent."

Accents, Now and Then

Having taken time to differentiate accents, dialects, and languages, let's revisit our earlier list of common observations and see where we stand:

- THEN: Accents and dialects are subsets of languages.
- **NOW**: While accents and dialects may emerge at a smaller scale than languages, it's more helpful to think of them through interrelationships and not in hierarchy.
- THEN: Dialects are "less proper" or "corrupted" versions of a language.
- **NOW**: Social inequity is at the root of dialects being perceived as "lesser than" or "improper." It would be more historically accurate to regard "languages" (Description C) as power-adjacent dialects.
- THEN: Dialects belong to a smaller geographic area (a state) than accents (a region); accents belong to a smaller geographic area (a city) than dialects (a country).
- **NOW**: Maybe! But rather than citing these relationships as categorical fact, let's stay curious about how different circumstances shape varieties of language.
- THEN: Accents include dialects; dialects include accents.
- **NOW**: These two concepts are inherently connected. Rather than "include" each other, they address different perspectives of the process of communication.
- THEN: Accents and dialects are the same thing.
- **NOW**: We can say now that this isn't true. While we understand how these terms can get confused outside accentwork, we'll develop our skills specifically for working with the physical embodiment of language: accent.

Are there any observations from Exercise 1.1 that you'd like to revisit and perhaps revise? Which of your previous observations still hold up?

The embodied nature of accent means that every*body*'s got one. You have a particular way of bringing your language variety into the world – and that's what we describe as an "accent." That accent may be one that feels entirely unique to you, or it may be one that identifies you as part of a larger group, be it family, friends, peers, community, city, or nation.

The way that your embodied communication matches up with others' is, as we've seen, a question of scale . . . but now let's zoom all the way in, to the personal level.

Exercise 1.3: Gradual Exposure

You'll need a memorized piece of text and an accent of your choosing to perform in (that isn't your own). You'll also take advantage of your skills in **Omnish** . . .

Check It Out!

For more on Omnish, see *Experiencing Speech: A Panlingual Approach to Actor Training*, by Andrea Caban, Julie Foh, and Jeffrey Parker (Routledge, 2021). Now would be a great time to review Module Seven in that book!

Web Resource 1.1 Gradual Exposure Exercise

When you're ready, navigate to **Web Resource 1.1** to find the **Gradual Exposure** exercise. You can listen to the audio file we've provided, or you can be guided through the written version of the exercise that we've made available for instructors.

Check-In

Reflect on what you learned from Exercise 1.3. What was it like to share, with the room, more and more of your voice, your text, and the accent you performed? Did it feel like sharing more and more of *yourself*? Or were you sharing something else? What felt easy in the exercise? What felt challenging? What surprised you? What did your experiences reveal about your preconceptions around accent?

Compare your observations here to your ideas from Exercise 1.1 and your descriptions from Exercise 1.2. What matches up? What doesn't? How is experiencing accentwork different from thinking about it?

Conclusion

You've given yourself time to explore the breadth of what accent *could* mean, what it means to you, and how those observations tie together. We've differentiated "languages," "dialects," and "accents," as both linguistic terms and as experiences in our lives. You also had a chance to enter, slowly and attentively, into the embodiment of an accent, through Gradual Exposure and a gentle interrogation of the preconceptions that surround accentwork.

Even as we explored concepts from a zoomed-out level, we've encouraged a process of *flow*, of allowing yourself to discover what you already know. Flow, freedom, and fluency are important because the art we're working on here only happens in conditions of flow – and all our efforts to manage that flow have a tendency to interrupt it. The strategy we've adopted so far is to support flow and then examine it *after* the fact. This progression from experience to analysis sits at the heart of all the work ahead.

We still have plenty of unanswered questions about how to describe accents, as well as what makes them so powerful – and so personal. In Module Two, we'll continue to zoom in and out, finding new points of view to illuminate and immerse in the complexities of accentwork.

MODULE TWO
UNPACKING

We described "accent" as the physical manifestation of a spoken language variety. Yet we also know that, in our lives, accents reveal information including our birthplace, our first languages, our educational experiences, our family, our friends, our peers, our residences, and how we wish to be perceived . . . even within a few seconds of speaking. The great promise of acting in accent is that you can reveal that same wealth of information about any character you play by modifying the sounds of your language. How do accents give us such rich, informative, and transformative potential, in our lives and in our art?

In Module One, we used zooming in and out to handle complexity without overly simplifying it. Another equally useful approach is to foreground certain parts of the holistic experience of accent while letting other parts slip away, if only momentarily. We could call this spotlighting of specific information a **perceptual filter**. Filters draw our attention to ideas and their relationships without reducing the complexity of the whole. As with scale, you may already be familiar with these types of filters through your experience with maps.

Imagine a map of the Indian Ocean. This map represents a real place, but what you notice about that place will change based on the filter through which you view it. While you could zoom in and out on it, if you don't have the right filter in place, all you'll likely see, at every scale, is

DOI: 10.4324/9781003314905-3

blue. Just blue. Apply a topographic filter to that map, however, and then you see soaring underwater mountain ranges, enormous basins, and bulky continental shelves. Apply a bathymetric filter and you see a psychedelic zigzag of water depths rendered in neon colors. Apply a filter for ocean currents, water temperature, aquatic life, shipping lanes, plastic accumulations . . . each one reveals a different set of observable facts about the same body of water.

A body of knowledge can be filtered and appreciated in the same way. The application of different perceptual filters to the idea of "accent" gives us the ability to organize our knowledge and experience in multiple ways. The territory we're investigating remains complex, but filters allow us to make "accent" comprehensible. With a better grip on the individual layers of our experience, we can assemble them into a practical and repeatable approach.

Let's start with five **Filters** that are especially useful for handling the complexity of accents in performance:

- Acting
- Communication
- Belonging
- Evolution
- Patterns

As we apply each of these Filters, notice how the highlighted information relates to your experience of accents. For each Filter, we offer some questions for reflection, which may be worth exploring again (and again!) as your skills grow.

Acting

Our thinking about accent, dialect, and language has taken for granted that this is something humans do. But the contexts in which we "do accent" is important. We can look at accent as it exists *in the world*, *in the self*, or *in performance*. We are, after all, focusing our work on accents in acting. But acting and "real life" overlap and relate to each other in meaningful ways.

When you act, there are aspects of your performance that are identical with your own "natural" human behavior. It is you that breathes, that listens, that grabs a chair and shifts its position. Those actions exist side by side with behaviors that are "artificial." You walk onstage because it's required by the text. You don't usually use the word "thou," but in *Twelfth Night* . . . thou dost.

In the same way, the embodied details of language that you employ in acting may be the same as those you use every day. Or the circumstances of the text may require some altered configuration of those details, with which you're less familiar. Accent resides in you naturally as a human being while it also serves a purpose in the story being told.

It's tempting to think of our behavior *in the world* in stark contrast to the natural-artificial hybrid of performance. We may distinguish as artificial those things done "with planning," whereas natural things "just happen." In other words, natural parts of our behavior are *unconscious*, while artificiality is marked by *intention*. Except this contrast isn't entirely true, either. Think of examples from your own life: is it artificial for you to intend to eat breakfast? Or to wear a flattering color? Or to pronounce a word in a way that you think will be admired?

These examples – and many others you can imagine – reveal that our lives *in the world* are not so different from our lives *in performance*, in terms of how we *act*. Accent, like all human behaviors, is a mix of the intentional and the unconscious, the natural and the artificial. In life, in acting, and in accentwork, the "artificial" is not an enemy, nor is the "unconscious" superior; we inhabit both as human beings, at the juncture of what "just happens" and what requires planning, intention, and goal-oriented action.

But it's also worth mentioning that the art of acting and behavior in the world are *not* the same thing, despite the fact that they involve the same human being (you!). When we look to the world for information about accents, we always need to consider the needs of our art as part of that process. The Acting Filter allows us to view accents as both organic human behavior (in the world and in the self) and as a powerful given circumstance (in performance). The skills we explore in this book give you a framework to build effective connections between art and life.

Questions: The Acting Filter

When acting in an accent . . .

- . . . how much of your own experience do you draw on?
- . . . how does accent resemble other given circumstances?
- . . . where do you get inspiration or resources for your accentwork?
- . . . what feels "natural" about accentwork? what feels "unnatural"?

Communication

Human communication is extraordinary. We take some aspect of our experience, known only to us, find a way to formulate that experience into a message (or *signal*), send that signal out into the world through physical actions, and then get that signal interpreted (hopefully) on the other end so that the receiver also knows about our experience. Our capacity to transmit our ideas is vital to our survival and the bedrock of our art. And accents are inseparable from what we communicate and how.

Challenges in Communication

We acknowledge that we're generalizing here. Human communication is a broadly shared ability that we can justifiably wonder at. However, communication is not always easy or, indeed, possible for all human beings. We want to take a moment to reaffirm the value, dignity, and humanity of those who might not share all the communicative skills we're investigating here.

While communication includes language, in all its varieties, there are also plenty of ways to send information that might not seem like language at all. Physical gestures, posture, eye contact, expressive noises (sighs, groans, grunts), touch, visual arts, music, dance, silence . . . we may find that there are other not-quite-language modalities of communication that feel deeply related to accent.

Let's tap into some of the communication skills you already possess.

Exercise 2.1: Layers of Communication

Find a partner. And select a "text" – a monologue, a poem, or lyrics to a song – in an **Acting Language** of your choice (see the following box). Make sure that you're able to repeat it – improvisation won't be as useful for this exercise. You may also want to have materials for notetaking nearby, because your observations throughout the exercise will be valuable for discussion later.

Revisiting Acting Language

In *Experiencing Speech*, we used the term of art "Acting Language." It's a language you know well enough for acting, be it your first language or an additional one. You may even have access to more than one Acting Language – choose what works best for you!

Start a conversation with your partner in Omnish. Warm up your articulatory possibilities while also engaging in the give and take of a light chat. After a minute or so, in Omnish, decide who will be the first Speaker and who will be the first Listener.

Speaker, share your text with your Listener in Omnish. That is, follow the ideas and impulses of the original text and let them emerge with specificity and personal meaning *through Omnish.*

Notice what your responses are to sharing a text you know in this improvised language. Do you feel like you're able to effectively communicate some part of it? All of it? None of it? Did you use anything besides Omnish to communicate information about your text or your relationship to it? (Take notes, but don't talk about your experiences yet!)

Listener, what do you receive from this communication? (Take notes! Don't talk yet!)

After sharing your text in Omnish, Speaker, get ready to share it again. This time, you're only going to use *gestures* – no speech sounds! You could physically reenact your text, but you could also use more abstract or expressive movements. You can take 10 seconds to imagine what sort of gestures you want to use, but no more than that. See what arises spontaneously in your physicality as you communicate through gestures.

Speaker, what were you able to effectively communicate in this version of the text? Listener, what did you receive? (Take notes! Don't talk yet!)

Speaker, get ready to share your text again, this time using only your face – no speech sounds or gestures! Your storytelling could involve a range of facial expressions, but you could also simply imagine your story and let your face organically respond. Again, take 10 seconds to prepare, if needed. See what emerges spontaneously as you communicate your text using only your face.

Speaker, what were you able to effectively communicate in this version of the text? Listener, what did you receive? (Take notes! Don't talk yet!)

Okay, Speaker, once more, prepare to share your text. You can still use facial expressions and gestures, but you'll start your text in Omnish. When you feel the impulse, during your sharing, shift into your Acting Language. Try to share at least half of your text in your Acting Language.

Speaker, what were you able to effectively communicate in this version of the text? Listener, what did you receive? Make note of it, and . . .

Discuss with your partner! What aided your communication? What impeded it? Was any version more frustrating than the others? Was any version more illuminating than the others? Make sure to include the experience of both the Speaker *and* the Listener!

After discussing, Listener and Speaker exchange roles. Run through the exercise again.

Notice, in Exercise 2.1, how Speakers and Listeners can have very different experiences of the same communicative acts. Communication involves both sending and receiving a signal – what linguists call **production** and **perception** – and the intentional and unconscious are again at play in both. While the content of our signal is often what we intend to communicate, what actually gets transmitted is heavily influenced by the expectations, beliefs, and habits of the speaker and the listener. The communicative environment – including surrounding noise and social context – also impacts what gets sent and what gets received.

Accent, as it appears through the physical manifestation of speech, is inextricably bound up in all aspects of communication. The Communication Filter allows us to view the impact accent has on our messages via production, perception, and the exciting areas in between. The Communication Filter also reminds us that accent itself conveys information and often does so independently of the words being spoken.

It's worth noting that, as an actor, you're always communicating with someone! While your fellow performers can receive the signals you send out, in words and actions, the very nature of performance means that the audience perceives *everything* you do as some sort of communication – intentional or not! When applied to accentwork, the Communication Filter reveals that we always have at least one set of listeners to keep in mind: the audience.

Questions: The Communication Filter

When acting in an accent . . .

- . . . what does the accent communicate to the other characters?
- . . . what does the accent communicate to the audience?
- . . . what does the accent communicate intentionally (for you or the character)?
- . . . what does the accent communicate unconsciously (for you or the character)?

Belonging

Belonging is essential to human well-being. We care deeply about fitting in with other humans, and our connections to others tell us something important about who we are in the world.

Our outward appearance, behaviors, belief systems, customs, and stories are crucial to our ability to interact with other individuals, maintain group memberships, and suss out who isn't like us. As a social species, we *seek* belonging, and we do so both intentionally and unconsciously. We may be aware of how we detect the stories of belonging around us, but often our judgments kick into action within the first few milliseconds of interaction, long before conscious awareness can catch up. We can also choose whether to fit in or not, deploying our conscious agency to associate with whom we please, when we please.

Accent plays a huge role in belonging by highlighting important information in our speech about our relationships to others. Does this person share my geographic origins or come from somewhere else? Are we of similar age, or are we speaking across a generational divide? What can I detect about gender identity, peer groups, socioeconomic markers, cultural fluencies, and personal history, all arising from another person's accent? Accents tell us who is like us and who is unlike us, where "we" end and where "they" begin.

As with communication, we'd wager that you're already quite skilled at figuring out belonging. Let's take those skills for a spin!

Exercise 2.2: Listen to an Accent

Web Resource 2.1 Accent Sample

Go to **Web Resource 2.1** and listen to the recording of a person speaking.

There's a lot of information to process in this sample, so we'll break the job down into three listens, each one focusing on a different task.

- **Listen 1**: Listen for what *delights* you about this accent. What do you enjoy about it? Are there sounds, inflections, word choices, or abstract impressions of it that you like?
- **Listen 2**: Listen for *identity*. What do you know or think you know about the speaker? Make an exhaustive, even redundant list.
- **Listen 3**: Listen for *judgments*. What might you imagine other people think about the speaker? These may not be views that you share or approve of. You may not think that these are accurate or polite or fair. Write them down. You won't be required to share them with anyone.

Collect your responses. What was the speaker talking about? What were you able to pick up about their relationship to their story that didn't show up in their words? What were you able to learn about *the speaker* that wasn't in their words? Bring these thoughts to a group discussion. Notice what seems easy to share. Notice what seems challenging to share.

This exercise may have made clear that we often negotiate our sense of belonging through **identity**, by being able to say that someone (including ourselves) "is" or "is like" something else. In Exercise 2.2, you may have had unconscious and readymade references to who "they" are, without even trying. Likewise, you may have been able to know, almost instantaneously, how they were similar to you and how they were different. Your responses may have obvious connections to your previous social and cultural experiences, or their genesis may seem more uncertain. Identities allow you to delineate your relationships to other people, and accent is integral to how you – and the characters you play – shape those identities.

The necessity of belonging highlights another interesting possibility: accent is a *survival skill* and plays a fundamental role in how we live and thrive. Our speech sounds communicate aspects of our identity, to which listeners bring their own judgments about how and where we belong. These interactions can sometimes present us with a possible *threat*, something that encroaches upon our sense of safety, physical, emotional, or social. As a result, accent can trigger *survival responses*, those deep, primal parts of ourselves that activate in order to keep us safe. Our nervous systems respond to not-belonging in the same way they respond to being attacked by a predator, with a rush of stress hormones and physiological arousal, such as the fight-flight-freeze reactions. And sometimes being "othered" by an accent *does* result in real, physical danger, so a survival response is entirely merited.

Exercise 2.3: Being Heard

Choose an accent different from your own to perform, in a text of your choice. You can use the accent you chose for Gradual Exposure in Module One, or a different one. You may feel confident in your ability with this accent . . . or not!

Find a partner. Choose who will share their text – in accent – first. That person will be the Speaker, while the other partner will be the Analyzer.

Remember the three listens in Exercise 2.2? The Analyzer will repeat that same process with the Speaker, in real time, using one listen.

Pause right here.

Speaker, notice: what are you physically sensing as you prepare to share? Where does your mind go? Does getting ready to speak in accent feel different from other ways of performing? Does it feel scary in any way? safe? uncomfortable? easy? Where do those feelings originate in your body?

Analyzer, notice if you have a response to these same questions in your role.

Speaker, you're going to share some of your text – but only as much as you want to. That means if you only want to share one word, one syllable, or one vowel, you have the agency to make that call. Speak some tiny part of your text (or all of it!), so you can experience being heard in accent and notice what physically happens.

Analyzer, you're going to keep your analysis entirely to yourself. Notice if you have any physical responses while listening to your Speaker.

Speaker, once you've shared as much of your text as you care to, collect your personal responses. Do this internally first, and then commit some of your thoughts to writing. Which of these thoughts would you be willing to share with your partner? Which would you want to keep to yourself? Are there any thoughts that you don't even want to write down?

After the Speaker has a chance to gather their experiences in writing, exchange roles with the Analyzer and repeat.

Once both partners have been heard in accent, if you're both willing, share some of your responses with each other. You get to be the manager of what you share. How does your internal experience of acting in accent connect with your sense of belonging, even in this intimate setting? What does it physically feel like to share your responses out loud?

When performing in a new or less familiar accent, it's not uncommon to experience a racing heartbeat, changed breath rhythms, sweaty palms, nausea, and blanking out. It can be a big experience! The Belonging Filter gives us insight into why performing in accent triggers such powerful responses in us. On the other hand, tapping into the primal potential of belonging can lead to dynamic and exciting possibilities in performance, if we're able to deal with it in a sensitive and consensual way.

Questions: The Belonging Filter

When acting in an accent . . .

- . . . how does the accent foster or hinder belonging in the circumstances?
- . . . how does the accent foster or hinder belonging for the audience?
- . . . how does the accent arise from or relate to the identities of the character?
- . . . what does the accent tell other characters about you?
- . . . what does the accent tell the audience about you?

Evolution

Everything we've touched on so far – accents, language, acting, communication, belonging – occurs in the context of time. No matter what we do, we're never separate from the ceaseless evolutionary movement from past to future. That movement has no "goal" or "target" – evolution is the gradual adjustment to current conditions. While we may like to imagine that evolution is always making things better, more efficient, or more fit, in truth, it usually just makes things *different*, again and again and again.

Languages and accents interact with their environment, human beings, and each other, changing over time in response to *selective pressures* that affect their evolution. These selective pressures are part of the linguistic environment, influencing which speech features thrive and which die out. Before we mangle Darwin any further, let's look at an example.

Have you taken in any old movies lately? As in, seventy to eighty years old. If you haven't recently, go ahead, treat yourself. We'll wait.

We'd hazard a guess that you noticed a difference between the way people sounded in these films and the way people sound today – something distinctly "old timey." Whatever that is, it's evidence that changes in spoken language have occurred over time.

You can find those changes closer to home, as well. A quick search of the term "oral history" and the name of your home location can often yield older recordings that show how your local accent has changed over the decades.

You may even be fortunate enough to experience this in your own life. Do you know anyone older than you who has "a different way" of speaking? You may also notice that the language of people younger than yourself sounds different with every passing year, no matter where they're from.

If we zoom all the way in, we may even notice that the accents of *individuals* shift over time in response to the selective pressures of their environment. The communicative tactics of childhood may adapt to the rigors of adolescence, or the language of home may shift to meet the needs of career advancement.

The same forces at work at the zoomed-in, personal level are also operating across the entirety of human history. As populations of humans move, grow, and coexist, their languages – and everything connected to them – change. At the most zoomed-out level, languages shift and branch and fade in a kaleidoscopic panoply that extends across the entire existence of the modern human species.

Check It Out!

Linguists have written *a lot* about the evolution of language, which we can't summarize in just a few sentences here. Look up some of these key terms: diachronic; synchronic; comparative linguistics; philology.

Let's zoom back in on accents. Maybe you've seen this phrase in casting notices, or maybe you've read about it in a novel: "the Brooklyn accent." We know there's a place called "Brooklyn" and it's one of the five boroughs of New York City. If we've watched a lot of Martin Scorsese or Mel Brooks movies, we probably have a distinct impression of what someone from Brooklyn sounds like. Were we to travel to Brooklyn right now, however, we would likely find that most people there sound nothing like mafiosos or vaudevillians. Varied populations have moved through the area known as Brooklyn for centuries, and the accents heard there today are not fixed relics from the communities of the 1950s or 1960s – nor will they be the accents we hear there in the 2050s or 2060s.

The relative isolation of human populations has been a key driver of linguistic difference over time. As groups evolve separately, their ways of

communicating evolve separately as well. Sometimes the causes of isolation are geographic – mountain ranges, bodies of water, urban avenues. If
we borrow from the etymology of "dialect" on page 9, where -*lect* referred
to a variety of speech, we could call these variations of language *geolects*
(*geo*- "earth") or *topolects* (*topos* "place"). Sometimes, divisions between cultural groups lead to variety in their "lects"; we thus end up with terms like
ethnolects (*ethnos* "nation"), *acrolects* (*akron* "summit" = upper classes), and
basilects (*basis* "base" = working classes). Complex layers of separation and
belonging have led over time to the seemingly infinite variability in language we observe around us today.

Within the past century, human beings have not only exploded in pop-
ulation, but we've also reconfigured our networks of belonging across vast
distances and times. Instantaneous communication technologies, globally
distributed media, and individual access to the Internet have collapsed
geographic barriers and realigned belonging-based divisions. The increasing speed of our technologies also means that linguistic evolutionary processes unfold at a faster pace than ever before. The way we're exposed to
accents is incredibly different than it was even twenty years ago. When all
it takes is an Internet connection and video app to gain access to almost
every accent in the world, we're striding boldly into uncharted territory for
linguistic evolution as we've known it. Our skillful deployment of the
Evolution Filter allows us to stay flexible and alert to change, building
skills to move with the times rather than sticking to accent models that
are outdated as soon as they're written down.

Questions: The Evolution Filter

When acting in an accent . . .

- . . . how does the accent reflect the time and circumstances
  from which it emerges?
- . . . what does the accent tell your audience about its
  circumstances?
- . . . how has the accent changed over time? How would you
  find that out?

Patterns

It feels easier to recognize a pattern than to know how to define one. The dictionary can get us started – Merriam-Webster gives us both "a natural or chance configuration" and "a discernible coherent system based on the intended interrelationship of component parts."

Let's make that easier to digest. A pattern is something we can recognize ("discernible") – if it can't be found by someone, *anyone*, it probably isn't there. A pattern needs to be *a thing* ("coherent") – it's got its own distinguishing characteristics that sets it apart from other things. A pattern expresses a relationship between parts: by zooming in, we can look at "component parts"; by zooming out, we can look at the "interrelationships" between them. Patterns arise because we intend them to (mosaics, codes, spelling), they arise organically from nature (snowflakes, fern leaves, weather cycles), and they can arise from intermingling of the two.

Accents possess all these pattern-based properties. We can recognize them when they happen (discernibility), we can identify them through their unique features (coherence), and when we zoom in, we can see that they're systems with interrelating parts. Accents also exist somewhere between "chance" and "intended"; they arise through a complex blend of social structures, identity, communicative need, selective pressures, intention, and unconscious influences.

We humans *love* patterns. We're also exceptionally skilled at detecting them, doing so incredibly quickly, often without conscious thought. In fact, in many ways, we're *too* skilled with patterns. We can find patterns where they don't exist, from imagining threats ("Is that a bush . . . or a bear?!") to crafting vast conspiracy narratives to explain the results of random chance ("Bears have taken over the landscaping industry to make us live in fear!"). Our extreme sensitivity to patterns can limit our ability to perceive new information; we favor data that support our internal models, and we ignore – or don't even notice – evidence that disrupts those models (**confirmation bias**).

We can also over-extend our patterning skills to determine what is true and false *before* we have an experience, in which case we can fall prey to *overgeneralization*. When we overgeneralize, we prioritize a pattern we've created over the evidence available to be gathered. Overgeneralization coerces reality to match our patterns, instead of crafting patterns to describe our reality.

Check It Out!

Social psychology and cognitive science offer an abundance of insight on the highs and lows of our pattern-finding and -making abilities. Helpful keywords to look up include: cognitive biases; cognitive illusions; fallacies; reductionism; overgeneralizing; stereotype; caricature; growth vs. fixed mentality.

Thankfully, we can counter our vulnerability to overgeneralizing with our ability to recognize and create **robust** patterns. These patterns maintain their coherence even as components or relationships shift – that is, robustness is the ability to respond and adapt to change. Languages are extremely robust patterns, able to evolve over time and in different environments, all while remaining recognizable as "English" or "Igbo" or "conversational Mandarin." And accents are a noticeably robust feature of languages, individually distinct yet interpretable across a wide range of same-language listeners.

Robust patterns are at the heart of the actor's art. We want to ensure that the roles we play are variable, able to live and breathe from scene to scene and day to day. In our acting, if we hew too closely to the same pattern, we might start to feel "stale"; if we deviate too much from the patterns of the circumstances or the script, we might confuse both the audience and our fellow performers.

We can encourage robustness in our work – and avoid reductionism – by seeking *possibilities* in patterns. Almost everything in human experience is **probabilistic**; aside from death and taxes, any pattern we observe is *most likely to occur*, or *likely to occur when . . .*, or *tends to happen if . . .* Engaging in this type of thinking allows us to maintain a healthy skepticism not only of our patterns but also of our evidence. Any accent pattern that seems 100% certain is probably too simple to be true. (See what we did there?)

Patterns also overlap across different scales. Smaller patterns are often parts of bigger patterns, which are themselves members of even larger patterns. As we saw in Module One, accents, dialects, and languages are examples of these scalar patterns. The more we remember our superpower of being able to zoom in and zoom out when it's helpful, the more adept we can be in our application of the Patterns Filter to accents.

Questions: The Patterns Filter

When acting in an accent . . .

- . . . what are the key components that seem to make up the accent?
- . . . what are the relationships between those components that make them a pattern?
- . . . how do your pattern-finding skills help you with accent-work? Do they ever hinder you?
- . . . can you think of instances when your work is robust? when it may be over-generalized?

Interactions Between Filters

Our five Filters give us a solid start on unpacking the complexity of accent-work. We gain even more insight when we observe their *interactions*. When we run our experience through multiple Filters, we produce combined views of accent that are greater than the sum of their parts. Potential interactions are too numerous to list completely. However, there are some combinations of Filters that arise early in accentwork and are worth identifying.

Scales of Identity

The way you communicate within your language includes not only the embodiment of your speech (your accent), but also your personal vocabulary, slang, and unique expressions (your dialect). Your most individual language variety is your **idiolect** (*ídio-* "own, personal, distinct"). As you zoom out from the individual level, you could find increasingly larger patterns of belonging that connect your idiolect to other peoples' idiolects, until you arrive at the largest possible group of people whom you could claim as having "the same dialect" as you do.

Because our patterns for belonging are robust, we can group together individuals who are otherwise quite different; for example, "actors" or "American English speakers." We also tend to find multiple patterns of belonging for each individual; for example, an "actor" could also be a member of groups that include "American English speakers," "Amharic speakers," "cellists," and "amateur botanists." Every person we encounter belongs to *networks of identity* that overlap, intersect, and influence each other, all of which could show up in accent.

Astoundingly, up to this point, we've taken for granted that we're able to *change* our accents. Considering all the factors at play – and that we're so often able to communicate through our many different identities – it seems nothing short of impossible that we could alter our accents at all. Yet we can . . . and frequently do!

Check It Out!

Sociolinguistics is a broad and exciting field that investigates the overlap between language and social interaction. We recommend looking up some of these keywords: code switching; shibboleths; linguistic accommodation.

Exercise 2.4: Accent at Scale

Write down your responses to the following questions. What's the largest group or groups that you could include yourself in, based on your accent? Besides this large group(s), are there other groups of intermediate size to which you belong? Can you identify which shared features (*markers*) of your accent create your shared identities?

Discuss your observations with a partner or the class. Where do your groups overlap with those of other people? Did anyone mention a group to which you belong that you hadn't thought of?

Standards

When we zoom out to the scale of a society, we can see that there's a social organization to identities. We apply different expectations and narratives to different groups, so that some groups are socially advantaged or disadvantaged. This differential valuing of identities affects people's opportunities in terms of access to power, resources, and social capital, which then tend to reinforce the advantages of those who already have them. The signals that a society reads as conferring advantage are often called **prestige**.

Accents are indicators of prestige and the complex circumstances that create it. How we communicate is essential to our social structures, our roles in them, and the benefits those structures provide. Our instinctive recognition of speech patterns can quickly tell us where a person sits on a spectrum of prestige relative to ourselves. Even so, those with prestige may not always be conscious of their status. Most people aren't fully aware of the advantages of prestige until they no longer have them.

Accents that become associated with socially entrenched prestige have tended to become *standards*, metrics to which other accents are compared. Standards are not "better" or "more correct" or "proper" – standards are standard because of their connection to power structures that lie beyond linguistics (such as government, commerce, or social hierarchy). You probably encounter standards fairly frequently; whenever you scramble to "correct" your pronunciation, you're referring to a standard.

We may feel attracted to standards because they're a useful tool for amplifying small efforts to much larger ends, allowing us to communicate valuable information consistently across large groups of people, just as we do with *standardized* measurements and *standard* time. Like all tools, however, the misuse of standards creates serious and lasting harm.

Standards are much, much less useful when studying accents, carrying all the hazards and none of the benefits. Accents exist in a state of continuous variation, and they can't be "objectively" measured or quantified. The best reference you have for understanding *any* accent is your own experience as a human being. Watch out for the undue influence of standards and examine the ways prestige might act as an obstacle to your freedom and creativity.

Check It Out!

Dudley Knight has written extensively on the topic of standards. We highly recommend "Standard Speech: The Ongoing Debate" in *The Vocal Vision* (Knight, ed. Hampton and Acker, Applause Theater Books, 1997) and "Standards" in *Voice & Speech Review: Standard Speech* (Knight, ed. Rocco Dal Vera, Applause Theater Books, 2000). Both are also available for free at ktspeechwork.org/readings.

Shifting Standards

Despite its self-reinforcing tendencies, prestige is not immune to change over time. Groups or social structures that were esteemed at one point might be forgotten – or vilified – at a later date. New trends arise, old fashions become passé, and certain habits that were endearingly quaint are unmasked as blithely oppressive.

Accents that once connoted wealth and refinement might come to represent snobbery or affectation. Accents that once echoed through factories and dockyards could easily become the voice of the morning news. The accent that defined "proper" elocution in 1940 sounds (to many) stilted and stuffy today.

As tempting as it may be to refer to a "standard accent" for quick answers of "right" and "wrong," the shifting nature of standards makes them just as unreliable as any other bias. In the pages ahead, we focus on building a framework for experiencing *all* accents. Instead of looking for a single truth, we rely on curiosity and cheerfully bid farewell to standards once they cease to be of use to us.

 Check-In

Look back on your notes and responses thus far. Go back to your list of ideas from Module One. And take another look at our list on page 5.

How do the Filters we named in this Module – and their potential interactions – show up in your thoughts about accentwork? Do some ways of viewing accentwork seem more prominent in your observations? For example, do you find that you've primarily thought about accent through the Belonging and Acting Filters? Are there any ways that the Filters make sense of your observations? How would you organize your observations – and ours – by viewing them through different Filters?

Conclusion

We've taken time to expand upon our initial description of accent – the physical embodiment of speech – and connect it to the impacts it has on our lives as acting, communicating, belonging, evolving, and pattern-seeking human beings. We're preparing ourselves to be more sensitive, flexible, and creative in our observation of the sounds around us.

We've also covered a lot of declarative ground in this module. In Module Three, we'll introduce a framework that provides direct connections between declarative and procedural understanding – in other words, how to *do* accents!

First, however, your homework: take a break. Go outside. Drink some water. Eat a delicious snack.

Let the ideas of this module settle, fall apart, recombine, and prompt new questions. You may need to revisit this module again, which is always a part of honing your process.

Curious? Excited? Bewildered? Good! Read on!

Reference

Merriam-Webster.com Dictionary, s.v. "pattern," accessed May 21, 2022, www.merriam-webster.com/dictionary/pattern.

MODULE THREE
THE FOUR PS

It's time to start talking about the *how-to-do* of accents.

In Module Two, we tried to honor the complexity of accents while offering solid ground to stand on. This balancing act required a flexible dance between zooming in and zooming out, as well as shifting the Filters through which we interpret accents. We're going to need those same skills for engaging with the work of accents, starting with *the Four Ps*.

The Four Ps are our way of summarizing a framework for *doing* accent-work. Each P describes a distinct and essential aspect of analyzing and embodying a pattern of speech. Those aspects are:

- People
- Prosody
- Posture
- Pronunciation

See? Four Ps!

The Four Ps are the perspectives from which we approach the overall act of accent. Any one of them is insufficient, in and of itself, to provide the whole experience we hope to create. It's only when you put all the perspectives together that you end up with something you'd actually enjoy performing and sharing with others.

DOI: 10.4324/9781003314905-4

The Filters from Module Two are *philosophical* and *social* views of accent as a whole, allowing us to understand how accents work within the larger tableau of human interactions. The Four Ps are *practical* perspectives, breaking down the process of performance and creating a framework for skills that lead to the authentic embodiment of accents in acting.

An analogy might help. Let's say you want to bake a cake. In a previous era, you'd only have a recipe to work with, written by someone else and relying upon whatever pre-existing culinary skills you already had. Nowadays, however, you can look up instructional videos online, browse message boards for advice, and comb through food blogs (if you're patient) to gain additional insight. By taking multiple perspectives on the experience of making the cake, you bring more depth and richness to it – and more flavor and artistry to the end result! Ultimately, only your actions make the cake a reality, as you assemble and synthesize the perspectives you gather.

Of course, you may ask why it's worth going to all that trouble when you could just follow the recipe – for a cake or an accent. Why bother with multiple perspectives when you can buy an accent guide, add audio, and stir?

With accents, the utility of a prepackaged formula quickly wears off. If you follow a step-by-step checklist for an accent, or if you just listen intently to a sample, over and over again, hoping to pick up the general "feeling" of the accent, you may get something serviceable that works for an audition or a few lines in a script. As soon as your lines change, however, or you find yourself auditioning for another role, or you realize that something sounds off and you need to make an adjustment . . . you'd be back at square one, repeating your previous technique and hoping it yields different results. In the end, a recipe or listen-and-hope approach to accent is most likely to be a pattern lacking in robustness; it's prone to becoming reductive or stereotypical, incapable of stirring up the full richness and flavor of a living, breathing, thinking, feeling accent. For that, you need more perspectives – and the adaptable skills to pull it all together.

The Four Ps aren't a recipe, and they aren't a checklist. They *expand* your opportunities for growth in performance, rather than reducing accentwork to a list of extraneous tasks. Let's examine them one by one and see what they each contribute as part of the holistic experience of acting in accent.

People

Any time you step into an accent, it comes from someone – or someones. The accent you investigate may come from real people, past or present, with sociocultural structures, patterns of belonging, and historical evolution that all play a role in the way they speak. The accent you pursue could also come from fictional people, characters who respond to the communicative needs of the writer, director, and design teams. Even the most fantastical of fictional accents, however, is highly likely to draw from real-world influences, so the distinction between the speech of "real people" and "fictional characters" requires sensitive calibration in accentwork.

Our goal when exploring *People* is to investigate, dig into, and *build empathy with* the speakers of our target accent. While another name for this aspect of accentwork might be *cultural context*, we want to emphasize the point well worth remembering throughout all our work: accents come from *people*. Accents come from human beings with emotions, dreams, fears, loves, insecurities, joys, and deep connection to their circumstances. When we spend time getting to know the people who live in our target accents, we not only get closer to understanding the forces that mold that accent, but we also create a sense of trust, respect, and nuance in our work. When we seek to understand an accent from the People perspective, stereotype, mockery, and reductionism are far less likely to ensnare us.

Another beneficial side effect of People is that we also *become aware of biases*. As we've mentioned before in *Speaking with Skill* and *Experiencing Speech*, we all have biases. In fact, our biases are often useful and energy-saving cognitive shortcuts, helping us process an abundance of information in the world around us. But when biases outlive their usefulness or extend beyond their initial applications, they may become detrimental or inhibitory to our learning process. Taking time to explore People in a personal and subjective manner allows us to acknowledge the biases inside and around us, ask which are actually beneficial for us, and let go of and forgive those that are unhelpful.

Prosody

Prosody describes the musicality of accents. It's the perspective from which we can view features like pitch, volume, duration, tempo, pauses, rhythm, and vocal quality, which exist in every part of our speech without being bound to the exact words we use. Prosody covers both what we can describe in the musicality of language and the purposes it serves in communication.

Prosody's two Greek roots are *pros-* ("to, toward, through") and *oide* ("song"), yielding *prosoidia*: that which comes "through song." If we translate those Greek roots to Latin, we get *ad* ("to") and *cantus* ("song"), which combine to form *accentus* – accent! So not only is Prosody an essential perspective on accent . . . it gave us the word we use today!

Despite the etymological head start Prosody has on the other Ps, linguistics is still grappling with how to contextualize and understand it in world languages. Linguists have formulated versatile systems for describing prosodic patterns, and modern technology has made recording, playback, and acoustic analysis more accessible than at any point in human history. But even with technological advances, we're still looking for terms, concepts, and descriptors that will allow us to efficiently and accurately describe the musicality of speech we hear in the world. Our approach to Prosody mirrors that of the other Ps: laying out skills, listening with care, and finding patterns.

Posture

The idea of *Posture* is one that Dudley Knight and Philip Thompson arrived at synchronously as they were pioneering this work in the late twentieth century. Mentioned briefly by Beatrice Honikman in 1964, "posture" remains relatively unexplored in linguistics. Since that time, KTS has independently developed a *practice* of Posture that provides a vital perspective from which to experience accent.

Variably called "oral posture" or "vocal tract posture" (VTP), Posture describes the physical alignment, tendencies, and movement patterns of the articulators in the production of speech. Posture both forms and is formed by accent. If we grow up hearing certain speech sounds around us and responding in kind, we begin to acclimate our muscles to actions that become habits. Those habits shape our vocal tract to find associated speech sounds more easily, while unused articulatory actions usually fall away.

Posture is a reflection of the process by which humans learn language, developing physical habits for the ease of effective communication. When we examine a target accent from the perspective of Posture, we get curious about the embodied "home base" of the accent, the relative positions of the articulators that make the accent possible. At the same time, Posture isn't static – our articulators need to *move* to communicate, so action patterns are also a key part of Posture. Using Posture, we build on the physical skills of speech (see *Experiencing Speech*) to "listen with our mouths," assembling an embodied sense of what it means to inhabit the vocal tract actions of another person.

Pronunciation

Even with a firm grasp of Posture, an intricate ear for Prosody, and a heartfelt connection to People, our realization of an accent would be incomplete if we didn't incorporate *Pronunciation*. If we deviate from the sounds a listener expects to hear in just a few words, we can quickly lose any sense of believability on the part of our audience . . . and ourselves.

Pronunciation focuses on the patterns of sound realizations in words. Our brains are so finely tuned to patterns that we sense which sounds to anticipate in which words, often unconsciously; even if we don't know the exact sound to expect, we usually know what *doesn't* belong when we hear it. Many approaches to accentwork often view accents *solely* through Pronunciation: "Figure out how to say each word in the accent, and you're set!" That outlook, however, tends to miss (or be frustrated by) the essential, expressive potential of musicality, physicality, and circumstances.

From our perspective on Pronunciation, we'll look at how we create patterns out of sounds and words through the lenses of *phones, phonemes,* and *categorization,* with particularly profound gratitude to the work of J.C. Wells. Wells's approach reveals how the historical evolution of words (in English) can streamline and expedite the process of recognizing sound patterns throughout and between accents. Pronunciation takes advantage of our pattern-seeking brains to efficiently group words by sounds while leaving room for all the idiosyncratic variations that occur with real people in the real world.

Put Them Together: The Four Ps

We hope it's obvious by now that each of the Ps – People, Prosody, Posture, and Pronunciation – is equally present and essential for every accent you consider. What's more, the skills you build by embodying one accent will transfer to the next one you work on, growing your proficiency over time. The goal of this text is not to develop "a good accent" or even "a couple good accents" – we want to give you the tools to develop *as many authentic, believable, and embodied accents as you care to learn.*

In subsequent modules, we'll be zooming in on the Ps, giving you time and experience with each. No matter how tight our focus, though, remember that accent isn't complete without the zoomed-out experience of all four Ps operating at once. People influences Posture which influences Pronunciation which influences People which influences Prosody which influences Posture which . . . and so on, *ad infinitum.* As you explore the individual Ps, we'll give you a sense of their interactions along the way.

And sometimes it's hard to ignore the other Ps. You may be listening for Posture and get pulled into Pronunciation, or you might want to learn more about People *but that PROSODY!* Again, your attentional super-powers come to your aid, helping you keep your focus tight on the questions at hand, even as you acknowledge the presence of another persistent P. Keeping your ability to zoom in and zoom out flexible, you can jump between and among Ps with ease and a sense of direction, organizing your perceptions around a framework that transcends any one accent.

Remember: The Other Ps

When it comes to the way we approach accentwork, the Four Ps will be our main focus and the bulk of the next eight modules.

Ultimately, however, our goal is to bring the Four Ps together into the P that integrates all of them: *Performance.* We're looking for a sense of flow in our accentwork, and the subtle contours of that experience are made approachable through People, Prosody, Posture, and Pronunciation. In a way, the Four Ps are **handholds** for maneuvering your way into flow, specific access points you can grasp to support your immersion in the lived experience of an accent.

Other Ps emerge as well from the practicality of our accentwork: *Personalization, Play,* and *Practice.* We'll explore these additional Ps more specifically in Modules Thirteen through Fifteen, but they'll come up again and again as we explore the Four Ps individually.

Also, as you see these terms in the coming pages, please know that we never intended to alliterate this much – it just happened. Promise!

Check It Out!

Now would be a great time to revisit *Experiencing Speech*, particularly the first four modules. We're about to play with activities from that previous book, so have it nearby if you find you could use some review.

Now that we've described our procedural tools, let's throw everything aside and *Play*.

Exercise 3.1: Playful Possibilities

Begin by *gurning* – you remember, the serious art of making silly faces. Move every muscle in and around your vocal tract. Breathe as you do this.

Think about this activity as resetting your Posture, pushing yourself away from the habits that define your everyday vocal tract posture. As you shift through muscular possibilities, let your gurning become **phthonging** by allowing voice to move through your gurns. For now, focus your articulators on *shaping* the flow of sound (not obstructing). Let the physical actions of your articulators lead – the sound is something you'll notice as an aftereffect of your gurning motions.

Gurn and phthong with your classmates. Start developing a personal connection to these other silly faces. *Let your facial expressions lead*, and use the resulting phthongs to say, "Hello," or, "How are you?" or, "What the heck is *that*!?" Respond to other gurns as they're addressed to you.

Bring your attention back to your own phthonging. Take some time, by yourself, to open up the Prosody (musicality) of your vocal production. Explore pitch variation and volume variation. Notice how the shifts around your larynx create different vocal qualities. Change the amount of time you spend in different gurns to play with duration. Alter the tempo. Explore pauses in your phonation (voicing), perhaps even creating rhythmic patterns in your phthonging. See how wide and open you can make your exploration of Prosodic possibilities, even as you continue to open up your Postural range.

Use your Prosodic and Postural variety – phthonging with lots of musical variation – to communicate with your classmates. How much *can* you communicate using Prosodic and Postural variety? Notice if you fall back into familiar patterns, such as familiar phthongs born of a habitual Posture, or Prosodic patterns that resemble phrases you know. Is it possible to communicate with your peers *without* using the familiar? What do you gain by tapping into the familiar again?

Bring your attention back to your personal Prosodic and Postural exploration. Now add **obstruents** to your flow of phthonging – in fact, add as much obstructive variety as you possibly can. Incorporate as many different phthongs as you can in that mix. You're speaking Omnish! Recall your previous experiences with phonetics – can you include non-pulmonic obstruents? central vowels? lateral approximants? co-articulations? every manner of obstruction? every place of articulation?

Building on your variety in Posture and Prosody, Omnish can reset your Pronunciation patterns. Omnish challenges you to use sounds you never use in places you never use them, without any sort of predictability or patterning at all. Omnish is maximally chaotic Pronunciation, rich in expressive potential. How can you use Omnish as an opportunity to shake up any associations you have in your daily Pronunciation? Can you keep Postural and Prosodic variety alive even as you expand your Pronunciation options?

Use this version of Omnish to converse with your classmates. Discuss the weather, your favorite current dance trend, or your preferred method of cake-glazing. Can you meaningfully communicate with others using this Omnish? Is it possible to keep Posture, Prosody, and Pronunciation as varied as possible? What makes variety fall away?

After some experimentation with maximal variety in Omnish communication, you can begin to relax your Prosodic, Postural, and Pronunciation innovation. Let yourself follow the sounds you hear around you. As you converse with your classmates, allow yourself to incorporate the sounds and shapes you receive from them. You can repeat phrases you hear, or you can relay an Omnish word or phrase from one person to another. Make sure you talk to everybody in the group.

Notice if your attention to the group's sounds has shifted your Omnish. Has your work with your class shifted your Posture? your Prosodic options? your range of Pronunciation? At this point, you may collaboratively arrive at a **Somenish** (you're no longer making all possible sounds, just *some* of them). Are these possibilities a result of the Posture, Prosody, and Pronunciation you absorbed? Or did the Somenish give rise to a Posture, Prosody, and Pronunciation?

Let's take one final step and name this Somenish . . . in Somenish, of course. (This is what linguists call an *endonym* – look it up!) Figure out a method for choosing a name for your group Somenish. No doubt, the process will be chaotic at first, since Somenish is always only somewhat organized. But as a semblance of order emerges, you'll collectively figure out a way to find a name, agree on it, and have everyone in the group repeat it at least once. Once that occurs, celebrate with a somewhat joyous cheer and express some gratitude to all.

That last step was an experience of People, because you both created and discovered a cultural context that influenced your Prosody, Posture, and Pronunciation. In truth, you were exploring People throughout the exercise, as you communicated with others, discovered successful strategies for relating, and felt the pull of familiar patterns arising from your own unique history. While Omnish and Somenish don't give the same experience of the Four Ps that an accent of an actual language does, notice how your need to communicate reveals your pre-existing familiarity with and reliance upon Prosody, Posture, Pronunciation, and People.

Note as well that working through the Four Ps produced experiences that were both individual and communal. In each perspective of accent, we'll find experiences that seem like they belong solely to the individual, like unique vocal resonances in Prosody or personal articulatory anatomy in Posture or idiosyncratic word choice in Pronunciation. At the same time, each of the Four Ps can help us identify patterns in speech shared by more than one person. Rather than limiting our observations to the description of idiolects, we can use the Four Ps to find the commonalities that unite groups of people through the features of their speech.

End of Part One Skills Celebration

Review your notes – at this point, they may be full to bursting with observations, digressions, unanswered questions, and objections. Now that we've built a cultural context with our five Filters and laid out a practical framework through the Four Ps, reflect on how your previous thoughts on accent have been challenged, reaffirmed, or changed by our work thus far.

Prepare a brief presentation (2–3 minutes) on your progress through accentwork up to this point. Where did you start? What's shifted? What do you hope to learn next? Is there anything in particular (the Four Ps, the Filters, an exercise) that gets you particularly excited? Is there anything that makes you anxious about the work ahead?

Use any form of presentation that feels most communicative to you. Speak it, move it, draw it, paint it, dance it, reenact it, sing it, or all the above. Give yourself – your full, embodied self – a chance to digest the knowledge of Part One and share it with your peers.

Then notice what your classmates share in turn. Where do their trajectories align with yours? Where are there differences? How could you collaborate in the journey ahead?

Projecting Ahead

The Four Ps set out the roadmap we intend to follow for the rest of this book. These perspectives on accent may make sense in the abstract, but as we zoom in, we'll find it beneficial to have a focus for our efforts going forward, so that you can see them all coming together, one P at a time. To that end, we suggest you find, acquire, or get assigned a *Big Accent Project (BAP)* (pronounced /bæp/).

Your BAP is an accent you'll develop, for performance, through each of the subsequent modules in this book. You'll apply the lessons from each module to your BAP as you progress, adding nuance and depth to the same accent over time. Your BAP could be an accent you need to develop for a production. Your BAP could be an accent your instructor has chosen to develop through classroom practice and participation. Your BAP could also be an accent you'd like to develop for your own personal repertoire – check out our note on *Appropriateness* in Module Four (page 58) if you're choosing your own project.

Ultimately, your Big Accent Project will gather together your insights and skills as you work through this book. We'll highlight those places in the text where you can apply your progress to your BAP, culminating with an Accent Celebration in Module Thirteen. It's our hope (as authors) that this investigation is richly rewarding and deeply practical for your work as an actor. You could, of course, repeat this process with *multiple* BAPs, though we definitely recommend pursuing one BAP at a time to minimize confusion.

Now, with our path laid out and a project in mind, let's dive in.

PART II
EXPLORING THE FOUR PS

MODULE FOUR

PEOPLE – ASKING QUESTIONS

We want to say this up front: People is the most important of the Four Ps.

Prosody, Posture, and Pronunciation are essential for exploring accent. But without sensitive care for and a deep understanding of the people who have accents, the entire endeavor of accentwork becomes shallow imitation at best and hurtful mockery at worst. A focus on People is the key to keeping our work vibrantly and compassionately human.

By concentrating on People, you come to understand the *given circumstances* of an accent, both in the world and in your art. Your goal is to skillfully embody the speech actions and patterns of a complete person, just as you aim to step into the clothes they wear, the words they speak, and the relationships they inhabit. And as with these other circumstances, scripts may contain information about accents, drawing inspiration from real people, real cultures, and real communities. Your focus as an actor – and, indeed, the focus of our work with People – is on bridging real-world knowledge with the needs of the story.

Another term we commonly use for the work around People is "cultural context." Unpacking "cultural context" gives us a good starting point for our approach to understanding people and their accents.

DOI: 10.4324/9781003314905-6

Culture and Context

"Culture" is as complex and multilayered a term as "language." Were we to try to define it, we'd need to draw upon anthropology, sociology, evolutionary biology, history, literature, and the arts – all of which lay outside the scope of our current efforts.

Instead, let's summon up our descriptions of "language" from Module One so we can understand "culture" in a similar way. If we modify our descriptions from page 8, we have:

A. *Culture* is something all human beings participate in. It's _everything_ we generate as a social species, individually or collectively, and all the meaning that comes along with it. If this sounds broad, that's because it is! Everything from fire-making to agriculture to social media is evidence of human culture. It is the stuff we do and make and think and say, as well as the meanings that are communicated by all that stuff.

B. *A culture* is a *specific collection* of artifacts, practices, and beliefs shared by a group of people. Examples include "Harappan culture" or "Late Incan culture" or "1990s Seattle grunge."

At the broadest level (A), culture takes into account most of what human beings do (including language). We can also zoom in and define culture more narrowly (B), according to parameters of belonging defined by a specific group of people. Our work with People keeps the focus tight on Description B as we seek to understand the way accents fit into the specific cultures in which they arise.

However, there's another common usage of "culture" that you've probably encountered. Some people may narrowly define "culture" as "*high* culture"; that is, as the culture shared by a group of people associated with high levels of prestige. When you stumble upon this erroneous description, you may hear things like, "Opera is so much more cultured than musical theatre," or, "Traditional kabuki is culture, anime is for mass consumption." This verbiage can also be applied to accents, claiming certain accents are "cultured" while others aren't.

This description is, of course, far too simplistic to be of use to us. It limits our ability to find depth in our work by reducing "culture" to only one (in this case, elitist and myopic) subset of expressions and practices. Rather than being restricted to one definition of culture, we cast a wide net and discover which aspects of culture are most important for the people we investigate.

Check It Out!

There's more to read on cultural history, theory, critique, and diversity than we can begin to recommend. Instead, we'll suggest a few key search terms to get you started: biocultural evolution; epigenetics; dual inheritance theory; engaged theory; cultural theory; structuralism; Stephen Gould; Charles Darwin; Trabian Shorters.

"Context" has a delightfully tactile etymology. The Latin root *texere* ("to weave") also gives us "text," "textile," and "texture," while *con-* indicates "together" or "with." "Context" is thus that which is "woven together," the fabric from which patterns emerge and through which important details can be revealed. When we dig into an accent, we want to understand how it's interlaced with the culture that informs and supports it, a distinct thread running through a whole cloth.

A deeper understanding of how an accent in the script connects to its context in the world allows you, as the bridge between them, to enrich your acting with nuance, detail, and creativity. Still, not every bit of culture you discover will be relevant, and you'll want to build efficiency in choosing which cultural threads to pull in your exploration. Allow your work with People to spark your curiosity and engage your empathy. Then coordinate with the needs of the performance to identify what deserves extra attention in your context-building and what you can trim away.

Exercise 4.1: Cultural Context Conversation

Find a partner and a space where you can converse with relative privacy.

One of you will be a Researcher and one of you will be a Source. Decide who will start in each role.

Researcher, your goal is to gather as much information as you can about the cultural context of your Source, as pertains to accent, so you can share that information with the class. We suggest you take about 15 minutes. You will *definitely* want to take notes!

Use these questions as a starting point for your investigation:

1. How would you describe the language/accent environment you grew up in? (Consider geography, language, culture, class, home, school, and any other significant influences.)
2. Did your language environment change along the way? If so, at what ages?
3. How do you think your accent is perceived by others? Has awareness of that changed the way you speak?
4. What are three to five things that you would like the people in this room to know about your accent and its connection to how you move in the world?
5. What do you need/want from the people in this room to understand about your accent and your relationship to it?

When time's up, Researcher, read through your notes and clarify any uncertainties with your Source. Great! Now Researcher and Source switch roles and repeat the process.

Now it's time to present your findings to the class. You'll take turns sharing your discoveries about your Source's cultural context, one by one. We're going to add two more parameters, however:

1. Limit your sharing to no more than *2 minutes*.
2. Share your research about your Source *in the first person*. That is, narrate your discoveries using "I," "me," and "my," *as though you were speaking as your Source*. One caveat: you are *not* trying to embody their accent. Speak in *your* accent as you offer *their* cultural context in the first person.

We acknowledge that this second prompt may have surprised you! You didn't know you were going to have to speak as your Source in the first person! Feel the weight of that. Breathe for a moment. Then, take the time you need to prepare by reviewing your notes – we recommend three to five minutes of prep. For now, avoid consulting further with your Source.

Then share! Volunteer when you feel the impulse to share. It usually helps to have partners share together, so if one partner volunteers, have the other partner reciprocate by going next.

After everyone in the group shares, discuss what you learned from this experience. What did you discover was important about your Source's cultural context? What was it like to step into the first person to share your findings? What was it like to hear someone else speak from your cultural context? Write down your reflections.

Building Empathy

Stepping into the cultural context of another person is an invitation to build empathy with their point of view. "Empathy" comes from the Greek *em-* "in" and *pathos* "passion, state of emotion," and it refers to the ability to "feel into" a situation, to put yourself into a set of circumstances and imagine what it would feel like to be there. This skill may already be familiar to you as an actor.

The questions in Exercise 4.1 are an invitation to enter into a deep communication with another person on charged topics – like acting, belonging, and evolution. We invited you to see what it was like to take care of the answers your Source provided. It's one thing to know what your Source says they think and feel and understand; it's another thing entirely to think and feel and understand those words as you would your own.

When it comes to accentwork for performance, we want to be similarly open to an empathetic experience of the people who gift us their accents. The care that you took in preparing to share the stories of a person only a few feet away is the same care you want to take in all your investigation and embodiment around accent. If you boil an accent down to "mere" sounds (Pronunciation) or a "simple" melody (Prosody), you risk thinking of the people behind that accent as "mere" or "simple." But those people have the same depth of experience, the same complex feelings and thoughts, the same range of hopes and dreams and fears as your Source did in Exercise 4.1. Remember what it felt like to be entrusted with the life stories of your Source and to entrust your story to someone else. That's what you'll be discovering every time you investigate People in your accentwork.

Another way we think about this empathy-building skill is to imagine that the sources of your accentwork are *always in the room with you* when you speak about cultural context. What would it be like to have your sources sitting beside you? Would they think you're really hearing what they have to say? How could you frame your explorations in ways that honor them as human beings, with all the complexities and contradictions that entails?

Remember that accent is a survival skill, and it matters in a primal way to all of us (see page 54). Working from empathy won't eliminate the energetic charge – be it fear, anxiety, or excitement – that arises from the interactions of accent and belonging. However, our capacity for empathy can direct that energy away from bracing, blocking, or defending and toward connection, communication, and understanding.

This aspect of empathy is particularly helpful when it comes to potential embarrassment, guilt, or shame when trying on someone else's accent. These stifling emotional defenses can be rooted in our sense of not-belonging, of not being right, of being "found out" – and they can be easily triggered when we're in the early stages of testing out a new skill. If you take time to build empathy with your sources – and yourself! – then you can enter into early learning with more ease and a sense of earned safety. Rather than hold back for fear of mocking your sources, or blaming yourself for messing up the gift they gave you, you'll know that you're attempting, adjusting, and learning from a place of respect.

Awareness of Bias

"Bias" comes to us from Middle French *biais* "oblique line," via Greek and Provençal (what an oblique etymology!). A bias is a slant, a path of least resistance taken when navigating a set of facts or judgments. Biases are made for efficiency. Biases reduce the demands on our brain's processing power by pre-consciously recognizing and extending patterns, so that we can work quickly and effectively in our decision-making. Many biases can be helpful: having a preconception of what will happen if you let go of a Faberge egg over a tile floor helps you avoid an *extremely* costly mistake. But biases that slant you toward old patterns in the face of new and potentially transformative information are less helpful and may even be harmful, to yourself and others.

Biases in general aren't "good" or "bad" – they're shortcuts used for helpful or not-so-helpful ends. We may call "good" biases "values" and "bad" biases "judgments"; in either case, we're finding a quick way to sort through the wealth of information that confronts us from moment to moment. We may find that some biases are *good for* certain contexts, though those same biases could be *bad for* other contexts. Importantly, however, many of our biases kick in below the level of conscious awareness, coming to our aid before we even have a chance to question their usefulness.

Unexamined bias is dangerous in accentwork – it risks undermining a listener's empathy for the humanity and complexity of a speaker, with a parallel reduction in the ability to understand and embody that speaker's accent. Biases about accents also contribute to larger-scale, societal patterns of inequity. All we need to work with and through biases is a little imagination. Whenever you encounter a bias, in yourself or in others, wonder what might make you feel that way. What assumptions, narratives, and personal experiences can you imagine that seem to lead to that mental shortcut? What alternative biases could you imagine that might relate to the exact same set of circumstances – and how would they come about?

In this process, you may also encounter a familiar theme: **prestige** (see page 31). The features of accent that we value, the narratives we employ to justify them, and the relationships we create to our sources can all interact with the perceived hierarchies of prestige. Take note if phrasings like, "That's not how English *should* be spoken," or, "That's not correct," or, "I trust it more because it's folksier," pop up in your examination of bias. Comparison to a standard – intentional or not – is a sure sign that a *prestige-based bias* is at play. Give yourself a reliable safety net by always converting "good" and "bad" (and all their variations) into "good for" and "bad for." This subtle shift in phrasing can move you away from implicit value judgments and toward context-based judgments of utility.

Exercise 4.2: Bias Workshop

Let's take time now to examine a few biases. Get together again with your partner from Exercise 4.1. Bring along your notes, too.

You're going to revisit your initial Cultural Context Conversations. We suggest giving each partner 10 minutes to discuss their experience as a Source while the Researcher listens.

As a Source, what biases arose in your responses to your Researcher? These could include biases you have about your accent, biases you have about other people's accents, or biases other people have about your accent. Remember that biases aren't intrinsically bad or good – there may be biases about your accent that you enjoy as well as ones that you find unenjoyable or even harmful. And note that you may be aware of biases around accent that you don't want to talk about – you get to manage what you share!

As a Researcher, listen with empathy to your Source. Take notes on the biases your Source mentions – and respect their right to manage their experience if they ask you not to write something down. Ask questions if you're not sure what they mean or if you need more context to understand the biases they mention. While listening, don't offer a "fix" or sympathy or your own experiences – just help them collect their reflections. This can take diligent focus on your part, but your role here is to offer a space where your Source can speak from their own experience.

After both partners have revisited their experience as Sources, look at the lists of biases the Researchers collected. As a Source, pick three of the biases you mentioned that you'd like to workshop in order to share with the class. Work with your partner to examine each bias. What beliefs, assumptions, narratives, and personal experiences might give rise to them? Can you imagine alternatives to these biases? Both partners should collaborate, so that each bias gets the benefit of two generous and compassionate imaginations.

Then, share your re-examined biases and their cultural context with the class. Notice how your classmates approached this task. What sorts of biases came up? How were they expressed? What was it like to take time to notice and examine biases in your understanding of your own accent? How could these skills come in handy for your future accentwork?

What's in a Context?

You've taken time to get to know a classmate. You've asked them some questions about language and accent, built some empathy, and maybe encountered a bias or two (or twelve).

But how does this relate to the accents you'll need for performance? How do you get the contextual information you need for an accent you hope to act in?

The approach isn't all that different, really . . .

 Web Resource 4.1 How To Collect an Accent Sample

Navigate to **Web Resource 4.1** to find a document titled **"How to Collect an Accent Sample."** Read through it – and download it for future reference!

Some of the questions in that document may look familiar – you've already encountered them in the previous exercises. But there are a lot of other questions you could possibly ask, all of which are aimed at fostering as detailed an investigation as possible.

We'd like to call attention to three important points from this Web Resource:

1. Biographical information is important to collect, and questions that circle around language and accent experience are especially useful. They help you create context for understanding where, when, how, and with whom the influences on an accent developed.
2. Asking questions beyond accent-related topics might lead sources to open up and find ease in expressing themselves.
3. We refer to people who share with us as our accent "Donors." Much as a philanthropist gives their time and resources for the betterment of society, your Donors grant you the gift of their voice, identity, culture, and accent for *your* betterment. Keep this generosity in mind in all your interactions with your Donors' gifts – and let them know how much you appreciate them!

While the process outlined in "How to Collect an Accent Sample" may seem technical, its overarching purpose is to engage a Donor in conversation. That's it – just get 'em talking. You want to establish a human connection and develop the empathy and bias awareness necessary to take responsibility for this sample in future accentwork.

So let's do it.

Exercise 4.3: Collect an Accent Sample

This exercise is designed to be a homework assignment. The point is to practice your People skills through primary source investigation. You may want to use this sample again for future exercises in this book and eventual performance.

Find a person, any person, who speaks with an accent you'd like to investigate – including the target of your Big Accent Project. Their accent should be one you can *appropriately* embody. Wait, what does that mean?

Appropriateness

We're using "appropriate" here as an adjective, but its relationship to the identically spelled verb is useful. "To appropriate" something is to make it one's own (Latin *ad-* "to" + *proprius* "one's own") – therefore, something that's "appropriate" for you is something you could make your own. We're in the territory of belonging and identity. When it comes to accent, ask, "Could this accent belong to me? Could I belong to it?" We're not asking you to put a limit on your artistic aspirations, but we *are* asking you to carefully and empathetically ask if a particular accent falls within your networks of belonging *before* you embody it. Bear in mind that systemic biases make it less acceptable for more privileged groups to appropriate the accents and culture of groups with less privilege. If you have any doubts about the appropriateness of an accent for your use in performance, reach out to a trusted coach or teacher before starting your preparation. You could also bring questions of appropriateness to your class – a conversation with evidence and well-reasoned support might be a way to build a classroom agreement about which accents are appropriate for your mutual learning environment.

Take care with this step in your accent-learning process. One of your primary goals is to make an accent your own – to *appropriate* it. By taking time to clarify what you can and cannot claim as your own, you learn how to avoid *mis*appropriation and communicate clear boundaries in your art.

Once you've identified the person whose accent you'd like to investi-gate, arrange a time to speak with them, following the protocol in "How to Collect an Accent Sample." You can meet in person, by phone, or by video – we recommend the latter, since having a visual recording of your conversation could prove helpful later. Follow the document's recom-mendations for recording sound, and make sure to send the sample pas-sages to your Donor before the conversation takes place.

Check-In

What did you learn about gathering information on People through Exercise 4.3? Were you able to build empathy through your investigation? If so, how did it register in you? Did working from empathy change the type of information you found interesting as you conversed with your Donor?

What information did you consider important to gather? What did your Donor find important to say? Did you become aware of any of your biases around accent that you wanted to shift? Did your Donor reveal any of *their* biases around accent that might be useful for performance?

Condense your experiences in Exercise 4.3 to a brief summary that you can read or perform. For example, a half-page of writing, one minute of audio or video, or a two-minute self-written scene. How would you summarize your investigation in, at most, 250 words?

Conclusion

Your work with People in this module has been centered on individuals, both yourself and your Donors. You've taken time to expand your empa-thetic awareness and to notice how biases may affect your perceptions. You'll continue to hone these skills over a lifetime of experience.

Accents don't emerge solely from individuals, however. Our perfor-mances often ask us to capture accents that transcend the idiolect of just one person. Whether we're prompted by information in the script, a blurb from a casting director, or requests from the production team, we're frequently asked to embody something that comes from a *larger* scale of accent. With all this time spent on just one person's accent and cultural context, how do we widen our focus without getting lost in a mass of information?

In Module Five, we'll zoom out and do some research.

MODULE FIVE
PEOPLE – DOING RESEARCH

We have a lot to juggle when it comes to stepping into the accent of another human being. Yes, we need to take account of our personal biases and maintain an empathetic connection to our Donors. But we also need to remain aware of the demands of the script, the expectations of our audiences, and the technical requirements of the medium (theatre? film? animation?) in which we're working.

On page 16, we applied the Acting Filter to consider how accent exists *in the world*, *in the self*, and *in performance*. Module Four focused primarily on your relationship to accent in the self – that is, in you. The next step in our work with People is to build more understanding of an accent as it exists in the world and in performance. Beyond empathizing with a single Donor, you also need to identify the group of people who speak with a particular accent, what it says about their culture, and what it signals to listeners inside and outside that culture. You'll also want to investigate the significance of the accent in performance – what story does the accent tell about a character's geographical, cultural, and social origins and aspirations, in relation to the other characters and the rest of the production?

To answer these questions, we'll engage in a type of research, a practical process of gathering information, asking questions, and testing hypotheses. As opposed to the first-person perspective your Donor offered in

DOI: 10.4324/9781003314905-7

Module Four, continued investigation of accent in the world may feel more removed, more analytical, or more declarative by nature. It may be tempting to call these different approaches "subjective" and "objective," but we'd like to offer another way of looking at them.

Emic and Etic

The linguist Kenneth Pike coined the terms **emic** (/ˈimɪk/) and **etic** (/ˈɛtɪk/) in 1954. He recognized that the distinction between *phonemics* and *phonetics* in language (which we'll re-encounter later) could also describe distinctions in other avenues of research, including sociology and ethnography. *Emic* research aims to understand its human subjects from *inside* their culture, prioritizing their point of view and values. By contrast, *etic* research studies its subjects from the point of view of the researcher, according to values and priorities from *outside* the culture. Both emic and etic understanding are needed, in conversation with each other, in order to understand cultural phenomena. Accent is no exception.

Check It Out!

We can only provide a taste of how these terms intersect with accent-work. You could also look for information related to the following: cultural anthropology; field research; ethnography; Kenneth Pike; jargon; argot.

In Module Four, you engaged in emic People research. By eliciting your Donors' narratives, you were empathetically figuring out what's important *from inside their experience.* One way to arrive at a wider understanding of People would be to conduct an enormous amount of emic research, gathering firsthand accounts about an accent from every perspective imaginable. It goes without saying, however, that doing that much work would be prohibitive for any actor, even under the most generous of extenuating circumstances.

Etic research and viewpoints accelerate our understanding of People in the world and in performance. By standing outside the context in which an accent occurs, etic research can identify tendencies, habits, and patterns that might take an insider years to notice – if they notice them at all. As actors, we can gratefully take advantage of the scrupulous work of experts in many fields without having to reinvent cultural context from scratch every time we perform.

Remember, though, that both emic *and* etic research are subjective, arising from personal worldviews, whether those of insiders or outsiders. Even the most rigorous scientists still approach their subjects from personal life experiences, which makes the questions they ask and techniques they use uniquely their own. As actors, our best bet is to embrace the subjectivity in our sources and – you guessed it – *remain aware of biases.*

Prestige ... Again

Emic-etic understanding also helps explain additional aspects of a powerful bias we've encountered before: prestige. As power and privilege accumulate to certain groups of people, their accents tend to become associated with **overt prestige**. This power imbalance can create a hierarchical relationship among accents, with overtly prestigious accents at the top. These accents are held up as the way the language "should" be, reinforced through standardization and social structures. Hierarchy is often propped up by **stigma**, the marking of specific speech actions as inferior, distasteful, or shameful. From the etic perspective, overt prestige gets encoded in cultural artifacts like dictionaries and school curricula; from the emic perspective, the hierarchy of prestige comes to be felt intuitively by individuals.

Yet a hierarchy of accent prestige also creates the possibility for **covert prestige** – that is, situations in which speakers prefer to use stigmatized or "inferior" speech features. Usually called upon in informal, conversational, and peer-group settings, covert prestige is another way to express belonging. It subverts the expectations of overt prestige and requires an emic understanding of societal norms and when to defy them.

Watch for the subtle interplay of emic and etic understanding when it comes to dealing with prestige. As you investigate emic sources, you may encounter phrases like, "I improved my accent," or, "She speaks better now than she used to," which reveal a hierarchy built into how speakers perceive themselves in relation to overarching power structures. But even etic sources can bring biased, prestige-based framing to their interpretations, especially through the implicit or unquestioned acceptance of standards and the social frameworks that buttress them.

Stick to the Script

As an actor, much of your performance starts with the script. The script provides your given circumstances, through dialogue, actions, and descriptions. You can also look to the script to guide you in your research for accentwork; it may specify an accent directly, and it might also give information that helps you assemble an accent's cultural context. Your first readings of the script lay out a path you can follow in seeking out emic sources and etic references.

Some clues to look for in the script include the following:

- Geographical location – Where does the story take place?
- Geographical origin – Where do the characters originally come from?
- Profession – Where do they work? What do they do for a living?
- Gender identities – How do characters see themselves? How do others see them?
- Time period – When does the story take place?
- Character age – In what time period did characters grow up?
- Languages other than English – Are they present in the script? Do characters mention them? Do we think that any characters speak other languages, even if they only speak English in the script? Is the audience meant to assume that the characters are speaking another language but that we somehow hear it as English?
- English acquisition – When did characters learn English? From birth? If later, when?
- Prestige (overt/covert) – Are there any hints as to the structures of overt or covert prestige in the world of the play? Do characters say or imply any value judgments about the speech of others?
- Dialect information (lexicon, grammar, etc.) – Does the vocabulary or grammar of the dialogue indicate a dialect that differs from your own? or from the dialects of other characters?

Sometimes the script leaves a lot of this work to us as actors. For example, we may know the story's location, but we don't have any information on where the characters originally came from. Or we see grammatical choices that seem to indicate that the writer expects the character to have a dialect, but we don't get any other hints to tell us what to look into.

Or how about this one: the script simply says a character is "from the city," which evokes for the writer a detailed, multi-layered context in its own (emic) way. To an outsider, though, this information feels insufficient or perhaps even useless. It's up to the actor – you! – to turn this description into circumstances that are specific, evocative, and, most importantly, aligned with what you know about accents in the world. These skills are especially important for auditioning, when casting breakdowns are often broad, unhelpfully simple, or inaccurate.

Building your knowledge and skills in the People perspective allows you to fill in the gaps between the script and the world. This practice supports a level of "cultural competence," a capability to recognize, relate to, and operate within a wide range of cultural contexts while also developing greater sensitivity to what you may appropriate and what you may not.

Exercise 5.1: Some Very Serious Research

Go back to page 63 and review the list of clues to look for in a script. Make sure you have something to take notes with as well – feel free to use a Professional Research Clipboard to make it official.

Choose a character in a play or film that you know really well. Feel free to reread the script or rewatch the movie – remember, this is Very Serious Research. Imagine that you were auditioning for this role – after all, nothing is safe from revivals or remakes these days.

Fill in the details you can gather from the script in response to the clues. Notice which questions you're able to answer and which ones you're not. Notice if your perception of the character's accent changes based on what you can find. No matter how many questions you're able to answer, where would you look next for more information about the character's cultural context? What sorts of emic sources would you seek out? What sorts of etic references would you want to find?

The Way of the World

Having unearthed clues in the text, it's time to connect them to an understanding of an accent in the world. So where do you find information about the way that real people speak?

Pretty much anywhere! Books, documentaries, articles, encyclopedias, online videos, interviews, textbooks, poetry, music, everywhere! Every clue is worth pursuing. It may be that you don't initially see why "profession" is on a list of accent clues, but after investigating the culture of 1990s yoga teachers or 1890s longshoremen, you discover nuanced connections to accent that add to the possibilities of your performance.

No two actors have identical processes, so you can pull together your People research in the way that suits you best. You could write timelines with copious notes to reflect the real-world conditions that shape a character's accent circumstances; you could assemble visual or audio collages that immerse you in the culture; you could write essays, journals, or poetry. The goal of the research process is to develop an understanding of a cultural context in the world that you can then embody through your performance. Though it may be of some benefit to summarize your findings in a way that others can interpret (for feedback or collaboration), your research is ultimately only in service to your acting.

If this research sounds similar to what you would ordinarily do for a role anyway – you're right! If you're working on a production that takes place in New York City in the 1980s, focused on the impact of AIDS on the Gay community, your research into the world of the play might already be leading you to research materials rich with information connected to real-world accents. By exploring these circumstances, you may accumulate clues about the way accent distinguishes one character from another, or how accent relates to stories of belonging, prestige, or persecution. Every bit of information you learn about how the culture is shaped by real people in real environments could bring you closer to knowing what it feels like to be identified with a particular way of speaking.

At this point, we might be able to say you've identified "an accent." The script has told you where to look, you've done research into places, times, and culture, and you have a pretty firm grip on the context that gives rise to the way you'll speak in performance. Great! You can celebrate your arrival at the naming of an accent, having developed a rich understanding of what that name communicates to your story and the world. However, your work with People isn't done yet! Even as you label the accent you want to embody, stay curious about the emic experience of *living in the accent*.

A Marked Improvement

Around this time, you may also encounter another idea that we'll call **markedness** (/ˈmɑɹkɪdnɪs/). An accent is *marked* (/mɑɹkt/) when it stands out in our perception. That is, we notice a mismatch between the way a speaker says things and the expectations of a listener or listeners. Mismatches of expectation are "marked" by the listener, and the more frequently they're aware of those occurrences, the more marked the speaker's accent will seem.

As always, context is key. An accent that seems completely unmarked amid London pubgoers might register as quite marked indeed in an Oxford lecture hall or on the BBC, even to fellow pubgoers. An American accent that sounds at home in a car commercial might be perceived as unmarked in a Des Moines grocery store and very marked at a Tallahassee barbecue. And while markedness might be the target of humorous ribbing from friends, it can also serve to stereotype, oppress, and persecute (as we saw on page 62).

To understand markedness, we need emic knowledge of the expectations and sensitivities of the people involved. A speaker from Yorkshire would most likely register as being simply "English" to both American and Australian listeners. However, the same speaker might register in a more nuanced way to a fellow Yorkshire listener, whose parameters for belonging are highly attuned to local distinctions. Thus, a listener from Sheffield would more easily mark a speaker as being from nearby Bradford, a distinction for which Americans and Australians usually lack the requisite context.

Accent "strength" also usually refers to some aspect of markedness. If scripts, research sources, or casting notices mention a "strong," "heavy," "light," or "weak" accent, then you'll need to do People research to triangulate the features of markedness for that accent in the world and in performance. It may be that one character's accent stands out in more frequent contrast to the accents of other characters in the production.

Or it may be that the world of the script is filled with accents that register as marked in relation to the expectations of the audience. As an actor, you step into the perspective of the production, real-world speakers, and your audience, in order to balance all their accent expectations with empathy. The more refined your attunement to nuance, the more possibilities you'll create for yourself that far exceed a limiting binary of "strong" and "weak."

Straight From the Source

So you've culled clues from the script or audition sides, you've expanded those into an understanding of how your accent works in the world, and you've investigated how this work will show up in the production's given circumstances. It's time to get some sources!

One way to gather accent sources is to go out and interview real people with the accent you'd like to embody – you went through that process in Exercise 4.3. But what if you don't know anyone who lives in the accent you'd like to perform? Or what if your research reveals that the accent you need to sample comes from people far removed in space or time, so much so that you won't be able to get direct access to them?

In that case, you're going to locate audio or video sources created by other people. Thankfully, the Internet makes available a truly staggering amount of primary accent sources, from audio archives to extemporaneous interviews to candid vlog entries.

 Web Resource 5.1 Sources for Sources

In **Web Resource 5.1**, check out "Where to Find Sources" and "Guidelines for Selecting Primary Sources." The first guide gives some tips for tracking down sources once you've gathered clues and know what you're looking for. The second guide provides general advice on what to look for in a source that will give you the most to work with in Prosody, Posture, and Pronunciation.

The wealth of information available online makes it possible to find accents "in the wild" that aren't as easy to locate in more traditional accent collections. The proliferation of streaming content also makes it possible to find voices in documentaries, broadcasts, and podcasts that were previously confined to much narrower audiences.

However, there are still plenty of instances when available sources are difficult if not impossible to come by. For example, productions that draw on accents that existed prior to the advent of widespread audio recording will likely lack the abundance of resources available to productions that take place in the twentieth century and onward. Access to early recording technology was also – and, in some places, remains – subject to the forces of prejudice and socioeconomic inequity, so that many accents without overt prestige have been lost to time. In these cases, you'll need to see which real-world sources best correspond to the demands of the given circumstances. While you may not be able to find historically accurate sources for every role you play, you can create an *artistic* cultural context that meets the needs of the story while also drawing upon real-world people and cultures.

Exercise 5.2: Let's Do a Research, Friend!

We've got a script (which we're making up) that says the story is set in Memphis, Tennessee. Frustratingly, it just says we're in the "early part" of the twentieth century, without giving us a year or even a decade. Half the characters are Black, the other half are White. The script has a fairly even balance of men and women. All characters are "working class," according to the writer.

Find an accent sample you could use to investigate an accent in this script. You won't be performing this sample's accent, so you can choose one that you could appropriately embody or one that could serve another actor for this script. The goal of this exercise is to run a trial of your People research skills, not to get to performance.

Note that we've arbitrarily chosen these circumstances, which reflect a few of the broad categories of identity that still predominate in most theatre seasons and casting notices. How does your research process interact with these oversimplified labels for groups of people? How can you frame your investigation to honor the complexity of your sources? And yourself?

Share your sample with your class. Describe how you found the sample, as well as the reasoning behind why you chose it. Listen to what your classmates found as well. How do the collected samples blend together? Do you get a sense of the cultural context of this imagined play? What

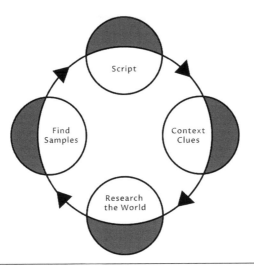

Figure 5.2 Productive People Process

surprises you? Do you perceive any differences in markedness? Do you gain any information about your own biases?

With the addition of samples to your understanding of People, you're ready to undertake a systematic study of the accent – via Prosody, Posture, and Pronunciation – and start applying that experience to your script. When you layer accent into the given circumstances, you may stumble upon or seek out more clues in the script, which could send you back into research and questing after even more sources. In this way, you set up an iterative process that productively moves towards an integrated understanding of People within the overall creative project (see Figure 5.2).

The more skills you build in this process, the more detailed and specific your research becomes with each accent you explore.

Culture Across Languages

In our discussion of cultural context, it may seem we've ignored a major dividing line in accents. In fact, for some of you, it may be the *most glaring* division of all: the difference between accents of "native" English speakers and the accents of "foreign languages."

Let's start by addressing these words in scare-quotes.

L1 and L2

Words like "native," "innate," and "natural" – connected by their Latin root, *nat-* "birth" – are problematic in reference to language and accents; they're too reductive for describing languages we are *born into* rather than *born with*. Likewise, "foreign" and "non-native" are equally inapt, because they reference geographic classifications that frequently don't adequately describe linguistic realities.

We prefer to borrow from linguistics and refer to **L1** and **L2**. For any given speaker, an L1 (/ɛl wʌn/) is a language they acquired in early childhood, in which they feel totally fluent, which arises from intuitive understanding, and with whose community of speakers they identify. For any given speaker, an L2 (/ɛl tu/) is a language with less fluency, less intuitive recourse, and/or less identification with a linguistic community than occurs with an L1. The "1" and "2" refer not to an order in which languages are learned, but rather to two tiers of integration and identity. An L1 is a language in which a speaker can seamlessly think, communicate, and culturally identify; an L2 is a language that's a little (or a lot) less easy to access.

The distinction between L1 speakers and L2 speakers doesn't change the fact that we *all* have accents. Instead, the L1/L2 distinction gives us cultural clues as to how speakers are perceived, how their accents evolve, and how they relate to other accents.

L1 English speakers are found in places as widespread as Australia, Singapore, South Africa, India, Ireland, and Canada. While they share an L1 (English), their accents might vary greatly. We would say that they have different *L1 accents of English*. Speakers who acquire English as an L2 deal with an additional layer of challenge; they need to translate the intuition of their L1 into L2 expression, which influences what we perceive as their *L2 accents of English*.

L1 and L2 accents of English are both subject to the fine perceptual distinctions of markedness (see page 66). For many L1 listeners, L2 accents are particularly prone to being described as "strong," "weak," "heavy," or "light." Yet again, though, those terms tell us more about listeners' expectations than they do about the skills of the L2 speaker.

L2 accents also tend to draw attention to some of the strategies human beings use to meet the expectations of a given linguistic context. In order to find fluid self-expression, L2 English speakers may *borrow* sounds, intonation, and grammatical structure from their L1 and apply them to their understanding of English. They may also attempt to *mimic* exactly what they hear in the speech of L1 English speakers, though without reference to the unconscious patterns that L1 speakers acquire through their language-learning process. Beyond borrowing and mimicking are an infinite number of other *adaptations* that L2 English speakers can implement, blending their L1 and L2 capabilities to make sense of – and embody – the English of their listeners.

Communication always involves real-time problem solving, and the problem being solved by an L2 speaker is a remarkably complex one. We can expect to find a great deal of variability in the strategies employed by L2 English speakers as they carve out their individual approach to the challenges of communication. Some speakers are able to mimic the sounds of English with incredible fidelity without being fluent in the language, while others have mastery of vocabulary and grammar but employ more noticeable and frequent borrowings from the sound patterns of their L1. And L1 English listeners have an equally complex set of (usually subconscious) expectations as well, which leads to variability in what they perceive as the markedness of L2 accents.

All these factors (and more) make it more likely that we'll find L2 accents more difficult to describe with uniformity. As you gather samples and sources, notice how L2 accents of English are likely to show variability between speakers – and that your skills equip you to celebrate those differences while still seeking out useful patterns for performance.

Exercise 5.3: Cost in Translation

Let's experiment with what it may be like to create an L2 accent – on the fly!

Web Resource 5.2 L2 Scenework
Navigate to **Web Resource 5.2** to find a recording of a short scene in a language you most likely don't speak. Two characters are speaking to each other about something very important. In

addition to the audio recording, we've also provided an English translation of the scene.

Get together with a partner and reenact the scene *in the original language*. The expectation is that you'll not only be able to speak this language for the scene, but that you'll also be able to commit fully to the circumstances and mean what you say. Use whatever skills you have available – from English, from other languages you speak, from this book or *Experiencing Speech* – but get as close to you can to realizing the exact sounds and patterns of the recording.

Once you've had a chance to rehearse with your partner and get off book, perform the scene for the class. Notice how each set of partners responds to the task of performing in an L2 and compare it to your experience. Where did you notice borrowing from available L1s? Did you catch any straight-up mimicking? What other adaptive strategies did you notice? How did different performers make different adaptations?

What was it like to perform in an L2? Did you feel connected to the meaning of the lines, as you understood them? What was challenging about this exercise? What did you enjoy about this exercise? Discuss your observations with your classmates.

Web Resource 5.3 L2 Scenework Variations

Check out **Web Resource 5.3** to find additional exercises for exploring L2 experiences. They all contain unique challenges, but, most importantly, they should be fun!

Under the Circumstances

We've gathered a lot of information in this module, and at this point, much of it may still feel oriented toward the etic, outsider perspective. So let's revisit our potential clues for research and exploration from the emic perspective. Reframe your People findings in ways that allow you to take ownership of them in performance. Answer the following questions in the first person:

- Geographical location – Where are you? Where do you live?
- Geographical origin – Where did you come from? When?
- Profession – What's your job? What's your professional identification?

- Gender identities – How do you see yourself? How do others see you?
- Time period – Is this in the past, the present, or elsewhen? Does this story cover a long period of time? What's your awareness of this moment in time?
- Character age – How old are you? How mature are you? How settled are you?
- Languages other than English – Assuming English is what you're speaking in this script, is it your L1 or L2?
- English acquisition – How new is English to you? How fluent are you? How did you learn to speak it?
- Prestige (overt/covert) – What social group(s) does your accent identify you with? What sort of powers does that give you? With whom?
- Dialect information (lexicon, grammar, etc.) – What words or grammatical constructions do you use that set your speech apart? Are others aware of these differences?

Ask these questions for any character and any accent; they're your People Gut-Check. If you can't answer these questions in the first person, or if you feel like you can't own some of the answers you do know, then you've got some more investigation to do!

These questions give you the grounds for a fruitful exploration of circumstances while also drawing well-resourced connections to the world as we know it. No matter how familiar or marked an accent seems to you, an empathetic and self-aware research process will add depth to your accentwork *and* your acting. And the more you practice it, the more accessible and reflexive it becomes.

A Gentle Warning

Enthusiastic and curious research may lead to some delightful discoveries and truly surprising connections. And that's a good thing! We just want to inject one delicate bit of caution: *context is not causation.*

Both emic and etic resources may seem to point to certain aspects of cultural context being "the cause of" accent features. This causal thinking often seems to arise in the relationship of geography and accent, with such doozies as "sweeping prairieland led to Americans' broad and open resonance" or "Irish accents roll and tumble thanks to the undulating hills of Eire."

While imagistic and perhaps inspiring, there is no legitimate backing for these claims. Even if these images are personally meaningful to an emic source or illustrative for an etic metaphor, they lead to a dangerous type of reductionism and determinism, one that seems to imply that geography (or any aspect of culture) reduces linguistic evolution to a foregone conclusion. Cultural context is a complex and ever-evolving combination of interrelationships, which can never be reduced to a few simple chains of cause and effect. Double-check your sources for this bias, and be willing to spot it in your own thinking as well, so you can forgive it and let it go.

Check-In

In Exercise 4.3, we gathered information about the cultural context of one particular Donor. When it comes to your Big Accent Project, you may need more than one source – or it may be that you aren't able to get access to a Donor whose accent suits the needs of your BAP. How will you source audio samples for your BAP? How will you gather cultural context information for your BAP accent and the people, places, events, and cultural forces that give rise to it? Run yourself through the People research process in this module, asking questions, doing research, finding (additional) samples, and investigating the connections to performance. Present a summary of your findings to the class in a way that feels interesting and exciting to you. Feel free to include visuals, music, and perhaps even a culinary sample.

Notice what your classmates share as well. What is inspiring about their summaries? What would you want to steal for your own research process? (And you should!)

Conclusion

At this point, you've opened up an enormous range of possibilities for your exploration of People. After gathering clues, following leads, pulling samples, considering markedness, and applying all this knowledge to the script, you're ready to weave a rich, interconnected tapestry of cultural context to support your embodiment of accent.

People sets all the other Ps in motion. If you start your investigation of accent with an indistinct or decontextualized sense of your target, then you won't have the resources or material you need for Prosody, Posture, and Pronunciation. All the Ps are necessary aspects of performance, but People sets the stage and primes your care for all the work to come.

Your work with your Donor in this module and in Module Four may make you feel closer to them and reluctant to let them go. That's great! They'll be coming with you as we explore Prosody, Posture, and Pronunciation, and you can use them as resources for future exercises. We hope you continue to practice your skills of empathy and awareness with every Donor you consult.

MODULE SIX
PROSODY – LISTEN AND SING

All human speech is imbued with music-like elements, and the same fundamental musical elements tend to appear in most languages. Different languages give rise to unique combinations of melody, rhythm, and emphasis. Accents within those languages can also be differentiated by those same characteristics . . . "through song," as it were.

The musicality of language conveys information in two major ways: the linguistic and the **paralinguistic** (Greek *para-* "alongside" + Latin *lingua* "language"). Linguistically, musicality contributes to the meaning of the words we speak. If you change your pitch while speaking, you might be indicating to the listener that you're asking a question, or that there's a particular word they should focus on, or that you're saying "curse" instead of "horse" (罵 mà versus 馬 mǎ). In this example from Mandarin, the exact same articulatory actions are distinguished by the movement of pitch; other **tonal languages** that make linguistic use of pitch in a similar way include Vietnamese, the Khoisan languages, and Navajo (among many others). Tonal or non-tonal, the linguistic structures of musicality are baked into the language(s) you speak. We'd wager you're already an expert user of linguistic prosody, though likely at an unconscious, procedural level.

The paralinguistic aspects of prosody provide a different type of information. We can gather information about a speaker's mood, their attitude

DOI: 10.4324/9781003314905-8

toward what they're saying, and when they'd like someone else to talk, all emerging from the melodic cadences of their speech. But beyond the words used or grammar constructed, we're also able to detect clues about belonging – about who is like us and who is unlike us – through the musical qualities of speech. Distinct patterns of musicality tell us about the age of a speaker, where they might be from, and even what other languages they may speak – in other words, musicality is an identifying feature of their accent. The paralinguistic cues for *accent identity* will be the subject of our exploration in Prosody (with a capital P).

Check It Out!

We're going to cut to the chase in this module so we can focus on what's most useful for accentwork. As such, if you find Prosody interesting, baffling, or anything in between, we recommend jumping down some hyperlinked rabbit holes by searching for any of the terms in this module. See where some of these words take you: prosody; acoustic; auditory; word; pitch; tone; duration; tempo; dynamics; timbre; syllable; mora; stress.

Here's the fun part: the linguistic *and* paralinguistic aspects of prosody are built with the same basic components. The music-like elements that communicate linguistic meaning also serve as the markers that help us figure out paralinguistic identity.

So let's start with the basics. We can use three main concepts to organize our understanding of Prosody:

- *Attributes.* The musical properties we employ in speech. The five basic attributes we'll explore are **pitch, loudness, length, quality** (or *timbre*), and **silence**.
- *Combinations.* Arrangements of attributes, either on their own (like swings in pitch) or together (like a simultaneous change in loudness and length).
- *Functions.* The meanings that attributes and combinations can communicate.

We'll work our way through the *attributes* in this module, taking stock of what you already know and sharpening your perception. In Module Seven, we'll explore how attributes accumulate into *combinations* and then get connected to specific *functions*. Then, with the basics in place, we can zoom out to the paralinguistic function that most interests us in accentwork: recognizing, analyzing, and embodying the patterns of prosodic identity.

But first, we need to define a few more terms, which will make it easier to understand how and where we perceive musicality in speech.

Prosody: The Suprasegmental Art

In linguistics, "prosody" specifically refers to the musicality of spoken language that communicates meaning at the *suprasegmental* level. Individual articulatory actions, such as obstruents and phthongs, are referred to as "segments." *Supra-* comes from the Latin for "beyond" or "above," which makes prosody something we detect "beyond" or "above" the layer of individual speech sounds. So what unit do we use that's bigger than a segment in order to measure out our perceptions of musicality?

Introducing: the **syllable**. Like individual notes in a piece of music, syllables are pulses of sound energy. They help us divide the flow of speech into smaller units and transmit information through their relative prominence. The organization of prosodic features into syllables occurs in many languages, including English, so you most likely already have an intuitive response to what a syllable is. For example, it may seem obvious to say that "English" has two syllables (making it *disyllabic*) or that "stress" has one syllable (making it *monosyllabic*).

Exercise 6.1: Bits and Beats

Let's put your intuitive syllabic wisdom to work – and in the process, let's see if you can describe what a syllable *is*.

Take a look at the words in Figure 6.1. Then speak each one of them aloud. Where do you create boundaries between syllables – *syllable breaks* – in these words? Mark them with the "syllable break diacritic" [.] (we've given you an example).

Look at the syllables you've created. *Physicalize* your syllables – which movements or gestures reveal your understanding of syllabification? Now,

po.ta.to	possibility	okay	gumption	superfluous
given	understand	perform	prompts	react
malarkey	little	athlete	stronger	gorgeous

Figure 6.1 Mark your syllable breaks

describe the structure of a syllable in words. Write down possible definitions, then pick your favorite.

Now test out your definition on the words in Figure 6.2:

immediately	steel	obvious	damn	comfortable
interesting	governor	fire	power	necessary

Figure 6.2 More syllable breaks

Find a partner in class. First, share your lists of syllabified words; then, share your movements. You could even engage in a friendly dance competition! Notice where you and your partner agree, and where you came up with different syllable boundaries. Discuss your reasoning with your partner – after presenting your case and hearing theirs, do you want to shift any of your syllable breaks? Do those potential changes influence your definition of what a syllable is?

Next, offer your definition of a syllable to your partner and hear theirs in return. Where do your observations line up? Where are they different? Can you reach a two-person consensus on how to define a syllable?

Finally, bring your two-person observations to a class discussion. How have other groups defined a syllable? Is it possible to reach a class consensus?

In English, syllables frequently feel like something we just *know*, while a definition only complicates things. It's ultimately an emic pursuit; there's no such thing as an "objective" syllable, only a language-by-language (or accent-by-accent) comparison of how sounds seem to be organized into musical units. We can use syllables to understand the suprasegmental organization of many languages, though for some – like Japanese and Ancient Greek – we might be better served by the **mora**.

All syllables seem to contain one essential part, which tends to carry its prosodic "weight." This central part of the syllable (the syllabic *nucleus*) is where we register most musical information. It's typically a vowel, though some consonants capable of being sustained can also serve in this role as *syllabic consonants*. Syllables can also contain more than one vowel shape, as is the case with *diphthongs* (two vowels in one syllable) and *triphthongs* (three vowels); a *monophthong* results when only one vowel shape carries syllabic weight.

The center of a syllable can have consonants that precede or follow it, though some syllables might consist only of vowels ("oh!" or "eye"). Different languages have different rules about how many and what types of consonants can begin and end syllables; English, for example, allows for consonant-dense syllables (like "strengths" and "prompts"), whereas Standard Italian permits far fewer consonants per syllable.

It's helpful to know how to break speech into syllables in order to make suprasegmental musicality easier to analyze and perform. Now that we have a way of organizing the music we hear, let's turn to its attributes.

The Attributes of Musicality

By the way, you're already outfitted with the most advanced prosody detection and analysis capabilities that have ever existed. Your senses and your brain have been training for prosody perception since before you were born. Musicality was your first experience of human speech *in utero*, starting with the melodic variations of the person who carried and gave birth to you. Linguists have conducted amazing research into babies' abilities to recognize their birth parents' prosody, even within a few weeks of arriving in the world. You were born into the music of speech, and your skills have grown and refined as you've continued to participate in the language environments around you.

Thanks to this early start, you already perceive the attributes of musicality intuitively. You understand what those clues are telling you without having to devote additional brainpower to describing what you hear.

However, in accentwork, we want to *expand* your current prosodic abilities, so that you can hear, analyze, and embody the Prosody of other speakers with agency and deliberateness.

The five basic attributes of prosody are borrowed straight from the vocabulary of music: *pitch, length, loudness, vocal quality* (*timbre*), and *silence*. Each of these elements is an **auditory** descriptor for what we perceive in the **acoustic** properties of sound waves. In other words, pitch, length, loudness, vocal quality, and silence are all ways of describing how we *experience* sound. While it may be possible to come up with alternative or additional attributes, these five provide an accessible approach to the musicality we need to access for accentwork.

Pitch

Pitch correlates to the acoustic **frequency** of sound waves. Higher frequency sound waves tend to be perceived as being higher in pitch; lower frequencies tend to be perceived as lower in pitch.

But what we perceive as pitch is relative! Pitch can only be "high" or "low" compared to other pitches, and the relationships between different pitches depend entirely on the listener's expectations and previous experience. For example, people who are accustomed to the **intervals** (differences in pitch) of Western musical composition may find the quarter tones of traditional Persian music surprising or difficult to describe. What we call pitch is thus highly dependent on the listener (perception) as well as the source (production).

Pitch in speech shows up in the highs and lows of the **fundamental frequency** of a speaker's voice, which is determined by the length, tension, and thickness of the oscillating vocal folds. This baseline vibration sets in motion an astounding array of overlapping **harmonic frequencies**, which we're often able to see on a spectrogram (see Figure 6.3). It's the fundamental frequency, however, that we tend to think of as the "pitch of our voice."

We notice pitch through ranges, intervals, and movement. In terms of range, pitch can cover different portions of the "scale" of the human voice, from wide to narrow (an exceptionally narrow range, limited to just one pitch, would be *monotone*). Intervals describe jumps between pitches, covering frequency changes from the very small to the very large. And

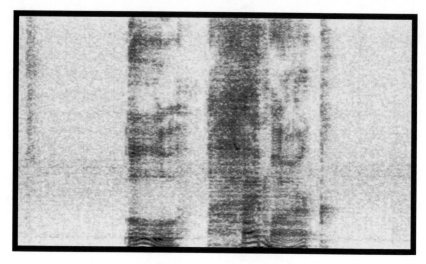

"Oh hi, Mark."

Figure 6.3 Spectrogram of a simple greeting

we can also perceive movement in pitch over time – rising, falling, and sequential shifts such as rise-falling, fall-rising, and more. Pitch movements can take place within syllables or across multiple syllables.

Exercise 6.2: Pitch Perception

 Web Resource 6.1 Pitch Perception
In **Web Resource 6.1**, we've provided sound samples that exemplify pitch variety in human speech. We've labeled each sample so you know what to listen for, and we've *removed the phonetic content* from these examples – you're just hearing the shifts in pitch, as filtered by a computer program. We've also included some visual representations of the corresponding pitch patterns, created by the same software. The vertical axis of the images measures pitch movement (higher and lower) while the horizontal axis indicates the passage of time.

Listen to each of the examples. Try to mimic each sample, without words. Move along with them – wave your hand in the air, wiggle your head, dance. Do any of these samples suggest words to you? Can you think of any examples from your own life that make use of these pitch possibilities?

Pick three samples that you find particularly interesting. Link them together into a *pitch phrase* by humming or phthonging. Practice this as your Pitch Phrase 1 – pitches only! No words yet!

Can you assemble your three examples in a different order to create a new pitch phrase? How does changing the order of the pitch elements change what you perceive? When you find a second combination that you like, make it Pitch Phrase 2. You may want to consider taking notes to remember your Pitch Phrases – or use the visuals or your movement to help you!

In class, find a partner. Start by sharing your Pitch Phrases, one at a time, taking turns. Once both partners have shared both phrases, have a "conversation" – exchange Pitch Phrases one at a time. Include movement if you find it helpful! Notice if any variety starts to seep in as you engage with your partner. How does pitch respond to being in communication? How easy or difficult is it to maintain your Pitch Patterns as you converse?

As a musical attribute of speech, pitch is one of the most prominent features used to create meaning in languages all over the world. However, it doesn't operate alone, and we're often only able to perceive shifts in pitch because of the time they take up.

Length

Length corresponds to the measurable time in which a sound occurs, also known as its acoustic **duration**. Duration can be measured with a timer in milliseconds; length is relative, ranging from very short to very long. Length is useful because it describes the relationship between sounds of different durations, and relative lengths are what we perceive as meaningful. Let's listen to this attribute in action.

Web Resource 6.2 Length Comparison

In **Web Resource 6.2**, we've prepared two samples for you. Give them both a listen.

In both samples, you should hear a speaker saying the same phrase. Notice that in each version, one word is *longer* than the others. However, Sample A took more time than Sample B. That is, Sample A took place at a slower **tempo**.

Tempo describes the *speed* of communication and is measured most often in syllables per second. Sample A's tempo is slower than Sample B's, which also means that Sample A's longest word takes more time than Sample B's. Yet that word in both samples feels *relatively* long in both, because it takes up more time *relative to all the other syllables*. Because length is a key marker for prosodic meaning, it's helpful to keep it distinct from duration and tempo in our work with Prosody.

Exercise 6.3: Length Perception

Web Resource 6.3 Length Perception

Web Resource 6.3 features samples that highlight length. Listen to each of the phonetically neutralized sound samples and look at their visual representations. Pitch variation is still on the vertical axis, while time (our reference for length) is on the horizontal. Try to mimic each sample, without words. Move along with them again: does focusing on length change the way you move? Do any of the examples suggest words to you? Can you think of any examples from your own life that make use of these versions of length?

Pick three examples that you find particularly interesting. Link them together into a *length phrase*. Practice this as your Length Phrase 1 – sound only! No words yet! Then create a Length Phrase 2 by reordering your chosen samples. Take notes or use the visuals to help you remember these two phrases.

In class, find a different partner. Start by sharing your Length Phrases, one at a time, taking turns. Again, consider sharing movement along with your Length Phrases. Once both partners have shared both phrases, have a "conversation" – exchange Length Phrases one at a time. Notice if any variety starts to seep in as you engage with your partner. How does prosodic length respond to being in communication? How easy or difficult is it to maintain your Length Patterns?

Of course, by playing with pitch and length at this point, you may also have stumbled upon the next attribute of musicality . . .

Loudness

It should come as no surprise that *loudness* is the perceived volume of a syllable. It corresponds to acoustic **sound pressure level**. Sound waves that produce more intense fluctuations in pressure are perceived as louder, while sound waves that are less disruptive are perceived as quieter.

Loudness describes the subjective perception of sound strength relative to surrounding sounds. A jet engine is inarguably very loud, no matter what the surrounding environment. But a whispered argument at a library can have much lower sound pressure levels while still registering as loud to surrounding readers. Additionally, patterns of relative loudness and softness can arise independent of the baseline volume, whether we find them in the hush of the fiction section or amidst the roar of a runway.

We can borrow the idea of **dynamics** to refer to loudness. In music, dynamics defines subjective levels of loudness, from *pianissimo* (very soft) to *mezzo piano* (medium soft) to *mezzo forte* (medium loud) to *fortissimo* (very loud). Movements in loudness between levels can *crescendo* (increase) and *decrescendo* (decrease), and loudness can also occur over a wide or narrow range.

Exercise 6.4: Loudness Perception

Web Resource 6.4 Loudness Perception

Web Resource 6.4 contains an array of samples that demonstrate possibilities in loudness. As before, phonetic information has been removed. Now our visual representations show *waveforms*, in which thicker parts of the shape indicate more relative loudness. Loudness is measured on the vertical axis, while time is on the horizontal.

Listen to each of the examples. Try to mimic them, without words. As always, feel free to move or dance, following the musical wisdom of your body. Do any of these samples suggest words to you? Can you think of any examples from your own life that make use of these versions of loudness?

In the context of accentwork, especially in English, it can be difficult to separate loudness from length. Even with lots of practice, it can feel counterintuitive to our lived experience to keep pitch and length constant while altering only loudness. For that reason, we're going to skip testing Loudness Phrases in conversation with a partner – though you're welcome to try if you'd like!

Vocal Quality (Timbre)

As part of speech musicality, *vocal quality* takes into account the types of vibration and resonance produced throughout the vocal tract's structures to give an overall description of a speaker's voice. Were we to look at the spectrogram (see Figure 6.2) of a given amount of speech, and were we able to process all the information it contains, the interplay of harmonic frequencies would create a distinct "sound-wave identity" for the voice we hear.

The musical term *timbre* (/ˈtæmbəɹ/) is often borrowed to describe vocal quality. An oboe and a saxophone are said to have different timbres, in that we can tell their sounds apart, even when they play the same note at the same volume. Vocal quality is perceived much the same way, wherein the same articulatory action produced at the same pitch, length, and loudness sounds different when produced with different types of voicing or resonance.

The term "vocal quality," as we've described it, may seem to be a vague description of the music-like features that make each person's voice unique (a so-called *vocal identity*). But vocal qualities can carry important prosodic information in many human languages, including English. For example, think of how switching from **modal voice** (or full phonation) to whispering provides an important paralinguistic cue in your experience.

Web Resource 6.5 Vocal Quality Perception

Web Resource 6.5 has some examples of prosodic vocal quality shifts. We haven't used any special software on these samples – otherwise, we wouldn't have any vocal quality information left to hear!

Read the descriptions of each and see if you can hear where the vocal quality changes. Have you used any of these prosodic strategies in your own speech? Where could you imagine these types of shifts showing up in your daily conversations?

The Rest Is Silence

In the richly layered flow of sound that makes up speech, silence plays an invaluable role. Like rests in music, silence delineates boundaries between chunks of prosody, it heightens contrasts between the other attributes, and it can even contain entire swaths of meaning. It's easy to imagine examples of times when silence answers better than speech could.

The alternation of silence and sound can help us build larger structures in spoken communication. When we zoom out beyond the syllable, silence allows us to notice things like **rhythm** and **connectivity**. Rhythm is a sense of semi-predictable timing produced by the interplay of lengths of silence and sound. Connectivity describes the sense in which speech feels smoothly linked (*legato*, in musical terms) or disjointed and separate (*staccato*). These larger-scale patterns are only noticeable when sound intermingles with silence . . . and even if the silences are momentary!

Exercise 6.5: Rhythm Circle

Web Resource 6.6 Rhythm Perception

Web Resource 6.6 provides one last tranche of sound samples. We've once again removed phonetic information – and this time, there are no images.

Listen to each sample. Notice the interplay of sound and silence and how they create a sense of rhythm over time. Move along with the rhythm – clap your hands, swing your arms, move your hips, tap your feet. Hum or sing along. You can notice and even repeat the pitch and loudness of the samples, but be sure to capture the alternations in length between sound and silence.

Pick two favorite samples and commit their Rhythm Dances to (body) memory. Create a circle with your classmates. One person steps forward and offers a Rhythm Dance. The entire circle repeats it together, as close to unison as possible. Then another person offers a Rhythm Dance, which the circle repeats in unison. Continue to explore until everyone has offered their two Dances. Notice how even students working from the same sample may come up with uniquely personal Dances to represent what they hear.

Exercise 6.6: Additional Ear-Training Opportunities

Web Resource 6.7 More Ear-Training Exercises

Web Resource 6.7 offers even more opportunities to increase your prosodic abilities through "ear-training."

Check them out for additional chances to practice your skills and eventually add Omnish, Somenish, and your Acting Language to your prosodic exploration.

Rise of the Machines?

Your human insight is ultimately your strongest asset for understanding and interpreting Prosody. Our work in this module has focused on naming the attributes you already know how to recognize.

Web Resource 6.8 Prosody Software

Computer software does exist for extracting acoustic information from audio recordings – you've witnessed it at work in the previous exercises. We've included in **Web Resource 6.8** a list of computer applications that are capable of creating various representations of prosody, often with impressive accuracy. However, these softwares aren't able to interpret the *meaning* of that acoustic input – that is, they can't tell us anything about the linguistic or paralinguistic information of the music they capture.

Software can be useful for double-checking your perceptions, comparing a computer's analysis of an audio sample with your own hypothesis as to what you think is happening. It can be really satisfying to perceive a rising pitch and then watch an ascending arc appear on your screen! However, try to refer to technology only after first giving it a go yourself. We encourage you to continue developing your perceptual abilities, not only by completing the exercises in this module but also by continuing your explorations in everyday life. By expanding your options in perception and production, you create more possibilities for the accentwork ahead.

Check-In

Go back to the audio samples you've gathered for your Big Accent Project and choose one to explore using your Prosody skills. Tune your ears to its musical attributes. Listen for pitch, length, loudness, vocal quality, and silence, as well as higher-level features like rhythm and connectivity. Write notes, draw pictures, dance, create helpful names for interesting combinations if you find them ("The

Thunderous Tumble," "Worried Robot," "The Aunt Josephine"). Get curious as to *how* you hear musicality arising out of your Donor's speech.

What did you learn about the musicality of this Donor? Which attributes seem most noticeable or prominent to you? Which attributes are the most difficult to perceive? Were you able to find instances where the musical elements of your Donor's speech communicated information that was separate – or even different – from the words being spoken?

Summarize your findings in a two-minute presentation to your class. Describe the musical attributes you scouted out and how you perceived them, using any means that feel appropriate: verbal description, visuals, music, dancing, movement, modeling prosody(!). Notice what your classmates share and how it compares with your observations.

Conclusion

You've given names to the musical attributes of speech and attuned your perception to detecting them. You've done a lot of listening, yes, but you've also done some modeling through exercises and conversations. In addition, you've explored the idea of the syllable, which provides a fundamental division for orienting to the flow of speech.

In Module Seven, we'll start combining attributes and connect them to functions, particularly in the context of accents of English. The skills we learned in this module are essential for understanding how musicality creates meaning, in languages and in accents. Once again, we've distilled a complex process down to simpler parts, which will make the applications ahead easier to navigate. Your work with Prosody is well underway, and rewarding patterns will come into sharper focus as you build your skills with the basics.

MODULE SEVEN
PROSODY – THE MEANING OF THE MUSIC

Pitch, length, loudness, vocal quality, and silence are hard to isolate in speech. As you may have found in Module Six, each of these attributes co-exists with all the others, and their mutual interactions are just as essential to our prosodic awareness as any one of them on their own. Our next step is to explore how attributes get arranged in speech and what those arrangements can communicate. Referring to our terms from page 77, we turn our attention now to the *combinations* and *functions* of prosody.

While most spoken human languages make use of the same few attributes of musicality, there are infinite ways to put those attributes together and connect them to meaning. If we were to attempt a compilation of every potential musical pattern and its functions in all human languages, we'd need multiple lifetimes to even get started.

Instead, let's zoom in on the linguistic and paralinguistic applications of musicality in English. We can always zoom out to notice thematic connections across languages, but our goal in this module is to develop prosodic skills for the performance of accents of English. This focus will then facilitate an understanding of how we use musicality to communicate belonging and identity – in other words, how we interpret and embody the Prosody that makes an accent distinct.

90

DOI: 10.4324/9781003314905-9

Check It Out!

With our focus on accentwork, we're going to be condensing a lot of valuable, interesting, and detailed scholarship. We recommend checking out J.C. Wells's *English Intonation: An Introduction* (Cambridge, 2006) for a thorough and accessible overview of English prosody. We remain indebted to Wells for so much of his lucid thinking and writing, some of which influenced this module.

Yes, but What Does It *Do*?

When it comes to the *functions* of prosody, we'd wager that you already employ quite a few of them already. Let's put what you know to work!

Exercise 7.1: Function Matching

Web Resource 7.1 Function Matching

Web Resource 7.1 provides some familiar samples of prosody – in fact, we used these in Exercise 6.2 (page 82), with their phonetic content removed. You'll also find a list of written phrases, in no particular order.

Working alone, in pairs, or in a large group, match each of the audio samples to one of the phrases. Each audio sample *does* have a written match, though we've offered more phrases than samples. Try speaking the phrases along with the audio – and test multiple phrases against each audio! You may be able to match one audio sample to multiple phrases – follow your intuition!

Once you've matched all the audio samples to a phrase, share your findings with the class. Notice where your classmates' matches coincide with your own – and where they differ. Discuss your strategies for matching prosody to words. How were you able to make connections between a prosodic pattern and its meaning? What does the musicality convey that the words on the page don't? What does this tell you about the roles that prosody plays in adding meaning to the words we speak?

Web Resource 7.2 Function Matches

Web Resource 7.2 contains the same audio samples with their phonetic content included. Listen to each sample and note which phrase was originally recorded. If you picked the same written phrase, notice which attributes of musicality helped you make the match. If you picked a different written phrase, notice that it may work just as well as the original – in fact, the same musical sample could add important meaning to multiple sets of words.

Discuss with the class what you've discovered about the functions of musicality. Can you name any of the functions that you or your classmates discovered? Would you be able to organize them into broader categories, based on the types of meaning they convey? Keep track of the functions that you find most familiar, most interesting, and most surprising.

Some of the more common functions of English musicality are listed here. How do these correspond to or contrast with your list?

Musicality can communicate information about:

- *What's important.* The way we use musical attributes in combination draws attention to the most important, newest, or most relevant information in a phrase.
- *Grammatical structure.* Pitch movement, silence, and changes in loudness and length can indicate boundaries within thoughts, as well as the contrast between questions, statements, and exclamations. In many ways, punctuation marks in writing are attempts to capture some of the experience of spoken musicality.
- *The speaker's attitude.* Everything from pitch movement to vocal quality can give us hints about the speaker's relationship to what they're saying. And there are lots of possibilities! For example, try saying, "I love it!" sarcastically, lovingly, and doubtfully. How does musicality help you create those distinctions?
- *Turn-taking.* The way we shape a phrase with musicality can let others know if we intend to keep speaking or if we're ready for them to respond. English paralinguistic cues can be purposefully tailored toward the social nature of communication.

So how do pitch, length, loudness, quality, and silence combine to indicate distinct functions? And with so many possible variations in musicality, how do we keep everything straight?

Make It a Combo

As an expert language user, you're already familiar with the *combinations* of musical elements that can carry meaning in your cultural context. As a very young person, you tested out prosodic options, copied those around you, and learned which ones were effective in meeting your goals. In fact, as we mentioned in Module Six, your exploration of prosody began *before* you were born, so you most likely discovered the interplay of prosodic attributes long before you mastered other aspects of speech. If you hear a "preverbal" baby chatting and cooing, much of their vocal musicality may sound recognizable, even though their articulatory actions have yet to become an intelligible language.

In English, we can identify combinations based on unique fluctuations in each of the five musical attributes. We could describe a prosodic arrangement through its pitch movements and intervals, its proportions of long sounds, short sounds, and silences, its ratio of loudness to softness, and its alterations in vocal quality. Silence can also serve as a *juncture*, creating pauses and breaks that make it possible to tell combinations apart.

Go back to your observations from Exercise 7.1 – and maybe even your notes from Module Six. If you noticed patterns in the musicality of speech, how did you describe them? It may be that describing a musical phrase in words feels futile – or, at least, extremely difficult. After all, how would you describe your favorite song? Or the voice of Ella Fitzgerald? Or the drumming of Dave Grohl? Awesome, obviously, but can words completely summarize what you perceive in a meaningful way?

So try this instead: *move!* Our bodies often know better what to do with music than our conscious minds. As you detect combinations in prosody, allow yourself to dance to them. Your movement can be a full-body endeavor. Or a tapping of your foot. Or a bobbing of your head. Or a gliding, twisting, tracing in your hands. Movement patterns often make prosodic combinations more obvious: the rising and falling of your hand may tell you something important about pitch, while the time it takes to trace that path gives hints about length.

You could also turn that movement into a *visualization* – just grab a pencil!

Exercise 7.2: Drawing Prosody

Web Resource 7.3 Drawing Prosody

Get a piece of paper and something to draw with. Navigate to **Web Resource 7.3**.

We've given you two options for each sample. One is the familiar (by now) de-phoneticized version. The other sample is the source audio – with real human speech! Listen to both: do you hear how the music-like sequences we've digitally isolated appear in the actual language?

Play each sample one at a time. As you listen, allow yourself to move; again, it could be a dance, a finger-tapping, a head-nodding. Give yourself at least three plays to just listen and move. When you feel like you've got a sense of the movement in your body, take that movement pattern onto paper by allowing your hand to draw a line along with the audio.

What do you end up drawing? Do your drawings feel impressionistic? Representational? Metaphorical? Analytical?

After you finish listening to and drawing the samples, look back at your collection. Do your drawings still make sense? Would you be able to vocally perform each sequence based on your drawing? And no worries if you can't! We're focusing right now on listening for, embodying, and then representing what *you* perceive; you can refine this tool through more experimentation.

Remember the visualizations from Web Resources 6.2 and 6.3? One way to arrange a prosodic visualization is with a vertical axis representing variation in pitch (and potentially loudness), while a horizontal axis represents the passage of time. As your hand (and thus drawing) moves up and down, you track the rising and falling of pitch. As you move from left to right, perhaps in continuous swoops or perhaps in hops and skips, you track your experience of length and silence. If you haven't already tried this format, repeat Exercise 7.2 using a pitch-vs.-time plot.

Web Resource 7.4 Prosody Visuals

Web Resource 7.4 contains visual representations of the samples in Exercise 7.2. Notice how we (the authors) each came up with different drawings, yet a pattern is visible across each sample. To keep ourselves transparent, we've also included a pitch-vs.-time visualization rendered by software. Again, it's not the same as our hand-drawn versions, and that's a good thing – we're not computers!

Ultimately, use the type of representation that captures what you perceive in prosodic combinations and helps you embody them in performance. Whether you prefer verbal description, movement, dancing, or drawing, find the approach that works best for you. The invitation is always open to wiggle, jump, tap, swing, conduct, trace, and scribble as you string together the music you hear.

Patterns With Purposes

So how do we connect unique musical combinations to functions? In other words, how do we produce and perceive meaning from distinct arrangements of attributes? In English, some combinations work for affirmative, declarative statements. Can we predict that another combination clearly indicates a yes-no question? (Read those last two sentences out loud to hear what we mean.)

To make sense of the relationship between combinations and functions, we'd like to borrow two terms from phonology: **inventory** and **distribution**. Let's make sense of these words with a metaphor.

The combinations of musical attributes we use in speech are our *inventory*. We could imagine them as a collection of tiny scraps of paper, all of which have written on them a particular prosodic sequence. Alongside these inventory items, we also have potential functions, which tell us the linguistic and paralinguistic information combinations can convey. In our metaphor, these functional categories are like the drawers of a filing cabinet, helpfully labeled and able to be subdivided further, should the need arise.

Distribution describes the system by which we sort scraps of paper into drawers; in other words, distribution tells us *how* to organize our inventory into functions. Or, rather, it *predicts* our organization – even the most comprehensive distributional plan still has to allow for anomalies, idiosyncrasies, and just plain weirdness. And these are arbitrary systems! Every language variety is unique in the subtly different ways it assigns combinations of prosodic attributes to communicative functions. But the governing philosophy remains the same: any language variety we investigate will have an inventory of prosodic signals (scraps of paper) and a system for distributing them to the functions they serve (drawers).

For example, your prosodic inventory could include patterns like (1) a low-pitched syllable jumping up suddenly to a high-pitched syllable, lengthened and rapidly falling in pitch; (2) three short, medium-pitched syllables leading to a long syllable that rises and falls gently in pitch; (3) two rapidly falling short syllables followed by one long syllable that swoops down and then up in pitch (see Figure 7.5). Note that we haven't connected these sequences to functions yet; for now, they're just combinations of musicality without meaning.

Your prosodic filing cabinet most likely contains drawers for statements, questions, interjections, parenthetical information, and other functions like those that you compiled in Exercise 7.1 (page 91). Most

Figure 7.5 Metaphorical prosodic inventory

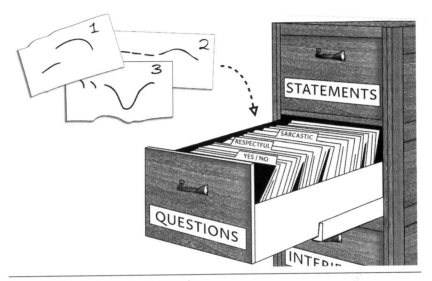

Figure 7.6 Metaphorical functional categories

of those drawers contain subfolders for more specific applications, such as variations that communicate sincerity, respect, sarcasm, or friendliness (see Figure 7.6).

Your prosodic distribution maps out the relationships between your inventory (paper scraps) and functions (drawers). Once a link has been established between a combination and a function, prosodic distribution allows you to perceive meaning in your otherwise arbitrary inventory items.

So, for some people, Pattern (1) in Figure 7.5 could be filed under "surprised disapproval" ("What? No!"). Pattern (2) could find a home under "tempting, open-ended offer" ("But if you want . . ."). And Pattern (3) could slot into "emphatic, continuing thought" ("I don't care, [but] . . .") or "affirmative statement" ("That's the truth.") – depending on the context.

And what determines the context? Why, the culture, of course!

Consider a well-known prosodic sequence: high-rising terminal (HRT). HRT is a pattern in which the final stressed syllable of a phrase starts at a relatively *high* frequency and then continues to *rise* through the end of the phrase (*terminal*). Almost all varieties of English have a

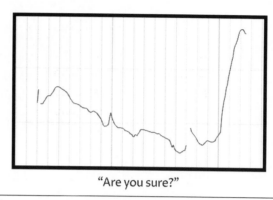

"Are you sure?"

Figure 7.7 HRT in a yes-no question

version of this sequence in their inventory. Many varieties of English also have a distribution that uses this pattern to indicate yes-no questions, like, "Are you sure?" or, "You mean, like this?" (See Figure 7.7.)

There are some prosodies of English, however, that also distribute HRT to affirmative statements, like, "Yes, I'm going," or, "I really like that." Certain New Zealand accents might use HRT in affirmative statements, at least occasionally, and younger speakers in the United States might use HRT frequently in statements. For many Kiwis, the use of HRT in statements is unremarkable – this arrangement of inventory and distribution doesn't draw attention within those accents' cultural contexts. In the cultural context of many US accents, however, the use of a combination associated with one function (yes-no questions) in another function (statements) can cause a mismatch in expectations – and no small amount of disapproval, particularly among older listeners (who may condescendingly call it "upspeak").

A Function of Identity

The example of HRT highlights the role of Prosody in accentwork. In relation to other varieties of English, New Zealand accents make use of the same music-like attributes and arrange those attributes into remarkably similar sequences. Compared to other varieties of English, Kiwi functional categories are largely the same and their prosodic distributions most likely overlap far more often than they differ. Some New Zealand accents simply assign the HRT sequence to affirmative statements as well as yes-no questions.

Yet that key detail in distribution communicates important *paralinguistic* information. When a professor from Auckland employs HRT in a class in Leicester, the students aren't likely to linguistically confuse the teacher's knowledgeable statements with a series of questions. Yet those same Leicestrian students will likely perceive the Aucklander's affirmative-statement use of HRT as a paralinguistic indicator of where their professor is from. In this case, musicality communicates information beyond the linguistic content of the speaker.

To understand the Prosody of an accent, zoom out to observe the inventory *and* distribution of musicality within a variety of English. Identify which combinations of attributes show up, then figure out how those sequences fulfill linguistic functions within the community of speakers who use them. Some accents may seem to differ in their inventory of possible patterns – for example, wide versus narrow pitch ranges. Other accents may differ based on their functional distributions of similar combinations, as we saw with HRT earlier.

Out of a speaker's prosodic inventory and distribution, we're often able to discern patterns that indicate a unique *accent identity* shared among a group of speakers. This is the key layer of prosodic paralinguistic information that differentiates accents: the relationship between the musical patterns they use and the functions for which they use them. Understanding the linguistic role of prosody is still essential, but your ultimate goal is to arrive at a sense of the complex identities encoded within the paralinguistics of musicality.

Exercise 7.3: Accent ID

Web Resource 7.5 Accent ID Samples

Web Resource 7.5 has stories gathered from three English-speaking Donors around the world. You're going to listen to a thirty-second excerpt of each. Thirty seconds isn't nearly enough time to comprehend someone's entire Prosody, and we're also withholding a lot of People information that could give you hints. So don't worry about "getting it right" – just stay curious!

As you listen to each sample, take note of prosodic patterns you observe (we've also provided de-phoneticized versions for comparison). How would you describe/dance/draw them? Then, can you identify what each pattern *does* – that is, what are its functions? Are there any categories into which you could group the functions: statements? questions? parentheticals? Do you get any paralinguistic information about how the speaker thinks or feels about what they're saying? You may want to listen to each sample a few times.

Once you've made notes on all three samples, look for similarities and differences. Do these samples share any prosodic combinations? How do their distributions of combinations overlap, if at all? Where do they differ? How do the inventory and distribution give you paralinguistic information about the speaker's identity?

Come up with a name for each accent (you might already be familiar with some of them). Take your observations and your names back to a class discussion. What did your classmates notice? What sort of paralinguistic markers did they discover? How would you organize your discoveries amongst attributes, combinations, and/or functions?

Do Stress!

There *is* one linguistic function of musicality that can be especially useful for analyzing Prosody, because it provides an accessible point of comparison across most accents of English. Almost every prosodic combination we assemble contains a syllable or syllables that are essential to what we mean to say. By changing the attributes of musicality on and around those syllables, we can highlight important information in our speech.

Stress, in general, is the creation of prosodic contrast to draw attention to a particular cluster of sound(s), usually a syllable. In English, stress is typically indicated by increasing a pitch interval jump, engaging in wider pitch movement, extending length relative to nearby syllables, and increasing relative loudness. We can find this relative musical contrast within words and also across multiple words.

Lexical stress is the inclusion of some degree of stress within polysyllabic English words (Greek *lexis* "word," derived from *legein* "to say"). Typically, one syllable in a word has *primary stress*, while others have secondary stresses or remain unstressed. Obviously, the more syllables a word contains, the more opportunities there are to include varieties of lexical stress. For example, "contain" is lexically stressed on its second syllable, "continent" on its first, and "condemnation" has secondary stress on its first syllable, primary stress on its third.

Lexical stress is built into an L1 knowledge of English and must be learned alongside pronunciation and meaning. English lexical stress also usually manifests through the specific phonetic qualities of vowels in stressed and unstressed syllables. For example, pitch, length, and loudness may distinguish the first syllables of the nouns "desert" and "dessert," but we'd also wager that the vowel shapes in those first syllables differ as well.

Beyond the level of lexical stress, we group our syllables and words into phrases based on the messages we hope to convey. In conversation, we mostly communicate in short bursts of words, which linguists call **intonation phrases** (**IPs**). These are the "chunks" of speech that carry us from one thought to the next as we express ourselves extemporaneously. Even in pre-scripted performance, we seek to embody the flow of thoughts as they roll out in IPs. When we notice that an actor's delivery sounds like it's "flat" or being "read from the page," we're often registering that they haven't found the natural prosodic divisions that characterize organic speech.

English intonation phrases create the context for **prosodic stress**, which can also be called *suprasegmental stress*, *sentence stress*, and *emphasis*. Within an IP, we almost always think we have something new, important, or relevant to say – otherwise, why offer that chunk of thought at all? We indicate this important information by adding stress (relative to the rest of the phrase) to the lexically stressed syllable of the most important word in the IP. This highlighted information forms the heart (or *prosodic nucleus*) of a phrase, and it's the defining element of so many of the combinations you've observed thus far. And it's usually something L1 English speakers can produce and perceive with incredible intuitive ability.

Exercise 7.4: Focus Shifting

Find a partner. You're going to put your intuitive knowledge of English prosody to work once again. One person starts as the Speaker, while the other is the Listener.

Here are four phrases, all of which could be a complete intonation phrase. Speaker, pick one of these phrases and memorize it. Read it as written at first; italics indicate where you should first place the prosodic stress.

1. I told you where those *books* were!
2. She said he had a cute *kit*ten.
3. They made two offers I couldn't re*fuse*.
4. What were they doing with my *loo*fah?

Listener, after the Speaker performs the phrase as written, take thirty seconds to jot down your observations on what you understood to be most important or meaningful. How does prosodic stress impact your perception of the Speaker's meaning? Which attributes did the Speaker use to indicate prosodic stress? You can ask them to repeat themselves if you'd like another listen (and don't forget to move to the music, if you want to).

Speaker, repeat this experiment six more times by shifting the prosodic stress to *each word in the phrase*. You can shift the stress in any order you like, but make sure you only use *one* stress per phrase – if you use two, you're likely breaking the sentence into *two* intonation phrases!

Listener, for each version of your Speaker's phrase, take notes on where you hear the prosodic stress, how it shows up, and how shifting **focus** through prosodic stress changes the meanings you perceive. After you've heard all seven versions of the phrase, share your observations with your Speaker. Speaker, share what it was like to produce different versions of prosodic stress.

Speaker and Listener then switch roles and repeat the exercise, with the new Speaker choosing a different phrase from the list. As a bonus, after both partners have acted as Speaker, experiment with adding *two* prosodic stresses to the sentences in the list. Two stresses create two IPs, so add a *phrase break* | to indicate the boundary between IPs.

Prosodic stress and its focusing effects are omnipresent in English. No matter what function a prosodic sequence serves, some part of it will be more stressed than another, which makes prosodic stress an easy feature to locate and analyze. Listening for prosodic stress often provides the most efficient route to recognizing the inventory and distribution of Prosody. By figuring out how prosodic stress is communicated in a declarative statement, a yes-no question, and a few other types of IPs in an accent, you form a snapshot of its defining paralinguistic features. You'll also build an easily accessible Prosody reference, which you can quickly compare to every other accent you learn to embody.

Adaptive Prosody

The prosodic experience of L2 English speakers can differ substantially from that of L1 speakers. L2 English speakers have to fill in gaps in their knowledge of English prosody by calling on whatever skills they have available, including those from their L1 experience. As a result, L2 English speakers may borrow their L1 patterns in unexpected ways in English, apply prosodic combinations to functions that defy listeners' expectations, or miss certain features of English prosody based on their own L1 expectations.

L2 speakers of English may also discover challenges in adapting to the ways L1 English speakers create stress. Some languages seem to favor the timing and magnification of stress at the expense of unstressed syllables – in this way, English seems similar to German and Russian as a "*stress-timed* language." Other languages seem to favor the even weighting of syllables, with stressed syllables receiving only slightly more prosodic exaggeration – French, Mandarin, and Turkish could serve as examples of these "*syllable-timed* languages." This concept of **isochrony**, first presented by Kenneth Pike (again!), has been challenged by more detailed acoustic research and may not actually exist. But Pike helpfully pointed out that the timing and patterning of stress differs between languages . . . and that can bleed over into L2 accents.

For example, consider an L1 French speaker learning English. Most of the ways that the French prosodic system handles stress are quite different from English. While it may be convenient to summarize these differences as "a syllable-timed prosody adapting to a stress-timed prosody," that doesn't actually tell us very much.

Instead, investigate how an L1 French speaker creates stress in their L2 English. Do they borrow musical combinations straight from French? Do they seem to use English prosodic patterns, but apply them to surprising functions? Start by breaking down what you hear into the attributes of pitch, length, loudness, vocal quality, and silence. Then listen for repeating combinations and see if you can connect them with any predictability to L2 English functions. With a well-researched sense of inventory and distribution, you could then draw some paralinguistic conclusions as to what creates the Prosody of a "French accent" in English – and how an L2 speaker's adaptive flexibility plays an important role in that process.

Check-In

It's time to exercise your skills in Prosody in your BAP.

Using your gathered audio samples, create a Prosodic Organization that includes at least ten prosodic sequences and their functions. Leave room for overlap – some functions might use multiple musical combinations, and some combinations may be assigned to more than one function.

Remember to use prosodic stress to your advantage. How is stress indicated using the attributes of musicality? Dance your combinations, draw them, describe them – and definitely model them ("listening with your mouth/vocal tract"). You could also use software to double-check your work. Call on the tools we've explored thus far to flesh out the prosodic inventory in as much detail as you can.

Which aspects of your Prosodic Organization seem to be most important (for you) to the paralinguistic identity of your Donor(s)? Is it the types of pitch patterns that repeatedly show up? Is it a particularly recognizable rhythm? Is it the feeling of connectivity – or lack thereof? Is it the way certain patterns get assigned to certain functions, such as statements, questions, or lists?

Reflect on what it's like to observe and document a Prosodic Organization. When does it help to zoom in and consider the attributes? When does it help to zoom out and look at paralinguistic patterns? How do you imagine your skills in perception and production will change over time with more experience?

Conclusion

Without Prosody, there is no accent – etymologically and literally. Embodying Prosody involves not only the production of musical elements in human speech, but also an understanding of what types of music get used where – and for what reasons.

So much of our understanding of Prosody is rooted in our L1 experience. Making that already inherent knowledge conscious can be the effort of a lifetime. However, our goal is not to internalize the entirety of the musicality of every accent we study, but rather to know what skills we can call upon when we want to learn more. We don't need to find more answers so much as come up with better questions.

Prosody skills grow with time, as they do in all Four Ps. Our work with Posture and Pronunciation in the upcoming modules will provide lots of potential connections to Prosody and the tools we use to illuminate it. Keep these insights with you as we shift our perspective on accent to yet another angle in the pages ahead.

MODULE EIGHT
POSTURE – LISTEN WITH YOUR MOUTH

At this point, you've done quite a bit of listening. Along the way, we'd also guess that you occasionally found yourself moving your vocal tract along with your sources, reproducing or mimicking some of the sounds you heard by feeling them out for yourself. It's sometimes hard *not* to follow along as you listen to others speaking!

In *Experiencing Speech*, we called this ability *listening with your mouth*. We described it as "a fundamental human ability" to *embody* incoming auditory information, immediately and intuitively. It's powerful and sensitive, attuned to tiny shifts in acoustic signals that give hints as to how you can approximate the speech actions of others. "Listening with your mouth" is a lifelong skill that not only aids in your initial language acquisition but also ensures that you're able to mold your sounds to negotiate belonging as you grow.

In Module Thirteen of *Experiencing Speech*, "oral posture" or "vocal tract posture" served as a comprehensive frame to hold together all the physical skills learned up to that point. Posture is also an essential contributor to the perception, identification, and production of accents. In fact, because accent is the aspect of language that results from embodiment, Posture holds our experience of accent together, like the glue of the Four Ps.

The skills of Posture can expand beyond your individual vocal anatomy to include all possible human speech configurations. Learning about the

DOI: 10.4324/9781003314905-10

specific athleticism of speech production augments the ability to feel into (or **interocept**) the vocal tract, its tendencies, and its movement patterns. But first, as always, let's take stock of what's already available to you.

Exercise 8.1: What Do You Feel Right Now?

Web Resource 8.1 Audio Anatomy Tour

We've provided multiple approaches for a luxurious exploration of the anatomy of the vocal tract. In addition to the following printed walkthrough, you can also find an audio version in **Web Resource 8.1**, along with video demonstrations of isolations and additional visual materials for reference. Feel free to use any combination of these resources as you work through this exercise – whatever serves you best!

Give yourself a brief physical warm-up of your shoulders, neck, face, and mouth. You could shake everything out, massage, explore gentle movement, stretch, or recall the articulator isolations in Module Two of *Experiencing Speech*. Allow yourself to experience movement and flexibility throughout the vocal tract and its surrounding anatomy. Make easy sound, if it feels right. Remember to breathe – frequently!

Allow the musculature of your vocal tract and surrounding areas to find whatever feels like rest for you. Stay curious as to what release feels like for you throughout this exercise.

Let your fingertips find the pads of muscle on the sides of your jaw, the *masseter* muscles (Figure 8.2). When you're at rest, how firm or soft do those muscles feel? Does one side feel different from the other? Can you release these paired muscles to allow your mouth to open?

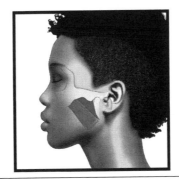

Figure 8.2 Masseter

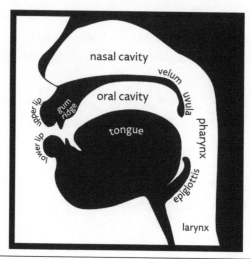

Figure 8.3 Oral cavity and pharynx

Notice the flow of breath into and out of your mouth. On the way in, the air of your environment is most likely cooler than your interior body temperature. Where do you feel that cooler air: on the roof of your mouth? On your tongue? On the insides of your cheeks? Around your gums? Around the *velum* (soft palate) and *uvula* (the little dangly bit hanging off your velum)? Into and around your *pharynx* (throat)? (Figure 8.3)

The flow of cool air might help you map the interior surfaces of your mouth. Feedback from nerve endings inside the mouth can contribute to the ability to interocept and visualize what you're feeling.

Shimmer your jaw a bit: explore micromovements of your jaw, not only up and down, but also forward, backward, and side to side. Let the movements be quite small indeed: if you know that your jaw requires care and attention, only explore those movements that feel healthy and safe. Then notice where your jaw moves to feel at rest. Does experimenting with a shimmered range of movement give you a different sense of where your jaw likes to rest, vertically, front to back, and side to side?

Next, bring your attention to your *buccinator* muscles, which run inside your cheeks (Figure 8.4). Thicken your buccinators as much as you possibly can, pulling your cheeks in toward your teeth. Rest them, and then

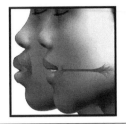

Figure 8.4 Buccinators   **Figure 8.5** Risorius and orbicularis oris

experiment with just shimmering them. Try to activate them one side at a time. Bring them back to rest. Blow out through your cheeks, allowing them to flutter in a rapid outflow of breath. Then let them come back to rest again. What does rest feel like now, relative to the range of activation and release that you just explored?

Pull your lip corners straight back, into a "creepy smile," by activating your *risorius* muscles. Try one side, then another. Find rest again. Then advance your lip corners, forming a loose-lipped pout, by activating the outermost corners of your *outer orbicularis oris* (Figure 8.5). Try one side, then another. Try different combinations of lip corner advancement and retraction. Add in some of the other muscles that lift and lower the lip corners, exploring facial expressions like smirks, genuine smiles, and frowns. Once you've got some variety going, reduce everything to a shimmer. Then come back to rest. What does rest feel like after exploring the possibilities of lip movement? How would you describe your lip corner resting position, between advancement and retraction, raising and lowering?

Play with trumpeting your lips out by using the entire outer orbicularis oris, as well as curling your lips in by using the *inner orbicularis oris*. Move between extremes, and then just shimmer, engaging in a subtle dance between pursing (bringing the lips together) and trumpeting. Then come to rest. Where do you feel your lips like to rest, on a spectrum from trumpeting to pursing?

Give yourself a big yawn – and the almost inevitably triggered real yawn that follows. Feel how the effort of yawning stretches your velum and pharynx. Try to come out of your yawns in slow motion. What does it feel like to let the muscles stretched by the yawn come to rest? These muscles might include the walls of the pharynx, the *palatoglossus* (an arching muscle that reaches from the tongue to the palate), and the muscles of the velum. Where is rest compared to the big activation of a yawn?

Stick your tongue out of your mouth by advancing your *tongue root* (which uses the *posterior fibers of the genioglossus*). Let your *tongue tip* and *tongue body* stay relaxed as you do this. Pull your tongue gently back into your mouth (using the *anterior fibers of the genioglossus*). Then, pull your tongue root straight back into your pharynx (using a combination of the *styloglossus* and *hyoglossus*) (Figure 8.6). Experiment with shimmering your tongue root, forward and back, with subtle movements that don't quite protrude your tongue from your mouth and don't block the back of your throat. Then come to rest. What does rest feel like for your tongue root, on a spectrum from advanced to retracted?

Clean the outside and the inside of your teeth using your tongue *blade* (*lamina*) and *tip* (*apex*). Go slow enough that you could imagine counting your teeth. Bring your tongue tip back behind your lower teeth. Next, reach up to the back of your upper teeth with your tongue tip. *Slowly* trace the roof of your mouth using your tongue tip as gently and easily as possible. Slide over your *alveolar ridge* (the bump of gum just behind your upper teeth), your *postalveolar* area, your *palate* (the hard, bumpy dome of the roof of your

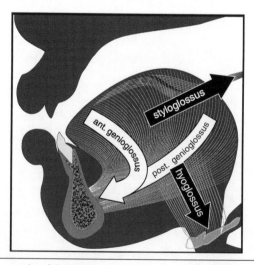

Figure 8.6 Extrinsic muscles of the tongue

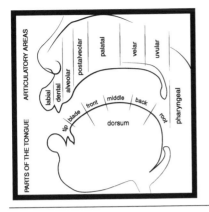
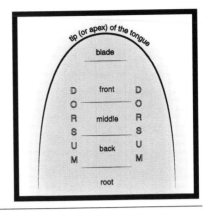

Figure 8.7 Mapping the oral cavity

mouth), and maybe even reach back to the velum (Figure 8.7). Reverse that process to let your tongue tip come to rest again. What does rest feel like, in terms of the relative height, tension, and availability of your tongue tip?

Bunch your tongue – make it thick and tall, by contracting the *transverse lingual muscles*. Then channel your tongue – make it thin and wide, by contracting the *vertical lingual muscles*. Shimmer between bunching and channeling. Then come to rest. What does rest feel like, when juxtaposed with bunching and channeling?

Pull the body (*dorsum*) of your tongue down. You can differentiate the *front*, *center*, and *back* of your dorsum to take the lead in lowering, or *cupping*. Pull all three parts down at once. Next, raise the body of your tongue, again differentiating between front, center, and back for different focuses of *arching*. Push all three up at once. Find the exact, vertical middle of your mouth with your tongue, a place that is neither arching nor cupping, with no muscular engagement of the dorsum (we called this position "Equator Tongue" in *Experiencing Speech*). Then engage in a shimmering tongue dance, arching and cupping subtly through front, center, and back. Then come to rest. What does rest feel like between arching and cupping, with an awareness of front, center, and back possibilities?

Can you feel the sides of your tongue interacting with your teeth? Do they push against your teeth? Or maybe just barely brush your teeth? You could feel the sides of your tongue making contact with the inner surface of your teeth, or you could be aware of the rough chewing edges of your molars. *Brace* your tongue against your teeth (simultaneous arching and channeling), and find different combinations of pressure on different surfaces of your teeth. Then let your tongue come to rest again. What does rest feel like? Are you picking up any tactile cues about your tongue from its proximity to your teeth?

Share some text – this exploration is for you right now, so no need to find a partner. Share it slowly at first, getting curious about how you move from rest into the actions of speech. Gradually speed up your sharing, noticing how you activate your muscles to create more sounds in less time. Vary the tempo and notice how the muscles of your vocal tract change to accomplish these shifts. Try adding effort to your sharing: what is it to add more muscularity to your language? Then take away some effort: what is it to communicate your text with as much muscular ease (or *laxness*) as possible? Vary the muscular effort between strong and lax: what do you feel in your vocal tract as you do so? Then come to rest: where is that after these lingual gymnastics?

One last time, let yourself breathe through an open mouth. Notice if the cool external air registers differently after you've moved through the possibilities of activity and relaxation. Did any parts of your anatomy stand out in your exploration? Did any of them seem more interesting after the comparison of motion and rest?

Postural Anatomy

Exercise 8.1 is both a refresher on the anatomy of speech and an exploration of what feels like "home base" in the habitual alignment of your vocal tract. By exploring the range of movement made possible by the finely tuned muscles of the face, mouth, tongue, and throat, you refamiliarize yourself with articulator isolations while also building an awareness of what we'll call your **Posture Zero** – the personal, habitual posture that you live in day to day.

And the previous exercise didn't even come close to exhausting your muscular options for Posture! In *Experiencing Speech*, we called the *vocal tract* the "flexible tube" that covers "the distance between your lips and nose and your voicebox." Let's get to know a few more of the muscular actions that can alter the shape of that tube.

When arching and cupping your tongue, you were most likely using a suite of finely coordinated muscles. Arching involves the *inferior lingual longitudinal muscles*, fibers that run through the underside of your tongue from front to back, on both the left and right sides. Cupping engages the *superior lingual longitudinal muscles*, mirroring along the top of the tongue their inferior counterparts. These *intrinsic* muscles – contained within the tongue itself – are also what you use to steer your tongue tip around. Moving the tongue tip up activates the superior longitudinals; moving the tongue tip down, the inferior. Steering your tongue tip to the left contracts the left superior and inferior longitudinals, while steering to the right contracts the pair on the right side. Go ahead – stick your tongue out and take it for a spin!

In order to use the longitudinal muscles for arching and cupping, you also contract *extrinsic* muscles – outside the tongue – to balance dynamic forces for sophisticated shapeshifting. When cupping your tongue, not only are your superior longitudinal muscles shortening along the top of the tongue, but you also use the genioglossus and hyoglossus to provide counterbalancing tension. Likewise, the arching of your tongue not only involves shortening the inferior longitudinal muscles, but also anchoring assistance from your genioglossus as well as some lifting from the palatoglossus. You can see the "arch" of the palatoglossus if you look in a mirror – it forms the first gateway between the mouth (*oral cavity*) and the throat beyond the uvula (*oropharynx*) (Figure 8.8). You can even tense the palatoglossus while keeping the tongue in place, which adds constriction to the oral cavity.

Other muscles also contribute to the constriction of the vocal tract, from the lightest of shimmers to vigorous tightening. We already encountered tongue bunching in Exercise 8.1, whereby the tongue thickens vertically to fill the oral cavity. Using different fibers of the

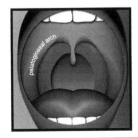

Figure 8.8 Palatoglossal arch

(intrinsic) transverse lingual muscles, you can focus bunching in different parts of the tongue, from the back of the dorsum all the way to the point of the tongue tip. Likewise, you can access different fibers of the vertical lingual muscles (yup, intrinsic, too!) to channel your tongue in distinct areas from front to back. Try channeling the front of your tongue while bunching the back – and vice versa. Is one type of action easier than the other?

Another noticeable form of shaping in the vocal tract involves the *pharyngeal constrictors*, which narrow the pharynx from top to bottom. The *superior pharyngeal constrictor* tightens the space around the upper pharynx (or *nasopharynx*), while the *middle constrictor* tightens the oropharynx and the *inferior constrictor* tightens the lower pharynx (or *laryngopharynx*). Also shaping the pharynx are the muscles of the velum, including those that lift the velum (*levator veli palatini* and *palatopharyngeus*), elevate the uvula (*musculus uvulae*), laterally stretch the velum (*tensor veli palatini*), and lower the velum toward the back of the tongue (palatoglossus). You can spot the palatopharyngeus in a mirror as the second archway in the oral cavity, just behind the palatoglossus. (Figure 8.9)

Some of the most visible constrictions you can make in the vocal tract occur around the lips and cheeks, whose near infinite shaping possibilities can be altered with only tiny degrees of effort or release. For example, the buccinators can contract along their entire length, effectively pulling the cheeks in between the teeth. They can also contract just around the outer ring of the orbicularis oris, tightening the lip corners and producing an effect called *lip pinning*. This firmness at the lip corners often forms a kind of anchor around which the other muscles of lip engagement move.

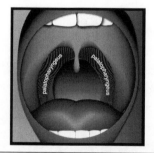

Figure 8.9 Palatopharyngeus

Even as one of the final articulatory shapes on the way out of the vocal tract, the tiny action of pinning can have a big impact on the sounds we hear and the postures we perceive.

Check It Out!

And still there's more to learn about anatomy! If you're curious about the physiology of the vocal tract, including the relationship of accentwork to voicework, we recommend *Speaking with Skill* (of course), in addition to anatomy apps and websites.

The Essence of Posture

It bears repeating, however, that our work with Posture isn't just about muscular tension. While we want to understand the muscles that shape speech and get to know them through isolations and selective activation, we're equally curious about release and motion.

Chances are, when you read "posture," your mind goes first to the way you hold your entire body, not just your articulators. Body posture may include aspects of your carriage that are consistent – for example, the distance between your feet or the height of your shoulders. Yet body posture isn't fixed – it changes as you move from standing to sitting to lying down, with different tendencies in each alignment. What's more, the way you live in your body is often a state of *readiness*, a blend of tension and release that's only witnessed in fleeting moments between actions.

The same is true of your vocal tract in its Posture Zero. Your articulators tend to find themselves in predictable degrees of activation over time, and Exercise 8.1 might have drawn your attention to which muscles are most **salient** through their actions. The word "salient" derives from Latin *salire* ("to leap"), so salience describes things that "leap out" to you. Generally speaking, you're more likely to notice actions that are less familiar or less practiced in your Posture Zero. On the other hand, you probably also found that certain movements were easier to explore or isolate than others, though you may not always be aware of the muscles that enable those actions.

Your current, habitual Posture Zero is a result of practice. The muscles you activate, the muscles you release, and the movements you find accessible arise from your previous speech experience. Your language environments have favored certain sounds over others, and your vocal tract finds the state of readiness that facilitates the most efficient production of those sounds. Efficiency is a key concept in Posture; so long as we can be understood by our desired audiences, we tend to conserve as much energy as possible in the actual production of speech. We build muscular familiarity with the particular kind of communication we need to survive and belong – and thus we develop a vocal tract posture.

Or, more likely, postures. We've suggested thus far that you already have one "home base," but it's far more likely that you have at least a few different versions of Posture Zero, if not multiple Postures Zero. For example, if you're multilingual, you may have a conscious or intuitive sense of how your L1s *feel* different in your vocal tract. You might even be able to identify what sort of articulatory shifts you make to transition from one L1 to another. And within any L1 posture, you may also be aware of slight shifts you make based on who you're talking to or the environments in which you find yourself. For example, imagine the physical changes you'd make in your mouth and throat to go from speaking to your friends in class to addressing a large assembly. How does your posture respond to social demands, even if in tiny ways?

It's also possible that you've built intuitive postural awareness through an L2 experience. Your L2 posture may not feel anywhere near as familiar as your Posture Zero . . . which is great! That lack of familiarity might help you build *more* awareness around the shift from Posture Zero to an L2 posture, since the latter requires more conscious effort. Whether you speak an L2 every day or haven't touched it in years, can you notice how you've got potential postural adjustments on call from previous L2 experiences?

Describing Posture

It can be challenging to put your intuitive, procedural understanding of posture into words. That challenge is compounded with every accent you explore – without declarative descriptions, how are you supposed to keep each of your learned Postures distinct and memorable?

Allow us to introduce one of our favorite tools . . .

Exercise 8.2: The Fifteen Listens

 Web Resource 8.2 Fifteen Listens

Web Resource 8.2 provides an audio sample of an L1 English speaker. Get it cued up, get some note-taking materials, and then get comfortable.

The Fifteen Listens are exactly what they sound like – you'll be listening to the sample fifteen times. Each listen will narrow your descriptive focus, zooming in on one aspect of posture that you can listen for with your mouth. By focusing your attention on one element at a time, you'll relieve yourself of trying to capture everything at once while also knowing you're accumulating helpful information with each listen.

Before we get to the list of questions, we should add that listening to this sample may activate the other Ps in your accent toolkit. You may identify with some of their cultural context, or you may really enjoy their prosody, or certain words' pronunciation may grab your pattern-seeking attention. You may also find that one aspect of Posture comes to predominate your experience, so that it's hard to focus on the targets of individual listens. That's okay! You can repeat as much as needed, and the invitation is to always let your perception – and your interoception – come back to the target again and again.

If any of the listens give you trouble, run experiments! If you're not sure what you're hearing-feeling, shift your vocal tract and see what effect that has. For example, if you have trouble interocepting what the tongue dorsum does, try arching and cupping while you listen with your mouth. Which actions get you closer to what you hear, and which seem to move you farther away?

Play the file all the way through for each question in this list. Listen with your mouth. *Take notes!* No need to keep all these in your memory.

Listen One: Where are the lip corners?
Listen Two: Is there lip trumpeting or pursing?
Listen Three: How mobile are those lips?
Listen Four: How open/closed is the jaw?
Listen Five: How front/back is the jaw?
Listen Six: How mobile is the jaw?
Listen Seven: Where's the tongue tip?

Listen Eight: How active is the tongue tip?

Listen Nine: Where's the tongue dorsum?

Listen Ten: How active is the dorsum?

Listen Eleven: Where's the back of the dorsum?

Listen Twelve: Where are the sides of the tongue?

Listen Thirteen: Where is the root of the tongue?

Listen Fourteen: Where is the velum?

Listen Fifteen: What food item might describe the shape in your mouth?

After the fifteenth listen, take a moment to breathe. Check in with your notes – do you want to reorganize them in any way? Did any of the features you observed seem most important (or salient) to you? Were any of the listens more challenging for you to engage in?

Now, try putting this posture on. Breathe through it. Shimmer it. Use your notes – you can also play the audio sample in the background for inspiration. It may be impossible to assemble and maintain all your notes at once, so which ones do you find most helpful for embodiment? Which parts of this postural description are most helpful for matching sounds from the sample? Which sounds give you the most useful clues for posture?

Share your observations and, if possible, your embodiment with your classmates. Notice how their descriptions of the sample's posture may differ from yours; everyone will have a set of instructions tailored to their own vocal tract. It's also possible that certain features of the posture provoke widespread agreement, based on the shared linguistic experiences of the class. You might be most interested to know how your classmates imagined a food item for the posture – that type of impressionistic description provides lots of room for personalization.

Comparing Postures

The Fifteen Listens are a tool, not a checklist. While we use them to get a sense of the minute features of an accent's posture, we often find that only some of those features are salient enough to aid in performance. You won't know which features are most important until you've had a chance to listen for all of them. Over time, you'll build skill in identifying which parts of *your* vocal tract respond most readily to other people's Postures. And the more you listen with specificity and care, the more quickly you'll identify and describe postural features in *all* accents.

It may also be evident at this point just how *subjective* a posture is. Salience is specific to your experience – what leaps out *to you*? The notes that help you describe your experience in the Fifteen Listens might not work for anybody else. Yet despite Posture's subjectivity, you can call upon your declarative knowledge of muscularity, articulation, and movement to connect your subjective experiences to those of others. In the end, it's not important if your postural description matches anybody else's – what's important is that each individual's description brings them closer to a shared sense of embodiment.

The subjectivity of Posture also means that you may find your personal notes are full of qualifiers. For example, in Exercise 8.2, how often did you end up using some version of "a little bit" or "a tiny amount" or "ever so slightly" in your descriptions? Some features of a posture are so slight that we really do need to call attention to how delicate our efforts are, which is also why we spent time shimmering earlier in this module. As you build skills in Posture through embodied listening, you'll likely find degrees of effort that are made clearer through the direct comparison of multiple postures.

In a similar vein, it may seem difficult to describe aspects of a posture defined more by movement than by a stationary position. For example, how do we describe lip corners that feel more pinned than our own, yet they're able to dance back and forth with surprising agility? One metaphor to explore might be a **center of gravity**, a point toward which the articulators tend to move without firmly landing. Just as celestial objects revolve around each other through space, so too might our articulatory efforts orbit around vocal tract shapes with more "mass" than others. A similar metaphor might be the idea of *magnet shapes*, or even *focal shapes*, both of which could also be connected to distinct sounds.

A particularly effective magnet is the **thinking sound** of a posture. When we allow voice to flow through the vocal tract in moments of uncertainty or reflection, the resulting sound is usually a reliable indicator of the overall tendencies of a posture at the ready. Thinking sounds can be invaluable for analyzing Posture, so listen for them carefully in your Donors' samples.

Thinking sounds usually bring up one other word that we'd like to call attention to: "neutral." Though certain parts of posture may seem to lack any noticeable tension or engagement, it only feels that way in comparison to your Posture Zero. What feels like no effort at all to you might, in fact, require quite a bit of effort from the vocal tract of someone else. This lack of absolute neutrality is what makes "objective" descriptions of any posture impossible.

If you do find the word "neutral" in your notes, could you reword your descriptions to reflect the tensed and released shapes that arise through your habitual posture? Always feel free to include "relative to my own posture" or "compared to my Posture Zero" in your descriptions – those phrases usually prove far more helpful than a hypothetical and impossible-to-define "neutral."

Exercise 8.3: Back to Zero

You developed a detailed breakdown of another posture through the Fifteen Listens in Exercise 8.2. Let's call that Posture One for the duration of this exercise. Revisit your notes to remember how to step into that posture again.

Let yourself play with a little Omnish in Posture One. Your Omnish may be limited in some ways by the shapes and tendencies of Posture One, resulting in less variety – go with it! For now, enjoy the free flow of obstruents and phthongs that arise most fluidly from Posture One.

Now just breathe through Posture One. Take stock of the sensations on the inhale. As you breathe, let your vocal tract slowly – *super slowly* – shift back to Posture Zero. Again, this may feel like "nothing" or "neutral," but it's simply another alignment of your vocal tract, reverting to its most familiar settings *for you*. How did you make that transition happen? In which muscles or movements or releasing were you most aware of the shift from One to Zero? Run some Omnish – full Omnish – through your Posture Zero.

Let the Omnish go. Feel your breath traveling in and out through Posture Zero. While maintaining awareness of your breath, transition super-slowly back to Posture One. Notice which shifts seem most salient or accessible for making this slow transition possible. Do you find it easier to focus on one feature for the entire transition (such as jaw height or tongue bunching)? Or is it easier to transition multiple features, one by one, until you've assembled a full embodiment of Posture One?

Repeat this process as many times as you like, noticing if you gain any additional information about Posture One *or* Posture Zero along the way. Eventually, allow yourself to Omnate *throughout* the transition, from Posture Zero to Posture One and then back again. Also try speeding up the transition, even to the point of an instantaneous shift, observing which parts of your vocal tract are most salient for different tempos.

For a final treat, conduct these transitions with a partner – literally! Take turns conducting each other by using your hands to indicate posture shifts for your partner: sweeping from right to left to indicate the speed of transition, or holding up one hand for Posture One and the other for Posture Zero. Then, hold a shape-shifting conversation in Omnish with your partner, alternating or transitioning between Zero and One. What's easy to hold onto in each posture when you add communicative intent? What slips away?

Check-In

What are you feeling right now . . . now? How has your experience of your Posture or Postures Zero changed? How would you describe your habitual posture to yourself for future reference? How would you describe it to someone else? How does having a Posture One for comparison help or hinder your exploration of Posture(s) Zero?

Present your observations, insights, and feelings about your Posture Zero to your class. Prepare a two-minute Posture Production. Describe it through words, but feel free to include other media of expression such as dance, poetry, visual arts, film, music, or demonstration. This is your chance to honor and rejoice in your personal posture experience – and to support your classmates as they honor and rejoice in theirs!

Conclusion

Posture often feels like the most magical of the Four Ps. By tapping into the procedural wisdom of our bodies, Posture frequently unleashes a sense of ownership in accent that we can't seem to find otherwise. But Posture is rooted in as much specificity, rigor, and attention as the rest of the Four Ps, and we still need all four to make the magic happen. Once you understand your personal approach to the shaping of the vocal tract, you can recreate a sense of wonder again and again – and explain it, too, if needed.

Indeed, it may already be evident just how many skills get tied into Posture. The more you listen with your mouth, the more you can discover in the perception and production of speech. The more postures you assemble, the finer you can draw your distinctions among them. All our work with articulator isolations and exercises has accumulated to create the physical precision needed to dig into Posture with thorough and powerful detail. These skills not only serve you in understanding your habitual articulatory settings, but they also prepare you for any and every accent you wish to investigate in the future.

MODULE NINE
POSTURE – SPEECH AS MOVEMENT

Vocal tract posture is better defined by movement than by stillness. That's because speaking is something we *do*. It's not a rigid form that we hold or lock onto. You spent much of Module Eight exploring the muscles with which you could make localized changes to your vocal tract. Your experiences also shed light on the balance and coordination of muscular actions that produce the sounds you use to communicate.

This process for learning the skills of speech is akin to a movement class or sports training. You started with the basics of anatomy and physical forces, the building blocks of movement. Then you drilled the fundamentals and took stock of your physical abilities for their dynamism, strength, ease, and malleability. Finally, you took time to appreciate the intuitive proficiency of your daily actions (Posture Zero) and how you can use your growing skills to analyze and embody another person's actions.

Now you're ready to put your Posture skills to work in more complex combinations. You can always return to the fundamentals, but it's time to zoom out and notice how your physical abilities contribute to the fluidity and coherence of performance. Were this a dance class, you're transitioning from barre and floor patterns to choreography. Were this a sport, you're transitioning from drills to scrimmage.

DOI: 10.4324/9781003314905-11

Theme and Variation

As we shift our focus from articulatory skills to the physical markers of an accent in performance, overlapping questions of identity tend to arise. When you're listening for Posture, how do you distinguish between the characteristics of an accent and the features that arise from the unique anatomical structures of the speakers you're listening to?

As much as your vocal tract is shaped through the acquired competence of language and accent, there are still features of your voice that are uniquely your own. On page 86, we briefly referred to this concept as *vocal identity*; the resonances, harmonics, and timbre of your voice are a result of the particular structures of your vocal tract, including the size, thickness, and proportions of your larynx, vocal folds, bones, cartilage, and tissues. This uniqueness may also arise through muscular action as well, such as laryngeal elevation and depression, or laryngopharyngeal constriction.

On the other hand, the postures of a group of speakers, when compared, may reveal a common pattern that hints at an *accent identity*, something we also identified as a key paralinguistic function of Prosody (see page 77). Despite individual anatomical variation in vocal tracts, we can perceive that a group of speakers has a similar accent posture due to shared muscular engagements and movement patterns. For example, we may notice that many English speakers in Gatlinburg tend toward tongue root retraction while many English speakers in Galway do not. The postural tendencies that reveal accent identity are what we seek out in our Posture work.

Stay curious about the overlaps between Posture, vocal identity, and Prosody (see Figure 9.1). It may be that some accents require you to shift the position of the larynx in order to find prosodic features you want to embody, which would have consequences for both Posture and Prosody. Or, in other accents, you could find that laryngeal height is a matter of personal vocal identity, independent of the prosodic or postural features of a larger accent group. While a muscular effort might be interesting and salient in an individual, compare it to other speakers to make sure it's part of an accent and not purely idiolectal.

As an example, imagine the voice of a favorite cartoon character. How much of that character's accent arises from Posture? From Prosody? And

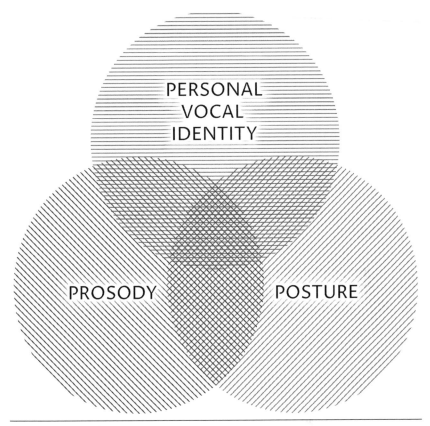

Figure 9.1 Potential Posture overlaps

from the structures of the actor's vocal tract – that is, their vocal identity? Sometimes the most fitting answer is "Yes!" to all three questions. It may be that we can't draw sharp distinctions between these three areas, so leave room for flexible and interconnected interpretations.

Exercise 9.1: From Sounds to Posture

You'll eventually be moving into conversations with your classmates. For now, find a space where you can explore on your own.

Start expressing yourself in Omnish. Add as much variety as you can – and include prosodic variety (pitch variations, tempo, durational shifts) as well as variety in the ease or effort of articulation. Do some **clinical Omnish,** too – momentarily forget about communicating meaning and make sure you're exploring as many obstruents and vowels as possible.

When you feel you've found your most expansive range of phonetic options, move into communicative Omnish again by finding things in the room that you like and telling them so.

Then, shift your Omnish into slow motion. You can keep your focus on communicating, or you could shift back to clinical mode. Just make sure a slower tempo doesn't reduce your phonetic possibilities.

As you savor the articulatory actions of slow Omnish, notice if there are any actions that feel particularly attractive today, including both obstruents and phthongs. Pick two of these actions to keep revisiting, albeit with as much variety as you can manage to include around them. Notice how you could physically describe these actions – with attention to the position, movement, and effort of your articulators. Remember these two actions as **centers of gravity** (see page 119) or through the **magnet sounds** they produce; your Omnish will bob and weave between them, never quite settling yet never far away.

Now turn the strength of those centers up to maximum – allow your entire vocal tract to shape itself around those actions. Let your jaw, lips, cheeks, and tongue shift to make your magnet sounds the predominant realizations of your vocal tract posture. While this may involve focused effort in some parts of the vocal tract, there are other areas that may need to accommodate by finding more release.

By letting your posture respond to articulatory centers of gravity, you may notice that your Omnish variety is reduced – and that's totally okay! Your focus on posture has brought your vocal tract to a particular alignment that now produces a **Somenish**. Your current Somenish is the range of actions and resulting sounds that are more accessible in this posture, while sounds that are difficult to find here fall away. Settle into this posture and its Somenish. Start by cataloging your articulatory possibilities in clinical Somenish, then use it to communicate with the world around you.

Remember to pause every so often and breathe in and out through your posture. What information do you gain about your vocal tract's physicality from the flow of breath? Take some notes on your invented posture. How are you shaping the entirety of your vocal tract, beyond the centers of gravity? Use the descriptors from the Fifteen Listens on pages 117-118 to gather more clues.

Take your Somenish around the room and use it to converse with your classmates. See what it's like to engage in the give and take of conversation while speaking *and* listening in your invented posture. Feel free to wander away and listen again to your Somenish – place your hands over your ears and mouth, if needed – in order to relocate your posture's centers of gravity.

Pair off with one partner. You can converse with each other in Somenish, or you can take turns exchanging longer Somenish monologues. Your goal, while listening and breathing in your posture, is to see if you can identify your partner's centers of gravity. You may get this information through the sounds you perceive, the muscle engagement you see, or perhaps even some listening with your mouth – just remember to find your centers of gravity again when it's your turn to speak!

When both partners have had a chance to observe each other, transition to another experiment: talk to your partner about this experience in your Acting Language *through your posture*. That is, speak a language you can both understand but maintain your invented posture as you do so. If needed, go back to your centers of gravity and Somenish to refresh your memory.

It doesn't matter if your observations exactly match your partner's experience of their centers of gravity. Instead, you may have noticed features that were salient to you but not the focus of your partner's conscious effort. Sometimes, what we notice is "articulatory spillover," wherein intentional changes in posture create unintended shifts in other parts of the vocal tract. That's a great thing to be aware of!

Continue this exercise with additional partners, or take your findings to a class discussion. Take notes for yourself as well. Which parts of this progression were useful for creating, maintaining, and describing a posture? What was it like to move into your Acting Language while retaining your invented posture? What was it like to listen and gather clues about someone else's posture – and keep your own throughout?

Exercise 9.2: Pass a Posture

Keep your invented posture ready – you're going to pass it to someone else!

Find a partner, preferably someone you didn't work with in the previous exercise. Decide who's going to be the first Guide, while the other partner acts as Learner.

Guide, start by modeling your invented posture. You can use any of our previous processes to do so – clinical Somenish, communicative Somenish, focusing on centers of gravity and **shimmering** around them, or speaking in your Acting Language through your invented posture. Play around with whatever you think will help your Learner perceive your invented posture. Your goal is to have them speak in a mutually comprehensible Acting Language while embodying your posture.

Learner, listen with your mouth and try on your Guide's invented posture. How far can you get before you need more guidance? Is modeling enough, or do you want more specific feedback? When you feel like you've got the posture, check in with your Guide – what do they think?

Guide, offer a "degree of thumbs" response – if they're right on, give them an enthusiastic thumbs-up! Learner, if you get less than a full thumbs-up, consider asking for posture-based notes (in your Acting Language) from your Guide. Which parts of your vocal tract should you engage? What should you release? Are there movement tendencies that help you zero in? Keep going until you get a full thumbs-up!

Guide, *can you offer guidance while remaining in the invented posture?*

When your postures are as close to matching as you can get, have a conversation in your Acting Language about your favorite times of year. Notice what it's like to listen, breathe, and engage from this shared posture.

Now, Guide and Learner, take your postures for a walk! Find another pair of partners. Greet them, ask how their day is going, chat about the weather – just don't talk about your invented postures! Notice what it's like to hear *another* invented posture as you and your partner communicate with other people. Do you notice similarities in the other pair's postures? Do you notice individual variation? Does your own partner help you stay grounded in the posture you share?

Say goodbye to that pair, and chat with your partner about what it was like to teach/learn a new posture, share it in conversation, and then encounter another posture in conversation. You can share this feedback in your invented posture or let it go – you deserve a break!

After discussion, Guide and Learner switch roles and repeat the exercise. The new Guide may need a little time to refresh their invented posture or consult their notes, but feel free to go through the remembering process as part of your modeling. And notice what it's like to encounter yet another set of postures on your walk!

Notice the progression from Exercise 9.1 to Exercise 9.2. Your invented posture arose from arbitrary sounds, as opposed to a real-world accent. Yet once you ran Somenish and then your Acting Language through it, it began to take on its own form of accent identity. Working with your partner, you found ways to transfer your accent identity to someone else, adapting to their personal vocal identity yet naming those aspects of Posture that you could share. Finally, you had a chance to experience a shared accent identity with your partner in comparison to another group – and all through innovation and play. Impressive work!

Moving Around the World

Of course, real languages are based on established patterns of sounds and meaning, which make them more predictable in Prosody, Posture, and Pronunciation than chaotic Omnish or only slightly more organized Somenishes. The greater predictability of actual human languages means that we can find postural patterns in them . . . even when we don't understand what's being said.

Exercise 9.3: Another Fifteen Listens . . .

Web Resource 9.1 Fifteen Listens L1

Web Resource 9.1 gives you a video sample of a speaker speaking an L1 other than English. The sample is relatively brief, but you'll be listening to it – surprise! – fifteen times. Take notes on how you would describe this person's posture using the questions from the Fifteen Listens (see Figure 9.3). Highlight the features that are most salient for you.

Then, put this posture together in your own vocal tract. You're *not* going to speak the language of the sample – because you may not know it! Use Somenish instead, transitioning from Omnish if useful.

If you find certain sounds serve as helpful centers of gravity, use them! But come back to the free flow of Somenish within the speaker's posture, rather than getting pulled into replicating what you hear, sound for

1. Where are the lip corners?	8. How active is the tongue tip?
2. Is there lip trumpeting or pursing?	9. Where's the tongue dorsum?
3. How mobile are those lips?	10. How active is the dorsum?
4. How open/closed is the jaw?	11. Where's the back of the dorsum?
5. How front/back is the jaw?	12. Where are the sides of the tongue?
6. How mobile is the jaw?	13. Where is the root of the tongue?
7. Where's the tongue tip?	14. Where is the velum?
15. What food item might describe the shape in your mouth?	

Figure 9.3 Fifteen Listens Questions

sound. We always seek to honor our Donors: rather than mimic their sounds, we're investigating their *posture* with specificity and respect.

Experiment with playing and pausing the sample as you speak in Somenish (Somenate). Which aspects of your embodiment seem most helpful for retaining the experience of this posture? Play the sample as often as you'd like, but take breaks to speak on your own – and breathe through the posture, too!

When you're ready, use your Somenish to communicate with something near you that you enjoy. Then, *move into your Acting Language.* Can you stay embodied in the posture while you switch between Somenish and your Acting Language? Does your Acting Language make any aspects of this posture *more* salient? Is it challenging to maintain this posture as you encounter your familiar Acting Language?

Web Resource 9.2 Fifteen Listens L2

Web Resource 9.2 provides a sample of this same speaker communicating in English. Listen to the sample with your mouth – do you still hear and feel the L1 posture in their L2? Which aspects of the speaker's L1 posture carry over? Which aspects fall away? Do the sounds you hear in their L2 English match your expectations from the L1 posture? How far could Posture take you in describing and embodying this speaker's L2 English?

Experimenting with a speaker's L1 gives you clues as to which familiar patterns they might call upon their L2 experience, but those patterns are *predictive* only. When moving into an L2, individual speakers make different choices as to how to adapt their L1 posture to meet their needs, including borrowing and mimicry (see page 71). And their strategies may shift over time, adding further variation among individuals as they spend more or less time honing their skills. Speakers of a shared L1 can produce shared postural patterns in an L2, but we shouldn't be surprised by large amounts of variability between speakers.

Also notice the value of Somenish in understanding an L2 posture. As a performer, you can't be expected to learn the L1 of every L2 accent you wish to embody. Instead, use the progression of Omnish into Somenish to gather information about an L1 posture and put it into practice. This path allows you to experiment with an L2 accent posture while treating your Donors with respect, curiosity, and specificity.

Overloading, Not Overwhelming

But maybe you didn't feel entirely at ease during Exercise 9.3, nor does using Somenish for L1 posture discovery always feel comfortable. You may feel, even in small ways, that this method of exploration brings you too close to mockery or caricature. That concern is a skill! Sensitivity to cultural context is something we very much want to encourage in all Four Ps, especially when you allow yourself to take on the physicality of another human being.

Your work with People should address worries about mocking. When you come from a place of empathy, the intent of mockery – to demean, belittle, or otherize – is interrupted. Caricature, on the other hand, might have some valuable lessons, if only in your solo explorations.

"Caricature" derives from Italian *caricatura*, meaning "an overloading," from Latin *carricare*, "to load a wagon." An exaggerated embodiment of speech actions, undertaken in a spirit of play and consent, may allow you to perceive and refine posture in ways that micro-adjustments do not.

If you take time to "overload" your vocal tract, you may find that your understanding of posture gets *more detailed*, before you dial it back down to the easy and shimmering efforts of your Donors.

The proper setting for that exploration, however, might only be in the privacy of your own work. While respectful use of exaggeration may build physical versatility, we *don't* advocate for the violation of consent, either in your relationship to your Donors, your fellow performers, or anyone who might be listening as you build skills. Exploring exaggerated postural options in public might cross social boundaries that are too complex to be safely negotiated in a classroom or performance environment. Refer to your work from People – if your empathetic understanding of cultural context hints that "now is not the time," heed that impulse and save your investigation for a more private setting.

And exaggeration is only one tool out of many! It may be a part of your process that you conduct as a thought experiment, without producing any sound, or one that you skip entirely. We just don't want to outlaw it from accentwork; it's a potentially useful step on a longer journey, but certainly not your final destination.

Inhabiting Posture

Ultimately, beyond the Fifteen Listens, Somenish, and exaggeration, our goal is to *inhabit a posture*. "Inhabit" comes from Latin *en-* + *habitare*, "to dwell in," which is related to the Latin root *habere*, from which English also derives "habit." We want a posture to feel like a familiar home, a place where you can breathe and listen and move with freedom and ease. Unlike exaggeration, an inhabited posture lives mostly in the shimmer, the tiny movements that flow and dance around articulatory centers of gravity. You should be able to move comfortably and spontaneously in your accents' postures, like well-fitted costumes (which, conveniently, is another Middle English meaning of "habit"). Whether with L1 or L2 accents, the postures you embody should feel like they do to the people who use them – authentic, organic, and responding in real time to your communicative needs.

Fortunately, the more work you do with Posture, the more familiar homes you'll have available! Thanks to your focus on the physicality of the vocal tract, you never gain skill for just one accent – you accumulate skills for *all* accents.

Are there ways to build Posture skills beyond analyzing one accent at a time? You bet! Test out these recommendations and see which ones work best for you:

 • *Back to basics!* Revisit the articulator isolations in Module Two of *Experiencing Speech*. While isolations may seem silly in, well, isolation, they add up to a highly detailed understanding of Posture, both in perception and production. If you encounter any aspect of physical exploration that feels unfamiliar or difficult to embody, find a related isolation to increase your awareness and dexterity. For example, if you're not certain how an accent you're listening to engages the tongue root, practice tongue root advancement and retraction. Then listen with your mouth again and test your new skills alongside what you hear. Visit **Web Resource 9.3** to find a copy of our Articulator Isolations Log (from *Experiencing Speech*) that you can use to track your gains.

Web Resource 9.3 Articulator Isolations Log

- *Give yourself permission to play!* Choose centers of gravity or magnet sounds at random, develop them into a posture, take the posture into Somenish, then move into your Acting Language (Exercise 9.1). Play with exaggerating and minimizing the strength of these arbitrary centers of gravity. Mix in parts of your vocal tract that are unfamiliar and see how effortlessly you can integrate them.
- *Ask, "Can I do less?"* Any time you create a posture, notice how little work you can do and still feel/perceive the accent. You could also work through the elements of the Fifteen Listens, one by one, and see which ones can be reduced in effort without noticeably impacting the overall posture. Of course, you may find that when you reduce the effort in some elements, the whole thing falls apart. It's worth testing all of them, just to see how much work is truly needed.
- *Always be in revision mode.* After arriving at a detailed understanding of an accent's posture, allow yourself to edit it later, especially as you acquire more postures. For example, it may be that what felt like a majorly arched back-of-dorsum in one accent is actually only

slightly bunched compared to another accent you discover later. You may also get helpful insights from other people describing the same posture, so borrow and steal freely. Your first observations aren't written in stone, and even tiny edits acquired through comparison can produce big and satisfying changes in performance.

And, as always, incorporate your own innovations! If you find a personal approach to Posture useful, make it into a game, share it with others, teach it to a classmate, or sing it in the shower. The more playful, the better!

Reference Postures

As you progress, you may find that postures for certain accents are easier to embody or are more consistent in performance. These postures can become *references*, providing ready-made models for comparison with less familiar vocal tracts you encounter in your work.

We've already explored the idea that your Posture(s) Zero can be a helpful reference. However, Postures Zero are usually so ingrained that they can be difficult to describe using declarative language. For that reason, learned postures can be potent references when your Posture Zero seems resistant to interrogation.

As your accent skills develop, keep track of which postures stand out as references. These postures could come from accents you found easy to learn – though they frequently also emerge from accents that proved most challenging! Reference postures should be ones that reach the level of unconscious competence, a form of "felt memory" stored in your procedural knowledge. Of course, the *most* useful references will be those that you also remember how to reconstruct through explicit, declarative description. It's that interplay of procedural and declarative that you can modify and manipulate to work your way into new postures, thereby expanding your skills ever onward.

Exercise 9.4: Shifting References

You'll need your posture and notes from Exercise 8.3 (page 120), which we'll still refer to as Posture One. And remember the accent you played with in Gradual Exposure (Exercise 1.3, page 13)? Let's bring that accent's posture back as a reference for this exercise and call it Posture Two. As always, have a memorized text at the ready, too.

Start by speaking a bit of text in Posture Two. How would you describe this posture? You're doing something new here – stepping into an accent posture you already feel at home in *and* putting your newly sharpened declarative skills to work! If you'd like, you can transition between speaking in your everyday posture (Posture Zero) and Posture Two. Which articulators and articulatory actions seem most salient as you transition between these reference postures? If you had to pick only three primary features for Posture Two, what would they be?

Keep Posture Two, but move into Somenish now – and keep communicating your text! What types of sounds seem to be favored by this arrangement of your vocal tract? If you'd like, you can shift between your Acting Language and Somenish to give yourself physical reminders for maintaining Posture Two. Take some breaths through it. Send your text to your environment in Posture Two Somenish. Listen to the room with Posture Two in your vocal tract.

Great. Let Posture Two go, but not far.

Repeat this process for Posture One, restarting your text as needed. Your goal is to communicate your text with Posture One Somenish, using whatever tools are most helpful. Breathing and listening are extremely helpful, as is distilling Posture One down to its three most important features.

Now, keep a steady flow of Somenish moving through Posture One, making sure to leave time for breath. At a moment of your choosing, without stopping your Somenish, switch to Posture Two – which will also change your Somenish. Give yourself time to settle into Posture Two Somenish. Then, again following your own impulse, switch to Posture One and its variety of Somenish.

Try slowing down the transitions between Postures One and Two. Notice what gets easier and what gets more challenging. At slow speeds, can you find moments when you feel like you're blending your postures? Experiment with other tempos. Play with this Somenish switching as much as you'd like, then take some notes.

How did you do that?! What does Posture One reveal about Posture Two? And vice versa? Are the same key features equally important in both transitions? Or do you focus on different aspects of your postures based on the direction of the change? How do these two references provide more detail on the shape and movement of your vocal tract?

Begin to Somenate your text in Posture One again. When you're ready, move from Somenish into your Acting Language. Then, when you have the impulse, switch to Posture Two *without interrupting the text*. The goal here is to focus on posture, so let your felt experience lead the way. Dip into Somenish again if it's helpful, but keep coming back to your Acting Language and text. Then experiment with alternating between Postures while speaking your text. Play with different transition tempos, and search again for opportunities to find a slow-tempo blend of both postures. Then take some more notes – what was it like to explore transitioning between reference postures in your Acting Language? Was it harder or easier than using Somenish? How did focusing on Posture impact your experience of your Acting Language?

Check-In

It's time to bring Posture into your BAP.

Revisit your Donors' samples – as many as you feel are helpful – and use the Fifteen Listens to analyze and embody their posture(s). If your Donor(s) speaks English as an L2, make sure to explore the posture of their L1 as well (like you did in Exercise 9.3). Practice embodying a posture that feels representative of your BAP accent. Compare it to your references. Then reflect on the experience.

What do you understand better about accents through the perspective of Posture? What still doesn't seem to click? Which physical skills do you want to practice more? Which physical skills feel well within your wheelhouse? Are there any accents you feel you already understand through an intuitive sense of Posture? Are there any accents you'd like to know better – or re-analyze – through the descriptive tools of Posture?

Summarize your observations, thoughts, and findings in a document and present it to your class. It could take the form of lists, idea clouds, a poem, or an essay. Be sure to include some modeling of your BAP accent, and see if you can name – and possibly teach – three salient features of that posture.

Conclusion

Exploring Posture allows you to enter into the feeling of an accent, to embody it. The incorporation of muscular actions, of movement tendencies, and of subtle, shimmering effort are reminders of just how physical accentwork is and how diligent we need to be in our conditioning for performance.

However, the interweaving of vocal and accent identity, of shape and sound, of resonance and musicality, are all reminders that the entirety of accentwork is physical, from People to Pronunciation. The specificity of your muscular skills forms the foundation for every aspect of your accentwork.

As we move into Pronunciation in the next two modules, it may be tempting to reconceptualize accents as groupings of words and symbols, as phonetic output resulting linearly from cognitive input. Remember that Posture illuminates the active, breathing, ever-moving foundation of Pronunciation. We'll soon zoom in on specific sounds and the patterns they follow, and you can use Posture as the framework upon which to hang the phonetic realizations of accent. You have an embodied sense of posture and articulatory finesse to build upon in the pages ahead, and your intuitive, muscular wisdom enlivens every sound you make.

Module Ten
Pronunciation – Categories

After People, Prosody, and Posture, we've finally arrived at the question that always seems most prominent in accentwork: how do you say the words?! Sure, the rest is important, but if we don't know how to say the words, will we actually be performing in accent at all?

Pronunciation *is* absolutely necessary for an accent performance that people accept as authentic – including ourselves! Our pattern-seeking minds are built to detect who belongs to our social groups by recognizing tiny variations in the speech sounds of others. Our intuitive abilities are so profound that we can often pluck a single word out of another person's speech and know that they are, somehow, *not like us*.

And we're *very* good at this type of recognition. Differences in pronunciation often seem to leap out at us, without requiring us to hunt for them. As we mentioned on page 115, this "leaping out" is what we refer to as **salience**. However, the intuitive processes by which we notice salience operate incredibly quickly. We can often leap to conclusions before we have a chance to check ourselves for reductive thinking, including biases, stereotypes, and the influence of standards.

The unchecked intuition of pronunciation has another limitation for us as actors: it hinders our ability to perceive and perform accents. If we don't slow down our understanding of pronunciation, then we rob

DOI: 10.4324/9781003314905-12

ourselves of nuance and subtlety. And, as we've seen, accents *live* in nuance and subtlety!

Be on the lookout for the limiting binary mindset of "correct" and "incorrect" pronunciation. The fact that we so often fall into this binary isn't our fault. In fact, there's a *long* history of it in the study and practice of accents, one that continues to reverberate today.

Traditions of Pronunciation

For most of their history, methods for teaching speech have dealt almost exclusively with the pronunciation of words. Traditional schools of thought around pronunciation, reaching back to antiquity, tended to be served up alongside a hearty helping of **prescriptivism**; that is, they focused on locating, analyzing, and teaching the prescribed or "correct" pronunciation of words. Closer to the modern era, many English-speaking accent teachers also saw themselves as guiding students toward "beautiful," "good," or "proper" pronunciation. What was "correct" was almost always centered on a standard variety of language with **overt prestige** (see page 62), which is what made it "beautiful," "good," and "proper" in the first place. Any pronunciation that differed from the standard was *ipso facto* substandard, inferior, or "wrong."

Check It Out!

Revisit Dudley Knight's "Standards" and "Standard Speech: The Ongoing Debate" for readable summaries of the role of prescriptivism and standard-based pronunciation in the history of accentwork. You can find these free articles at ktspeechwork.org/readings.

Many English-speaking actors in the twentieth century learned accentwork that inherited a hierarchical worldview and devalued non-standard accents. Standard accents – like **Received Pronunciation (RP)** in the UK or "Mid-Atlantic" in the US – were the first goal of actor training. Other accents were taught through comparison to standard pronunciation, usually via the concept of "sound substitution." This process required students to triangulate a target accent between the standard and their personal accent, adding complication and reducing authenticity. The result was a system of accent training that was corrective, prejudicial, incomplete, and, in most cases, oppressive.

But perhaps the biggest issue with prescriptivism and sound substitution is that *they don't reflect how accents actually work in real human beings.* The way that we hear, produce, and attach meaning to speech sounds is not determined by ideal templates of languages, floating outside the people who speak them. Accents emerge from the complexity of our very much embodied minds, forming and re-forming organic patterns that don't rigidly obey rules frozen in time.

Enter linguistics – and a revolution in our understanding of language. During the twentieth century, linguistics made enormous advances in assembling **descriptive** tools for understanding human language. Though many linguists, like all of us, operate under the prejudices of their times and cultures, they've laid the theoretical groundwork for a non-prescriptive understanding of languages, dialects, and accents.

Check It Out!

KTS owes a huge debt of gratitude to the field of linguistics for its descriptive tools and techniques. Among the many of our heroes whose work we'll be all too briefly touching upon are Daniel Jones (a driving force behind the IPA), William Labov (who almost single-handedly pioneered sociolinguistics), and J.C. Wells (you'll hear a lot about him soon). We recommend learning more about the work of those individuals, as well as a few of our other favorites: J.C. Catford; Lera Boroditsky; Inger Mees; Beverley Collins; Kenneth Pike; Linda Shockey; Peter Trudgill.

Our goal in Pronunciation is to combine the best of our accent-training legacies, uniting non-hierarchical descriptivism with process-based performance. Instead of looking for "right" pronunciation, remain curious about how certain sounds can be *right for* a given set of linguistic circumstances.

The Language Process

We said on page 9 that language is "a process of encoding ideas into a transmissible form which is then reconstituted by a listener/receiver." We could represent this process with a simplified diagram, as in Figure 10.1.

Let's go through this process and describe what happens when you communicate your ideas through language:

(A) First, you need ideas! Your inner experience arises in some form (thoughts, concepts, emotions); this often, though not always, precedes their formation into language.

(B) Your ideas get translated into *units of meaning*: words and grammar. "Grammar" in this case refers simply to the arrangement of multiple words into larger contexts. "Units of meaning" translate your inner experience into chunks that you can send to someone else.

(C) Words are further broken down into **phonemes**. As we'll see, these phonemes are the sounds you think you'll need to make to transfer your words to another person.

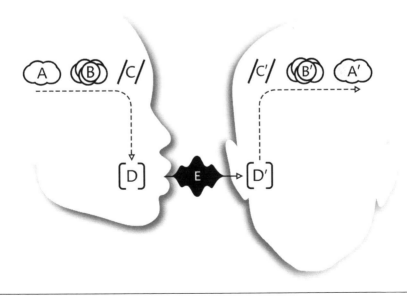

Figure 10.1 A model for speech

(D) Phonemes are realized by your articulators, executing the physical gestures which give rise to your intended sounds.

(E) Your articulatory gestures produce *actual* sounds. These intricately nuanced pressure waves created by your vocal tract are also known as **phones**.

Notice how the left and right side of the diagram are almost mirror images of each other – what gets encoded by the speaker is decoded by the listener. A listener picks up the sound waves (E); their auditory framework (the ears and associated neural pathways) deduces the articulatory gestures that created those sound waves (D'); those hypothetical gestures get decoded into phonemes (C') and then into words and grammar (B'); and the listener reassembles those units to (hopefully) understand what the speaker means (A').

If even this simplified process seems much more elaborate than your experience of spoken communication, we should remind you that it happens *unbelievably* quickly when speaking your L1. The transition from idea to words to phonemes happens entirely within your mind, almost instantaneously and unconsciously. And the physical transition from phonemes to sounds is also mostly immediate, with no noticeable gap between thinking the sounds and making them (with exceptions that deserve honoring – see page 18). How do we get a better grasp on this process when so much of it happens outside our conscious awareness?

Let's start with the part that's identical for the speaker *and* the listener: the sound waves themselves.

Phone-ing It In

When we consider (E) in Figure 10.1, the sounds involved could be described as a *signal*, with *no inherent meaning*. After being compressed by the speaker, speech sounds need a listener to determine what thoughts they signify.

In Figure 10.2, notice how there seem to be divisions in both the waveform and the spectrogram, places where the quality of the signal seems to change. In fact, we could probably divide the signal into chunks at these boundaries, delineating distinct speech sounds and linking them to specific articulatory actions. These chunks are **phones**, which we

WAVEFORM

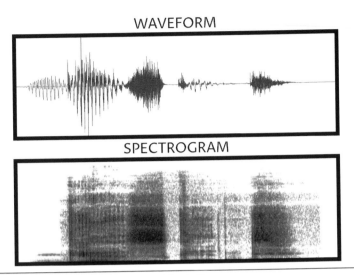

SPECTROGRAM

Figure 10.2 Visual representations of the word "gasket"

summarized in *Experiencing Speech* as "a single unit of speech, regardless of its function in language" – that is, a piece of a signal, regardless of the context that gives it meaning.

Measurable qualities in the flow of sound – like harmonic frequencies, turbulence, and timing – point to the physical actions that shaped them. In fact, the association between articulatory gestures and sounds is so close that we often consider them together, describing phones through the physical actions that created them. We describe **phthongs** (vowels) as close or open, front or back, rounded or unrounded. We describe **obstruents** (consonants) based on the nature of the airflow, voicing, and the place and manner of articulation.

Listening for the properties of phones and describing them in a way that others can understand is the goal of **phonetics**. For our work with Pronunciation, we develop a sensitive and detailed phonetic understanding of speech so we can understand *what's being physically produced*, independent of the speaker's intention or the listener's expectations (see "etic" on page 61). Phonetic awareness provides an opening to examine an otherwise automatic process: the two-way conversion between what we mean to say and the phones we produce to say it.

The growth of your phonetic skills – including a wide variety of Omnish – slows down the process between (C) and (C') in Figure 10.1.

Omnish asks you to listen attentively, find nuance through specificity, and appreciate phones apart from their potential meanings. When it comes time to attach linguistic meaning to phones, though, we need a different system of description . . . and a different way of thinking about speech sounds.

Phonemenal

As you've hopefully learned from Omnish, you can create and hear an infinite variety of phones, and all of them are potentially valuable for transmitting information to other human beings. Even with a palette of sounds considerably reduced from Omnish, such as English or Hindi, you most likely encounter more distinct phones every day than you could ever hope to remember. It's easy to imagine how overwhelmed we'd become if we had to remember the meaning of *every single phone we hear*, and yet, somehow, we hear thousands and thousands of phones a day and understand all of them.

Here's where another of our human superpowers comes to our aid: *categorization*. We, as human beings, like to put things in groups. Creating a group out of distinct elements is efficient for our brains, allowing us to more easily identify and manage large amounts of data. We create categories intuitively as well as consciously, in our thought processes, physical surroundings, and social lives.

We also categorize phones. Our grouping impulse smooths over tiny variations in phones and focuses our attention on the shared identity of sounds within larger categories. These larger categories of phones are what we called **phonemes** on page 141. A phoneme is a collection of phones that share an identity in a language user's mind. The way we categorize phones as phonemes is dependent on the way we understand the expectations embedded in our language variety (see "emic" on page 61).

We can see how phonemes work through the comparison of **minimal pairs**. Consider the English words "meet" and "mitt." For most L1 English speakers, the consonant phonemes in these two words are the same, which allows us to more readily perceive that the vowel phonemes are different – hence, they *contrast*. On the other hand, a large number of L1 English speakers would consider the vowels in "meet" and "meat" to be *non-contrastive* and group them into the same phoneme (making the two words *homophones*, from Greek *homos* "same" + *phone* "sound").

Notation Convention

Now would be a good time to remember a helpful convention in notation. When you want to indicate that you're talking about phones, use brackets – [fɤʊ̯nz]. When you want to indicate that you're talking about phonemes, use slashes – /ˈfoʊ̯nimz/.

Every phoneme has countless variations in the exact contours of its phonetic realizations. For example, the vowel in "meet" could be realized as [i], [ɪ̯], [e̞], [ɹi], and [ɨ], and all could fall under the phonemic umbrella of L1 English /i/. In this case, we would call [i], [ɪ̯], [e̞], [ɹi], and [ɨ] **allophones** of /i/ (Greek *allo-* "other, different"). Yet there are also times when seemingly miniscule differences in phones are *phonemically* important; phonemic categories have blurry boundaries at best, and they shift from language to language and accent to accent.

All spoken languages include phonemes. When we learn to speak a language (which, of course, comes with an accent), we also acquire expectations around which words use which phonemes – and we often do so through trial and error. An explicit framework of phones and phonemes could actually make it much easier to learn a language, especially when compared to the usual way we learn pronunciation: "No, don't say it like *that*! Say it like *this*."

Another word may come in handy at this point: **phonology**. Phonology is the systematic, linguistic organization of the sounds of a language or accent, as well as the study of such systems. Phonological systems describe which phonemes are present in an accent or language, which allophones are associated with those phonemes, and how those phonemes show up in words. An understanding of an accent's phonology helps us understand both sides of the communication process – how words are translated to phonemes and then spoken as phones, and how phones are heard as phonemes and converted back into words.

In your L1(s), you largely commit to memory the phonological organization of your daily vocabulary, which can number from 20,000 to 40,000 words. Most L1 English speakers internalize that "running into someone" and "cuts of steak" are realized with the same phonemes ("meet" and "meat" /mit/), whereas "a type of hand protection" differs by one contrastive phoneme ("mitt" /mɪt/). Likewise, many L1 English speakers take for granted that "great" and "mate" rhyme, while "great" and "neat" do not. We may not always be able to *describe* why this is so, but the phonological scheme we acquired within our accent is a system we're masterful at intuitively putting into practice.

Exercise 10.1: Group These Words!

Grab a sheet of paper and something to write with.

Look at the list of words in Figure 10.3. Group together words that use the *same vowel phoneme*. We highly recommend saying each word out loud as you sort.

Pretty easy, right? Do you feel confident in your ability to sort these words into categories based on your existing understanding of their vowel phonemes? Compare your groups to your classmates' and discuss any differences that may arise.

Next, sort the words in Figure 10.4 by their initial *consonant* phoneme.

This round of sorting might have felt easy as well, though you might have noticed that saying the words aloud was more helpful than their spelling. Compare with your classmates again and discuss any words that you sorted differently. We suspect that "thanks" might occasionally produce differing results, depending on the speakers present.

way	bet	cent	hey
neigh	help	bay	wet
cake	sell	safe	neck

Figure 10.3 Group These Words: Round One

think	these	Thor	there
third	them	thoughts	then
this	thespian	thou	thanks

Figure 10.4 Group These Words: Round Two

Now try sorting the words in Figure 10.5, again using the *vowel phoneme* as your guide.

How many groups did you create in your sorting? Was this round easier or harder to sort, compared to the other rounds?

Compare your groups from Figure 10.5 to your classmates'. Did you create the same number of groups? On which words does there seem to be broad agreement? On which words or groups of words does there seem to be disagreement?

It may be that everybody in your class agrees on how to group these words. Listen in **Web Resource 10.6** to some volunteers from different places in the world speaking *their* groupings of these words; how are they similar to or different from your class groupings?

Web Resource 10.1 Volunteer Pronunciations

Finally, sort the words in Figure 10.7 according to their vowels.

How did spelling impact your ability to sort by phoneme in this round? Compare your groups to your classmates' and see where there may be potential disagreement.

cross	bop	cough	thought	moss
long	dock	law	on	hot
chalk	broth	cod	awe	watch

Figure 10.5 Group These Words: Round Three

dough	flow	plough	drought
beau	cow	enough	honey
jump	though	done	sew

Figure 10.7 Group These Words: Round Four

Here are some potential takeaways from Exercise 10.1:

- You make use of categories to understand which words have similar sounds and which words do not. Phonemes, phones, and phonology are something you already do!
- Spelling – also known as **orthography** – is not always indicative of phonemic categories. Some languages have a more "phonemic" orthography – that is, the association between spelling and phonemes is consistent and predictable. But for languages like English, spelling can be an unreliable guide to pronunciation (looking at you, *plough*, *though*, and *enough*), and we have to make sense of phonological patterns obscured by the written forms. The disjunct between spelling and sound can lead to **orthographic interference**, instances when spelling clues lead to unexpected pronunciations. This type of interference is especially likely in L2 English.
- Not all L1 English speakers realize the same words with the same phonemes.
- Even those people who think they're using the same phoneme may use different allophones – which may or may not be salient to their listeners!

Mapping the Middle

If a speaker converted their thoughts into phonemes and then phones, and then a listener converted those phones back into the exact same phonemes and arrived at the exact same meaning, then we'd guess that the concept of "pronunciation" would never come up. Information would flow between these two people using utterly predictable sound patterns, with phonemic expectations and phonetic realizations perfectly aligned.

The word "perfectly" should be a giveaway – this idealized scenario almost never occurs. What we perceive as "accent" arises in pronunciation because the encoding and decoding systems – the phonologies – between speakers and listeners are *rarely exactly the same*. The middle zone in any communication – between (C) and (C') in Figure 10.1 – is where our work in Pronunciation emerges. Let's zoom in on a simplified view of this part of the process.

In Figure 10.8, we assume that the speaker and listener share the same language, so the words that both call upon in daily conversation are roughly the same. Where these individuals may differ is in their phonological systems – that is, they may have different ways of organizing the relationship between words, phonemes, and phones. When those differences begin to "leap out," the speaker and the listener will most likely notice a difference in their accents, specifically in that aspect we call Pronunciation.

Let's look at a visual example.

In Figure 10.9, a speaker of L1 English thinks of the word "bath" as the phonemic sequence /bɑθ/. They send their physical realizations of

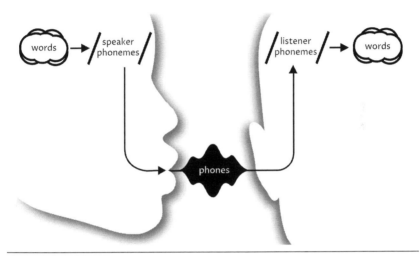

Figure 10.8 Zooming in on accent phonology

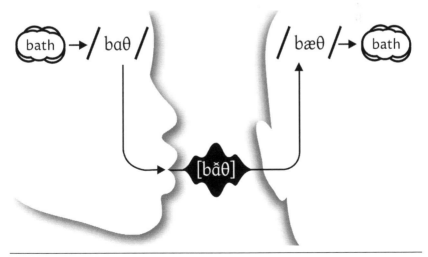

Figure 10.9 Accents as phonological difference, part 1

those phonemes out as the phones [bǎθ]. A listener hears those phones, in that order, and reassembles them according to their own phonemic organization; they connect the phonetic signal [ǎ] in this context with their phonemic category /æ/. This decoding allows the listener to hear the word "bath." Notice how **robust** this process is – the speaker's message came through, even though the phonemic categories of both people are different. This robustness is what allows communication across all varieties of a language to occur, though differing phonologies will likely lead the listener to think, "Gee, that speaker has an interesting accent!"

Of course, even a robust phonological process can result in translations that don't match.

In Figure 10.10, the speaker thinks of the word "faith" as the phonemic sequence /fe:θ/. A potential allophone of /θ/ for this speaker happens to be [t̪], which is what they produce with their articulators. The listener hears the phonetic string [fe:t̪] and makes two phonemic translations: [e:] as an allophone of the diphthong /eɪ/, and [t̪] as an allophone of /t/. As a result, the listener thinks they've heard the word "fate," which is still an incredible phonological feat, but not what the speaker intended to communicate. No doubt, the speaker and the listener could quickly clarify the confusion, but their experience shows how different phonological expectations contribute to the mismatches we sometimes perceive in accents.

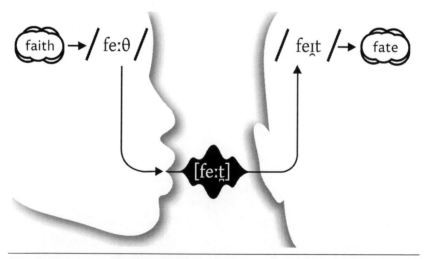

Figure 10.10 Accents as phonological difference, part 2

Check It Out!

Of course, the complexity of our phonological experience is so intricate that it's bound to contain confusions and curiosities. Try looking up these amusing examples from English: mondegreen; eggcorn; spoonerism; pun; folk etymology; holorime; homophone; malapropism.

Your goal for working with Pronunciation is to understand the phonological organization and phonetic realizations of the accents you want to embody, as both a speaker *and* listener. You're seeking out the underlying phonological map for an accent that tells you not only which phoneme shows up in a given word, but which allophones you can use to realize it.

We could imagine this mapping of words, phonemes, and allophones as a relationship between **targets** and **realizations**. When analyzing an accent, figure out which phoneme to target in a word – which phoneme is *right for* that accent context? Then, as your articulators move to shape those phonemes, the allophones that result are the realizations you actually produce. How your allophones get interpreted by your listeners will depend on *their* phonological map, as they reverse-engineer your realizations into targets that make sense for them. Work in Pronunciation trains your ears to listen not only for individual sounds and how they show up in words, but also for the logic that organizes the entire system.

That may seem like an immense undertaking, as though you're trying to get an exhaustive knowledge of all speakers' and listeners' thinking. Luckily for us, one phonetician has already given us a head start . . .

Lexical Sets

When it comes to figuring out the hidden architecture of phonology, we just so happen to have a handy tool that's premade for incredibly efficient phonological analysis: *lexical sets*.

> ### *Check It Out!*
>
> Here's where we, like others before us, defer to J.C. Wells. His book, *Accents of English* (in three volumes), is a seminal work in the study of accents and has influenced almost every subsequent researcher since its publication in 1982. In summarizing his contribution, we're likely to gloss over the rigor of his thinking, depth of his evidence, and generosity of his good humor, so we highly recommend reading at least the first volume of *AoE*. We also highly recommend *Lexical Sets for Actors*, KTS Teacher Eric Armstrong's open-educational resource that provides a step-by-step introduction to Wells's work and its applications.

As we saw on page 100, "lexical" comes from the Greek for "word," so "lexical sets" are groups of words. J.C. Wells surveyed *many* accents of English, and he arrived at a system of word-grouping that holds together across many L1 English-speaking communities.

Wells offers twenty-four "standard lexical sets," which organize the overwhelming majority of words in English according to their stressed vowels. Wells's system doesn't provide for the organization of consonants and most unstressed vowels, but even with this limitation we can create descriptive maps of pronunciation centered on a relatively small number of categories. Wells came up with his sets by comparing **RP** and **"General American,"** since they were widely accessible references for most specialists at the time of publication. He traced the words in his standard sets back to their roots in Middle English, whence he could follow their evolution throughout the world. The result is an adaptable and easy-to-use system that can be applied to most accents of L1 English.

Web Resource 10.2 Wells's Lexical Sets

Navigate to **Web Resource 10.2** to find a document that lists and gives examples of Wells's standard lexical sets. Each set is named after one representative word from that set, conventionally written in ALL CAPS. The twenty-four standard sets are shown in Figure 10.11.

KIT	BATH	THOUGHT	NEAR
DRESS	CLOTH	GOAT	SQUARE
TRAP	NURSE	GOOSE	START
LOT	FLEECE	PRICE	NORTH
STRUT	FACE	CHOICE	FORCE
FOOT	PALM	MOUTH	CURE

Figure 10.12 The standard lexical sets

Let's zoom in on a set to see how this tool works. The KIT set contains words like "pit," "sick," "milk," "business," and "women." Based on these words' evolution from Middle English origins, Wells groups them together because, for the majority of L1 English speakers, *they all contain the same phoneme.* This shared group tendency is ostensibly true of the other lexical sets; see if you agree that most of the example words from **Web Resource 10.2** use the same stressed vowels in your accent of English.

BUT! Note that the set doesn't tell you *which* phoneme they contain – it just tells you that these words are part of the same category based on the way they behave in accents of English. So, while the /ɪ/ phoneme may occur in KIT words in an accent from the USA, those words could end up with /ə/ in an accent from New Zealand or Scotland. Likewise, North American speakers might target /æ/ in BATH words while some London speakers target /ɑ/ – and Australians do a little bit of both! The words in the BATH set remain the same – it's the phoneme targeted in those words that changes from accent to accent.

The utility of the lexical sets arises not so much from the twenty-four words but from the logic that Wells laid out to develop them. Once again, categorization is the skill tucked inside lexical sets. Lexical sets give you an evidence-based approach for quickly unearthing phonological organization. If you're able to determine the phoneme in *one* member of a lexical set, chances are high that you'll know the phoneme for *all* the words in that lexical set.

The constant evolution of language does mean that the lexical sets Wells devised can't capture every detail of an accent's pronunciation. Some words defy categorization and are thus not included in the standard sets. Wells also readily acknowledged that his sets described but a single moment in linguistic history, a late twentieth century snapshot of the grouping and regrouping of English words that continues to this day. And it bears repeating that Wells's sets were developed for L1 accents of English – L2 accents require adaptation of this tool, which we'll explore more in Module Eleven (page 170).

Thankfully, the principles underlying lexical sets make them very flexible indeed. If we discover we need a new way to arrange words in an accent, we can gather evidence for new categories and redesign them to suit our needs. For example, since Wells didn't create standard lexical sets for consonants, we can apply his philosophy to create groups when they're useful; to that end, some linguists have coined new groups like the THIN set or the STREET set.

We'll use Wells's lexical sets as a starting point, a way of getting to know – and, with time, intuit – the tacit phonological structures of L1 English. By coming to understand Wells's sets, you gain practice in categorization and can look for opportunities to make your own improvements and modifications along the way.

Exercise 10.2: Fun with Lexical Sets

Web Resource 10.3 LexSet Fun!

Web Resource 10.3 has lots of opportunities to get to know Wells's standard lexical sets. We've compiled documents and images you'll need to play a variety of games, along with written instructions. From Lexical Set Bingo to Word Gardens, we encourage you to enjoy your intuitive intelligence in phonological organization – and discover surprises along the way!

Remember, though, that lexical sets still don't lead to a "right answer." Even as you engage in friendly competition, you're still using the sets as a way of finding the phonological organization that is *right for* your accentwork. In the process, you'll also strengthen your abilities to work categorically with sounds – phonemes and phones – in the future.

Check-In

After you've had a chance to play with Wells's standard lexical sets, take them right into your BAP. Choose one Donor for this Check-In – you can always visit others later. Organize the words your Donor uses into Wells's standard lexical sets – it's like a scavenger hunt, where every word's a treasure! You can listen for one set at a time: for example, you could listen for KIT words, then DRESS words, etc. Or you could start from the beginning and identify each word by its set. Of course, completely sorting even one Donor's speech sample may be time-prohibitive, so consider analyzing only sixty to ninety seconds. It may also be worth taking a little time to write the text out, so you have a chance to find and label the words on the page.

At this point, you're *not* trying to come up with the phonemic target for each set. Your Donors may not realize words in the same set with the same sounds! You're just trying your hand at identifying and organizing words into Wells's standard sets. We'll build more on this foundation in Module Eleven.

Map out your lexical sets so you can share them with your classmates. Name each lexical set and then give examples of the words in that set that your Donor used. For example: "My Donor said these words from the THOUGHT set – 'call' and 'small.'" If you'd like to add aesthetic flourishes to your presentation, feel free to include visuals! Have a discussion afterwards, and be sure to mention words about which you were uncertain. Notice what your classmates came up with as well.

Conclusion

Categorization can be extremely efficient for accentwork, particularly in the case of lexical sets. If you hear one word from any given set, you've got a likelihood of knowing how other members of that set will be phonemically organized and phonetically realized. The task of identifying phonemes and connecting them to words is reduced from the scale of tens of thousands of words to gathering clues about twenty-four groups. Rest assured, categorization is not as abstract as it sounds – it's a skill that has big impacts on how we find ease, efficiency, and authenticity in accent.

We've left some important Pronunciation topics for Module Eleven: how to approach L2 English accents, how to address variability in phonemic targets and allophonic realizations, and how exactly we turn this conceptual structure into a personal process. In many ways, these concepts simply add further refinement to your already impressive categorization abilities. With practice and application, you'll be able to effortlessly apply your formidable Pronunciation skills to the pragmatic needs of performance.

MODULE ELEVEN
PRONUNCIATION – PARTICULARS

Imagine you hear someone talking. What arrives to your auditory framework is a stream of sound vibrations that have been carried through the air. Amongst those vibrations, amazingly, you're able to perceive a sequence of three phones: [pʰæn]. You then recognize them as allophones of three phonemes in English: /p/, /æ/, and /n/. Those three phonemes in that order, nestled between word boundaries, conjure immediately to your mind a flat container, probably made of metal and most often used for cooking, baking, or prospecting. (It's also possible you imagined a flying youth, a flute-playing satyr, or a terrible review.)

Notice how we seemed to race from the detail of the phonetic transcription – [pʰæn] – to arrive at the broader meaning encoded in the phonemes: /pæn/. Phonemes are robust because they cast a wide net. We can hear a range of extremely specific phones and still arrive at the same meaning. Yet the phones, with their rich, acoustic detail, are essential for tapping into our phonological sound recognition.

When it comes to observing, analyzing, and performing in accents, phonetic details create the patterns we hear and serve as the medium through which we perceive phonemic meaning. The richness of phonetic realization is the means by which we convert our categorical understanding of phonology into something we can practically perform.

DOI: 10.4324/9781003314905-13

Narrowing It Down

In *Experiencing Speech*, we advocated for the skills of *narrow phonetic transcription*. Learning to use the consonant charts, the wide-open spaces of the vowel quadrilateral, and the precision of diacritics expands what it's possible for you to notate and, through careful attention, to hear.

In accentwork, narrow transcription reliably provides the clues you need to get a practical understanding of Pronunciation. Patterns in the narrow transcription of an accent can tell you which phones are realizations of which phonemes – and how they might be surprisingly different from your own! You can also learn which circumstances predictably impact the realizations of allophones.

For example, when listening carefully to a speaker, you might notice that they pronounce the word "let" as [lɛt], but the word "tell" as [tɛɫ]. You've detected a difference in two realizations of the phoneme /l/. In the first instance, the speaker's tongue touches the alveolar ridge, and the dorsum and root of the tongue are lax (and possibly lowered). In the word "tell," however, the realization of /l/ seems to involve a more raised dorsum, and the tongue tip may be barely elevated.

These articulatory differences could indicate that the phoneme /l/ has two allophones – if you swapped the two variant sounds ([ɫɛt] and [tɛl]), the meaning of those words wouldn't change, but the details of their realizations would. With a bit more digging, you might find that this variation is predictable: the speaker uses [l] before a vowel, and [ɫ] in final position. You'd miss this useful pattern – which could be a key marker of the accent – if you assumed that all instances of the phoneme /l/ were realized with the unvarnished phone [l].

Many kinds of conditions that can make allophonic variations predictable. For example, as we saw on page 150, the phonemes /θ, ð/ have realizations that are dentalized plosives [t̪, d̪] in some varieties of English. Those same accents may also realize /θ, ð/ as [θ, ð] in the context of greater emphasis or increased speech consciousness on the part of the speaker. Narrow transcription can detect these socially sensitive patterns, revealing that these speakers have unique allophonic realizations for /θ, ð/, subject to phonetic and sociolinguistic conditions. You would only learn this predictable phonological distinction through the specificity of your phonetic perception.

Exercise 11.1: Say These!

Check out the narrow transcriptions in Figure 11.1. Refer to the IPA (also available in our **Web Resources**) for any symbols or diacritics that look unfamiliar – there's no need to work from memory for this exercise.

Find a partner, and read these transcriptions out loud, one at a time. Both partners should read aloud before you move to the next transcription. Feel free to give each one a few tries and discuss how you're approaching the physical actions the symbols describe. When you've had a chance to work through all the transcriptions, you may have discovered that some of them had you *embody an accent!*

Discuss your experience with your partner. Which transcriptions were particularly evocative for you? Were there any transcriptions that took multiple reads for you to recognize an underlying meaning – and if so, what was it like when you made those connections? How did speaking and listening to a partner help you organize your understanding of the phones and phonemes in the transcriptions?

Narrow transcription can trigger our subconscious ability to categorize. Granted, the samples in Exercise 11.1 were brief, but even a handful of segments is enough to conjure up a familiar accent's Pronunciation. You can intuitively recognize another accent's phonological underpinnings through the practice of nuanced phonetic perception.

A. [ˈpʰaːkn̩ ɬ̬ʔ]	D. [ˈĩ̃ndiə̯ ɹɪn ˈʧã̃ɪ̯nə]
B. [fəʃ n̩ ʧəp⁼s]	E. [ˈwəʧü θĩ̃ŋkən]
C. [ˈɑːftəwədz]	F. [jə ˈfëːtləs bəm]

Figure 11.1 Narrow transcriptions

Organizing an Accent

As you gather phonetic clues and useful patterns, how do you put all this information together? How do you combine the categories of Module Ten with the particulars of narrow transcription to make a practical map for your work as an actor?

When working with an L1 accent of English, the standard lexical sets provide a guide for listening to, transcribing, and organizing your observations. After consulting a Donor or gathering audio samples, make successive passes through them. Tune your attention towards words that seem indicative of the behavior of each set. You can work through the sets in Wells's order, KIT to CURE, or you can first tackle the words that seem most salient – that is, the ones that stand out the most according to *your* expectations. Or you could ignore vowels and focus instead on consonants. Or you could figure out what's happening around /R/ – a very wide-ranging English phoneme!

At this point, you're becoming a phonological detective. Listen to your sample(s), identify words by the lexical sets they belong to, and play them back (again and again) to arrive at a narrow transcription that represents the phones you're hearing. Once you've done that work a few times per set, you'll have a high probability of knowing how almost *all* the words in that set get realized. The lexical sets make note-taking easy – simply write the set name (in ALL CAPS), draw an arrow, and write a symbol. For example, if you listen to a Donor say "ask," "path," and "dance" with [a̰], [ä], and [a̤], you could write BATH → /a/.

record scratch A phoneme?! Yes! In the example just given, your narrow transcriptions for BATH words are all different, yet you might deduce they're all aiming for the same **target**, namely, an open, front, unrounded vowel /a/. You'd want to make sure you have enough examples of BATH words to back that up, but a phoneme gives you the target for an entire lexical set, with allophonic variation arising organically during performance. Of course, if you feel squeamish about making a phonemic assertion, you could just write BATH → [a] and leave it at that.

Sometimes, however, you may want to blur the lines between phones and phonemes – we're performers, after all, not linguists. In our example, you may find with more listening that "answer," "can't," and "chancellor" all tend to use [æ], whereas other BATH words use a more centralized [ä]. It may be worth your while to create a category for BATH + /n/ words and call it the DANCE set. While your Donor may still think of all BATH words as using /a/, your Pronunciation notes can account for the realizational distinctions you want to recreate in performance. Whether you think of this organization as "BATH → [ä], DANCE → [æ]" or "BATH → /a/, except DANCE → [æ]" is secondary to finding a model that serves you as an actor.

It's worth noting that **mergers** and **splits** of lexical sets are a normal part of the evolution of English pronunciation. Mergers occur when two lexical sets come to use the same phoneme. For example, in many accents of English, FORCE and NORTH words are both assigned the same phoneme and are thus merged – is that the case in your accent? Splits occur when a formerly unitary lexical set develops two contrastive phonemes and divides into new groups. For many American speakers, TRAP is splitting into two new sets, creating TRAP and TRASH. Wells's sets are themselves the results of mergers and splits in the past, historical processes with epic names (the Great Vowel Shift, the NURSE Merger, the TRAP-BATH Split) that have resulted in the current diversity of L1 English accents heard around the world.

If you detect a predictable, rule-based variation that isn't covered by the standard sets, you can create a category that serves you better and give it a name. If GOAT words seem to be pronounced differently when followed by /l/, then you may find it useful to add a GOAL set to capture this variation. The sets you use should create a reliable, consistent model that you can uncover in a relatively short period of study.

You may have noticed in "How to Collect an Accent Sample" (page 57) that we included texts that you ask your Donor to read aloud. If you've searched online for accent samples, you've undoubtedly heard similar texts, under bizarre titles like "The Rainbow Passage" or "Comma Gets a Cure." These types of passages are known as *elicitation texts*, and they're written to evoke a wide array of English phonemes and their allophonic variations. However, it's worth remembering that reading aloud frequently produces more careful and standard-conscious pronunciation, quite distinct from the realizations we hear in conversation. For that reason, elicitation texts are best used to test hypotheses gathered from extemporaneous speech, a means of double-checking your work while staying aware of their limitations.

Exercise 11.2: Transcribe These!

Web Resource 11.1 Narrow Transcription Samples

Our **Web Resources** contain brief audio samples of a few different L1 English speakers. Pick one, and get ready to take notes.

Listen to your sample – as many times as you need to – and group the words you hear according to Wells's standard sets. Then narrowly transcribe the words in each set. Consider using audio slowing software, if you have it available.

Notice that you're performing two related tasks here. You're recognizing phonological distribution by placing words in groups, and you're taking stock of the phonetic realizations of those words in the process.

Label each set, in all caps, and transcribe how the vowel in each set (as a whole) is pronounced. You can represent that pronunciation with either a phonetic realization or a phonemic target. Then, find a classmate and share your sets and transcriptions with them. Coach your partner to speak out loud a few words from each of your sets, using your notes – and then share those words with the class!

What did you learn about your sample's phonetic realizations? phonemic targets? How did listening for the sets aid or impede your transcription? How easy was it to find a phonetic or phonemic marker for each set? What was it like to use your partner's notes for performance?

A Descriptive Pronunciation Guide

One of the many reasons we appreciate linguistics is that it's already done a lot of valuable legwork. If we, as actors, understand the concept of phonemes and their manifestations in speech, then we can take advantage of the phonological maps created by others and save ourselves potentially hours (if not days or months) of research. Phonologists and phoneticians have already gathered and analyzed much of the information we need for performance.

However, we still need to exercise caution, as we would any time we follow a map provided by a stranger, no matter how friendly and helpful they may be. When linguists draw up a guide for "Canadian English phonology" or "Swahili phonology," they're zoomed out to a wide scale. The broad scope of their research focus might favor accents with prestige, power, or standard status. Even a more narrowly focused phonological map is still going to generalize features of individual speech into larger patterns, which may be missing some of the subtlety we need for performance.

Thankfully, we have individual sources we can compare these broader analyses to – our Donors! Before you grab an accent guide or an online phonological breakdown, listen with your mouth to your Donors. Then compare your observations to those of other researchers and notice where your perceptions align.

Let's look at a sample phonological map in Figure 11.3, similar to those we often find online, in print, or when working with coaches. Remember that these tables are **descriptive**, meaning that they portray patterns observed among real speakers and not authoritative rules for how words "should" be said.

It's helpful to see phonemes mapped out so cleanly, but you still need to compare this map against a real Donor's speech before you can step into it in an authentic way. What does Figure 11.3 suggest you might want to pay attention to in this Donor's sample?

An interesting pattern we want to double-check against an actual speaker is the suggested four-way merger between LOT, CLOTH, PALM, and THOUGHT – is that true for all those English words? Or are there instances when the Donor might deviate from that pattern? The table also suggests that CURE words are merged with NURSE, but, again, we might want to check to see where *poor* and *tour* end up. You might also notice that NEAR, SQUARE, START, NORTH/FORCE, CURE, and lettER are all **rhotic** (realized with an articulated postvocalic variety of /R/), yet would those realizations of /R/ all be the exact same? We need to know more about how a speaker with this accent handles rhoticity before we can use this table as a guide to performance.

KIT → /ɪ/	FLEECE → /i/	NEAR → /iɚ̯/
DRESS → /ɛ/	FACE → /eɪ̯/	SQUARE → /ɛɚ̯/
TRAP → /æ/	PALM → /ɑ/	START → /ɑɚ̯/
LOT → /ɑ/	THOUGHT → /ɑ/	NORTH → /ɔɚ̯/
STRUT → /ɐ/	GOAT → /ɤʊ̯/	FORCE → /ɔɚ̯/
FOOT → /ʊ/	GOOSE → /u/	CURE → /ɚ/
BATH → /æ/	PRICE → /aɪ̯/	happY → /i/
CLOTH → /ɑ/	CHOICE → /ɔɪ̯/	commA → /ə/
NURSE → /ɚ/	MOUTH → /æʊ̯/	lettER → /ɚ/

Figure 11.3 An L1 English phonological map

By comparing your own findings against those of other research-ers, your work with Pronunciation doesn't remain abstracted on a table swiped from the Internet or dug up in an accent guide. Instead, test your perceptions *and* the perceptions of others against the speech of a real human being. Finding a blend of pre-existing patterns and sponta-neous adaptability is a familiar goal for most actors when approaching a script and its given circumstances. You can take the same spirit of curiosity, specificity, and playfulness into your skillful understanding of Pronunciation.

Clouds in the Head

Of course, human beings are far more complicated than Figure 11.3 suggests. As they reach for their phonological targets, people manifest far more phonetic realizations in actual speech than can ever be captured by a single symbol. This reality is especially vexing when it comes to vowels.

Slight shifts in tongue arching or cupping, bunching or channeling, and advancement or retraction foster a huge amount of allophonic variation among vowel phonemes. Adding further challenge is the fact that the most minute shifts in production can trigger important shifts in perception. For example, a slight elevation of the tongue dorsum could register as a shift between phonemes for some listeners, whereas others may hear that same adjustment as allophonic variation within one phoneme.

To help us navigate this complexity, we could imagine the relationship between allophones and phonemes through the metaphor of clouds. A "vowel cloud" is the phonetic territory covered in the vowel space by a particular phoneme. Unlike the more discrete phonetic labels of Figure 11.3, vowel clouds tend to make more intuitive sense of the fuzzy boundaries between phonemes and allophones in actual communication.

As an example, look at Figure 11.4. We've mapped out potential vowel clouds for the /i/ and /ɪ/ phonemes in So-Called General American (SCGA). The clouds indicate that the potential phonetic realizations for SCGA /i/ cover the close-front-unrounded space, while /ɪ/ could be perceived anywhere from near-close to abutting mid-central. And there may even be overlap between the two phonemes! For example, a mid-centralized [ï] might be an allophone of /i/ in "feel" and of /ɪ/ in "king."

"Vowel clouds" are a useful metaphor. They acknowledge the complexities of production and perception that allow us to realize vowels with limitless variation while also recognizing that larger categories still exist. The differing phonetic contours of vowel phonemes – the wisps and bulges of the clouds – give us insight into how accents with similar phoneme inventories can still have different allophonic realizations. Furthermore, the same concept also aids us in understanding L2 accents. A speaker's L1 vowel clouds may give us hints about how they map familiar phonemes onto their experience of English (see page 171).

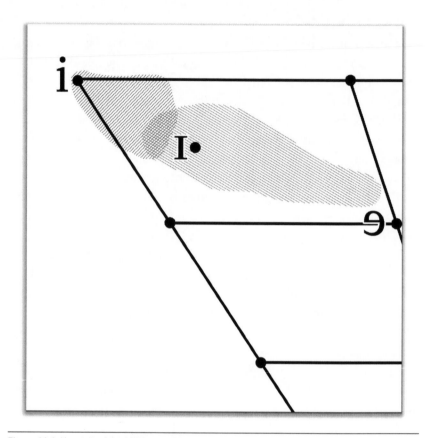

Figure 11.4 Vowel cloud for SCGA /i/ and /ɪ/

A phonemic meteorological map can shift in response to many conditions, such as stress, surrounding consonants, or sociolinguistic factors. As we saw earlier, clouds can overlap, so that one phone can be an allophone for two phonemes under certain conditions. Even diphthongs can flow through clouds, with variation in where they begin, where they end, and how they move in between.

We can also reimagine consonants through the idea of "phonemic clouds," noticing how the boundaries between consonant phonemes change based on the phonologies involved. As an example, in Figure 11.5, we've traced out clouds for /t/ in SCGA and Hindustani on a zoomed-in portion of the IPA's pulmonic consonant chart.

So where are your phonemic clouds?

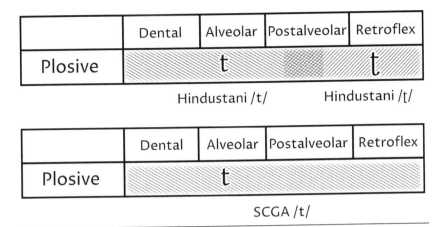

	Dental	Alveolar	Postalveolar	Retroflex
Plosive		t		ʈ

Hindustani /t/   Hindustani /ʈ/

	Dental	Alveolar	Postalveolar	Retroflex
Plosive		t		

SCGA /t/

Figure 11.5 Phonemic clouds for SCGA and Hindustani /t/

Exercise 11.3: Pin the Phoneme

Web Resource 11.2 Pin the Phoneme

Pull up or print the graphic included in **Web Resource 11.2**. It should look familiar: it's an empty Vowel Space, with the phonetic symbols removed.

Next, navigate to the audio snippets we've provided. We've organized the snippets into two groups; we recommend focusing on one group at a time. Each snippet contains one English word, and the words in each snippet are different.

As you listen with your mouth to each snippet, place a mark for approximately where in the Vowel Space you perceive the stressed vowel in each word. Try to be as specific as possible – let the position you mark carry all the information you would normally add through diacritics in narrow transcription. Label each mark with the number of the snippet (for future reference). In a separate location, write the number and a symbol in slashes that you feel best represents the *phoneme* you're hearing. When you've worked through one group of snippets, take a look at your map.

What does your distribution of vowel phones look like? Are they clustered tightly together, or are they spread further apart? Do certain sounds that you marked as close together in the Vowel Space have different phonemic representations for you? Were there certain snippets to which it seemed hard to assign a phoneme? If you had to draw boundaries around your vowel clouds, where would you draw them? Are there places where your vowel clouds overlap?

Compare your map to your classmates'. Were you placing marks for the same snippets in the same places? Were your classmates perceiving the same phonemes in the same snippets? Where did your classmates draw their vowel clouds? How might the differing linguistic experiences of you and your classmates influence the way you perceived, labeled, and drew your vowel clouds?

Notice how you and your classmates were all working from the same audio but may have come to different conclusions about phonemes *and* phones. The way you perceive vowel sounds is influenced not only by the words being spoken, but by the phonological framework you bring to your listening. The subjectivity of perception is ultimately why you need some understanding of the insider's (emic) experience of your Donor's vowel clouds. You may be blessed to work with Donors whose allophones are phonemically grouped very much like your own. But you also want to question your personal phonemic assumptions, so you can better step into the Pronunciation experience of *any* speaker you encounter.

Set Limitations

The utility of lexical sets is manifold in accentwork. Instead of asking a Donor to read your lines in accent, you can listen for words which reveal underlying categories. Instead of hoping you find an audio sample that has the words you need to mimic for the script, you can use lexical sets as a tool to reassemble the sound patterns of a believable and authentic accent.

But all tools have their limits. The efficiency and predictive power of lexical sets cannot meet every challenge we face in Pronunciation. Any endeavor as complex as accentwork is going to resist complete systemization, and we always need to leave a little room for chaos – after all, that's where the fun stuff is!

As in all languages, English contains outliers, words whose evolution led them down unique paths, singly or in groups. Wells was transparent in this regard, frequently pointing out words that cannot be phonemically lumped together with others. The common word "dog," for example, diverges from predictable patterns too often to be placed into a standard lexical set. Even more famously, two words that inspired a *song* about accents – "tomato" and "potato" – don't fit the historically rooted structure of the standard lexical sets and thus form their own tiny sub-category. As helpful as the sets are for creating maps for Pronunciation, more than a few words are islands unto themselves.

Even within the more reliable sets, pronunciation is *predictable*, not predetermined. And unpredictability is always an option! For speakers of most accents, some words use phonemes or allophones in a state of *free variation* – that is, no predictable pattern governs their occurrence. For example, for some L1 English speakers in the USA, the lettER set exhibits free variation between rhoticity and non-rhoticity; the unstressed syllable is sometimes realized with postvocalic tongue-bunching and sometimes without. Free variation means we can't figure out a predictive pattern – guessing would serve us just as well as trying to come up with consistent "rules."

The good news is that our ability to categorize is robust enough to tackle the possibilities of free variation. As performers, we can celebrate the predictably unpredictable nature of speech and follow the creative freedom of Posture without being rigidly locked to unchanging realizations. The lexical sets help us figure out where pronunciation patterns are predictable and where we can allow ourselves the artistic license of free variation.

A more glaring issue with the standard lexical sets – and perhaps one you've already encountered – is that they're, well, *standard*. Wells deliberately built his sets around RP and GenAm. The choice of these standards as "reference accents" leaves room for glossing over patterns in other varieties of English that didn't follow the evolutionary paths of RP or GenAm. To be fair to Wells, he openly acknowledged that the reference accents had pre-existing advantages in prestige, which also place limitations on their overall utility. While the standard sets can, in theory, be applied to any variety of L1 English, they favor the phonemic structures of the reference accents and occasionally miss out on the systemic sophistication of other L1 English speakers.

This brings us to a final, major limitation of the standard lexical sets: assumed in Wells's title of *Accents of English* is that we're interested in *L1 accents* of English. If you want to take on the Pronunciation of a fellow L1 speaker, you can get remarkably far using only your intuition to connect their sounds to your own phonological understanding. But what about the Pronunciation patterns of L2 accents of English?

L2 Considerations

Lexical sets often seem to reflect an innate truth about accent phonology for L1 English speakers. The language varieties these speakers use to meet everyday needs arise amidst the same linguistic trends documented by Wells in the late twentieth century.

L2 English speakers, however, face a much different challenge. These skilled humans grew into language amid the phonology of *their* L1, be it Cantonese, Ukrainian, or Quechua. They structured their linguistic expectations around the phonemes of their L1 and categorized words according to a phonological scheme that they learned implicitly from their fellow speakers. As L2 speakers acquire English, they're usually not learning the phonemes of English and how those get realized in everyday words. Instead, most pedagogies of English-as-an-L2 focus on vocabulary and grammar, far removed from the phonemic pronunciation patterns that L1 speakers seem to "just know."

As a result, most L2 English speakers attempt to bridge the gap between their L1 and English phonologies. For example, they may borrow phonemes from their L1 to apply to English words. Or they may modify their L1 "phonemic clouds" to account for the patterns they notice in English. Or they may find it easiest to mimic and memorize common English words, regardless of their phonological consistency with other, similar words.

While it's amazing that this process can occur at all, it also leads L2 speakers' phonologies to appear less systematic in comparison to L1 speakers' expectations. L2 speakers' phonologies also tend to be less uniform across speakers, since each individual makes their own adjustments based on their experience, practice, and skill. And L2 speakers often have to deal with more **phonemic interference** – that is, their L1 expectations influence the targets and realizations of their L2. Though, since many of their phonemic assumptions are quite reasonable, it might be more fair to call this "phonemic inference."

We've provided a visual example of phonemic inference in Figure 11.6. Imagine that the listener has Standard Italian as an L1 and English as an L2. If the listener is still relatively early in their process of deducing the phonological organization of English, they're likely to rely more frequently on their knowledge of Italian phonology. When the listener hears English realizations of "meet" [mĭt] and "mitt" [mɪt], they may group [ĭ] and [ɪ] together as allophones of /i/ – a categorization that occurs in Italian. That may lead to confusion, however, about which English word is being targeted by the speaker.

This phonemic inference can work in a similar way when speaking. An Italian L2-English speaker might want to distinguish "meet" and "mitt" in meaning but may not have separated the English /i/ and /ɪ/ phonemes from their experience of Italian /i/. Thus, both could emerge sounding like [mĭt], somewhere between the /i/ and /ɪ/ phonemes of an L1 English listener. Similar tendencies can also lead L2 English speakers to be more sensitive to orthographic "inference," assuming pronunciation from a spelling that is phonemic in their L1.

But L2 English speakers frequently come to recognize patterns in English phonology, just as they do in their L1. For the Italian listener in our example, they may figure out that [ĭ] and [ɪ] represent two different American English phonemes. Then, they may deduce the FLEECE

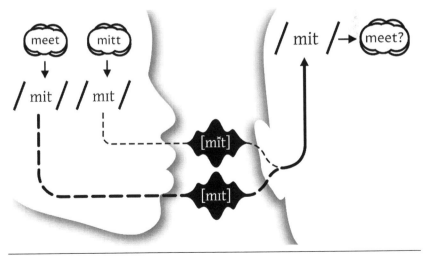

Figure 11.6 An example of "phonemic in(ter)ference"

words that make use of an adapted /i/ and the KIT words that use a more novel /ɪ/. Each Italian L2 English speaker would have to chart their own course through this process of differentiation and deduction. Therefore, while we may find a certain consistency arising among Italian L2 English-speakers – in this case, potential merging or free variation between FLEECE and KIT – we also shouldn't be surprised to hear a lot of variability between "Italian accents" when we consider them as a group.

For most L2 English accents, then, the standard lexical sets give you a starting point, though less precise in application than in L1 accents of English. L2 English speakers, even those coming from the same L1, tend to apply highly individualized strategies to their acquisition of English. Be ready to reorganize the words you hear in an L2 accent, taking into account the phonology of the speaker's L1, their inferences about English (including spelling), and the cultural context of their L2 learning process. The subtle interplay of categorization and particularities allows us to appreciate the stunning versatility and genius of L1 *and* L2 English speakers.

Check-In

Using your word lists from the **Check-In** in Module Ten (page 155), propose a phoneme for each of your Donor's lexical sets. If you sampled more than one Donor for your BAP, figure out which phoneme best represents your analysis overall. Feel free to arrange the sets in any order you like – and modify your sets as needed to match the phonemic inventory and allophonic realizations of your BAP accent. Use slashes // around symbols to indicate phonemes. Take note of exceptions as well – are there individual words that defy categorization? Are there particular members of a set that need to be accommodated? Include examples and notes as needed!

If you find that you need to account for consonants that differ from your expectations, map out those patterns, too. You can refer to consonant phonemes in general terms, or you may find you need to tailor sets to account for specific conditions. For example, the /θ/ and /ð/ phonemes might have different allophones only at the beginning words, which could be addressed with THIN and THIS sets.

Feel free to research the phonological patterns that may influence your Donors' speech, from accent guides to the phonologies of other languages they speak. Remember, though, that any patterns you discover through research should be compared against your Donors' actual speech. Which researched patterns hold up to what you hear? Does any of your evidence seem to refute what others say about this accent? Is there anything that surprises you about your Donors' phonemic and allophonic inventories?

Present your findings to your class – visual aids are always welcome. Start by playing a brief excerpt of one of your Donors. However, your presentation should also include your *modeling of the phonemes*. That's right! Produce the sounds of your Donors using your own vocal tract! Feel free to use sample words taken straight from your Donors' speech. Include exceptions and outliers as well.

Remember, if you find any aspects of your classmates' presentations interesting, useful, or effective – steal them!

Conclusion

As we cycle down our exploration of Pronunciation, we've pulled together the final threads of the Four Ps. Far from being prescriptive and rule-bound, Pronunciation reminds you to follow your observations, revel in individuality, and remain curious about patterns. Descriptive Pronunciation work leaves room for free variation, for ambiguity, for uncertainty, and for evolution, allowing you to find consistency while acknowledging the variability of real-world speech.

Your skills in Pronunciation are ultimately far more powerful than the pat answers of prescriptivism. Rather than determining how an accent *should* sound, you unearth pattern-based options for how you *could* sound, based on your knowledge of accents in the world. Lexical sets and categorization allow you to efficiently dig into the phonological understanding of an accent and its speakers, without reducing everything to a list of words or a set of substitutions. And for all those places where a descriptive approach doesn't give you an absolutely "correct" answer, you can take advantage of your artistry to find the phonetic realizations that feel consistent with People, Posture, and Prosody – just as real speakers do in conversation.

Of course, it's the interconnection and relationships among the Four Ps that bring your accentwork to life in performance. Now that we've examined them all through a descriptive lens, we'll turn our attention to the ways they inform and bolster each other. It's time to weave the Four Ps together, allowing you to celebrate the complexity and richness of their interactions.

MODULE TWELVE
THE FOUR PS COMBINED

The Four Ps are a thorough approach to accentwork that allows you to enter into the complexity of performing in accent by zooming in on its component parts. At the same time, complexity arises through the interaction of a system in motion; when examined one by one, the Four Ps provide only a partial view of the art of acting in accent. It's worth reminding ourselves of something we said all the way back on page 40: "No matter how tight our focus, we need to remember that accent isn't complete without the zoomed-out experience of all four Ps operating at once."

As you've spent time with each of the Four Ps, you've likely found that their interactions pop up spontaneously and organically. By embracing the inevitable overlaps between People, Prosody, Posture, and Pronunciation, you're preparing yourself to incorporate all four perspectives into your process with ease and reliability. The trust you build in your ability to combine the Four Ps allows accents to *emerge* through your performance as an intentional discovery you set up through preparation and practice.

Pursuing a Personal Process

Because they're not a one-size-fits-all approach to accents, the Four Ps depend on *personalization* to culminate in fully embodied and authentic accentwork. Our goal in zooming in on discrete aspects of accent, one at a time, and then bringing them back together is to provide a scaffold upon which you can build your skills. You may find that your intuition, pre-existing talents, and preferred learning styles allow you to move more efficiently through some parts of the Four Ps while turning to others only when you get stuck. Or one of the Ps may provide a reliable entry point from which the rest of your performance consistently unfolds, with the other perspectives providing helpful reminders.

Follow the paths through the Four Ps that make the most sense for you. If one perspective seems more approachable, follow it! In all likelihood, your first forays will soon branch off into areas that fall under the canopy of the other perspectives – so follow those branches. For example, it may be that Pronunciation provides ready access to an accent – certain sounds catch your attention, and you find yourself listening with your mouth before you're even conscious of making the effort. Go for it! Allow Pronunciation to lead you into Posture (how do sounds influence muscular habits?), Prosody (what musicality arises with these sounds?), and People (who else makes sounds like these?).

As you bring the Four Ps together, you'll find plenty of opportunities to zoom in and zoom out. You may benefit at times from focusing tightly on one perspective, or its subcomponents and skills, soaking up fine details. In the next instant, you may find yourself zooming back out to notice how your new discoveries interact with all Four Ps in flow. Directing the specificity of your attention is a skill you've been building throughout this book, so remain flexible in your focus even as you grow closer and closer to fluency.

In the remainder of this module, we suggest some possibilities for drawing explicit connections between the Four Ps. These suggestions are starting points, just a few of the interrelationships we imagine between the various aspects of accent performance. For several of the following exercises, you'll need an accent sample, and for that, we recommend three options: 1) use the samples we provide in **Web Resource 12.1**; 2) consult Donor samples from your Big Accent Project; or 3) refer to your instructor for a sample. There's a lot of value in deepening your understanding of your BAP, of course . . . but there's also value in mixing things up and listening with fresh ears to some new friends!

Web Resource 12.1 Accent Samples

Connecting to People

As we mentioned in Module Four, your work with People sets the stage for all your work with Prosody, Posture, and Pronunciation. Not only does People help you precisely identify the accent you want to work with, but your understanding of cultural context also provides information about how that accent fosters belonging in the communities where it arises.

The influences of cultural context on the other Ps can be incredibly subtle. Slight shifts between speakers and listeners in the balance of prestige, power, and identities can impact the intonation of our speech, the way we use our articulators, and the way we choose (or not) to realize sounds.

Exercise 12.1: Contextual Circumstances

You'll need a piece of text in your Acting Language and a partner. One of you will be a Performer while the other acts as Audience. You *could* perform this exercise in any accent you already know, but it may be easiest to simply use your own accent.

Performer, share your text twice. Choose two different scenarios from the options in the following list, but *don't* let your partner know what they are. Imagine sharing your text with:

A. your boss at work
B. your family on a picnic
C. your family during an extraterrestrial invasion
D. your family on a crowded airplane
E. your ancestors
F. your descendants
G. a joint session of Congress/Parliament/legislature of your choosing
H. a judge in court before sentencing
I. a romantic partner on your first date
J. a romantic partner before you propose marriage
K. a romantic partner as you're breaking up

    L. someone you very much want to be your romantic partner
    M. the audience during your Oscar acceptance speech
    N. a news broadcast
    O. a former bully, over a phone/video call
    P. your favorite stuffed animal
    Q. a baby or toddler
    R. someone who doesn't share your L1
    S. the givens (of the text itself – no added circumstances)

Audience, listen for how your Performer's circumstances impact Prosody, Posture, and Pronunciation. The more specific you can be, the better. For Prosody, notice how your Performer makes varying use of the basic attributes and if they create different combinations depending on the circumstances. For Posture, notice if there are shifts in muscularity, range of movement, or articulator salience that respond to changes in context. And for Pronunciation, notice if sound realizations in phonemes or lexical sets change to meet the needs of the circumstances. It would definitely be beneficial to take notes!

Once the Performer has shared both versions of their text, they can reveal which circumstances they chose, if they like. Then switch roles.

When both you and your partner have performed, discuss your experiences. How does varying the context of communication show up in the rest of the Four Ps? Do those strategies arise consciously or unconsciously? Do you and your partner share any similar adaptations to changing circumstances?

Our ability to make these adaptations, and to hear them in others' speech, is a social skill as well as a linguistic skill. Some of these changes might register on a scale of **formality** – that is, the degree to which we mold our speech to meet the expectations of a standard of some kind. In many cases, formality in speech is associated with the expectations of overt prestige, while *informality* connotes the benefits of covert prestige or familiarity. Our perception of our listeners causes cascading changes in Prosody, Posture, and Pronunciation that can produce a marked difference in accents between "formal" and "informal" (or "conversational") settings.

Exercise 12.2: Reading Between the Lines

Pull up an accent sample. Remember how we ask Donors to record pre-written passages as well as improvisational speech? Listen to a decent chunk of both (say, forty-five seconds of each).

Take notes on the shifts you observe between the read-out-loud portion and the conversational portion. What changes in the accent of the speaker? Get as specific as you can for each P.

Do you sense a difference in the speaker between a more "formal" context (reading out loud) versus a more "familiar" context (talking to another person)? Are there even shifts within the conversational portion, as the speaker touches upon different subjects? Do any of the Ps seem particularly salient for marking that shift in context? Do any of the speaker's strategies feel familiar to you? Do you perceive shifts between reading and conversing as a change in formality, or would you call it something else? Discuss your observations with the class, and notice how your classmates' may differ from your own.

Follow the Music

The musicality of an accent can affect us at a physical level, tapping into our body wisdom around dance, motion, and synchronization before we even know what's happened. Prosody therefore gives you a deeply felt opportunity to connect to the other Ps and to follow your intuition into greater descriptive specificity.

Prosody's connections to Pronunciation are most often observed through the ways in which the musical attributes (particularly length and quality) interact with the shapes of the phones we produce. Shifts in Prosody can show up in the modulation of Posture, as muscles constantly respond to our articulatory efforts and to the rhythmic patterns running through them. Prosody can also be a bridge for connecting to cultural context; how many of the circumstances in Exercise 12.1 have clear prosodic markers, both linguistic and paralinguistic?

Exercise 12.3: Who Could Ask for Anything More?

Grab around a minute of an accent sample. Choose three **intonation phrases (IPs)** – the actual words and their prosodic pattern – from your

Donor. Remember, an IP isn't necessarily a whole sentence; it usually only includes one prosodic stress or important piece of information (see page 101).

Speak the three phrases, trying to match your musicality as closely as possible to your Donor's. Notice how the other Ps respond. Does your Posture change to make these shifts possible? How do your Pronunciation skills support you? Does the context of communication inspire your musicality?

Next, find a partner. Let them hear your three IPs, and listen to theirs as well. You can play the original audio if you like, but also let your partner enjoy *your* version of these IPs. Now one partner will act as Musician, while the other will be the Audience.

Musician, test out your three IPs by altering the musicality of each. Try to isolate just one aspect of Prosody to change – it may be impossible, but make a worthy attempt! We suggest modifying your IPs by making them:

A. faster (*presto*)
B. much faster (*prestissimo*)
C. slower (*largo*)
D. much slower (*larghissimo*)
E. louder (*forte*)
F. much louder (*fortissimo*)
G. softer (*piano*)
H. much softer (*pianissimo*)
I. more separated (*staccato*)
J. more connected (*legato*)
K. more regular (straight rhythm)
L. more irregular (syncopated rhythm)

Audience, notice what changes from the original IPs to the new versions. How does the shift in Prosody lead to changes in Posture? in Pronunciation? in what you understand about the cultural context? Take notes! Then switch roles.

When both partners have had a go at being Musician, compare your experiences. How did alterations in Prosody impact the other Ps? Do changes in Prosody seem to cause macro-level changes across the entirety of accent? Or do prosodic changes seem to be more localized? What was most salient as Musician? What was most salient as Audience? Take your observations to a class discussion.

Exercise 12.4: Prosody Coaching

Take your three IPs from Exercise 12.3 and write down the words in their original language, *without* punctuation. Then find a new partner, who hasn't yet heard these IPs in action. One partner will be the Coach, while the other is the Performer.

Coach, give your written IPs to your Performer. Allow them to read the words. Then, coach your Performer to match the Prosody of your speaker – *by using only notes about the attributes!* You can direct their attention to pitch, length, loudness, and vocal quality, as well as movement and ranges within these attributes. Don't give them *any* information about People, Posture, or Pronunciation – including how to say certain words, where your speaker is from, or how to move the articulators. This also means you'll want to avoid modeling the Prosody for them – stick to describing, drawing, gesturing, or dancing.

Set a time limit – we suggest around ten minutes for each coaching session. As a Coach, your goal is to get your Performer as close as possible to the Prosody of your speaker by the end of the session. As you get to the final three minutes or so, you can both model and play the audio from your speaker. Notice, however, that modeling and playing the sample reveal other information about the Four Ps – what does that do to your Performer's experience?

Once both partners have had a chance to take the role of Coach, discuss your experiences. Did coaching through Prosody alone give hints about the other Ps? Where did you run up against the limits of Prosody-only coaching? At the end, did information from another perspective really help you learn more about Prosody? Take your observations to a class discussion.

Exercise 12.4 reveals not only the interrelationship of Prosody and the other Ps, but also the limitations of working solely from one perspective. When it was your turn to be coached, the last few minutes might have felt revelatory as you were able to hear your Coach's modeling and the original samples. Stay curious about the individual contributions and limitations of each perspective while also appreciating the way their combinations bring everything together.

In Module Seven, we explored the idea of *stress* as an important function of musicality, especially in English (see page 100). We also hinted at how stress often involves phonetic changes as well as prosodic changes. While this connection between Prosody and Pronunciation is most noticeable in lexical stress (for example, *content* as an adjective versus *content* as a noun), it also shows up in prosodic stress. Prosodic stress can change the phonetic quality of stressed words, and it can alter the realization of unstressed words and the muscularity required to make them. The change in effort from a stressed version of a word or syllable to its unstressed version(s) is often referred to as **reduction**, and it's a phonetic change linked to prosodic considerations.

Exercise 12.5: O Brave New Focus . . .

Find a partner. Remember these sentences?

1.   I told you where those books were!
2.   She said he had a cute kitten.
3.   They made two offers I couldn't refuse.
4.   What were they doing with my loofah?

Pick one to share with your partner. As you did on page 102, test seven different versions, with prosodic stress falling on each word, one at a time. You might want to speak a little slower for this round. Not only are you and your partner listening for changes in prosodic stress, but you're also sensing shifts in Posture and Pronunciation.

Rather than formalize this exploration into Performer-and-Listener, both you and your partner act as Researchers. Experiment together through the free exchange of your sentences and their varying focuses. If, while speaking, you notice a change in your Posture or Pronunciation based on where you place the prosodic stress, share it with your partner and see if they perceive it, too. If, while listening, you detect a change in your partner's Posture or Pronunciation related to prosodic stress, make note of it and see if they agree.

After you've both had a chance to perform your seven trials, discuss your findings. How did prosodic stress impact stressed vowels? unstressed vowels? stressed consonants? unstressed consonants? Do you perceive a reduction of articulatory effort in unstressed syllables, resulting in audible phonetic change? Were there any sounds or words that seemed especially susceptible to this Prosody-influenced alteration? Bring your findings to a class discussion, and notice what other groups discovered as well.

Exercise 12.6: ... That Has Such People in It!

Listen to thirty to sixty seconds of an accent sample. Notice how your Donor makes use of prosodic stress. Then listen again, this time taking note of how Pronunciation and Posture respond to your Donor's prosodic focusing strategies. Pay special attention to unstressed syllables: does your speaker reduce them in any way? Take notes of what you observe, and feel free to write down or transcribe specific examples.

Does your Donor have any predictable prosodic strategies, either for stressing or unstressing? Do unstressed vowels all tend to a certain phonetic realization? Or multiple sounds? Do unstressed consonants disappear or blend into nearby sounds (*assimilation*)? Does reduction lead to the elimination (*deletion*) of sounds or syllables? Do your speaker's stressing and reduction strategies match your own? How would you summarize these Prosodic tendencies? How would you describe associated shifts in Pronunciation and Posture?

Back to the Shape of Sounds

The connection between the sounds we make and the muscles that shape them is a central pillar of our work. Careful listening is necessary for careful embodiment – and vice versa! Listening with your mouth cultivates your phonetic precision and improves your kinesthetic awareness. Pronunciation and Posture perpetually interact and, hopefully, engage in a positive feedback loop of ability and perception.

Exercise 12.7: Narrowing in on Posture

Grab an accent sample, and choose a three- to five-second excerpt to narrowly transcribe.

Get as detailed as possible! How would you help someone who's never heard your Donor speak this text using only your transcription? We recommend spending at least twenty minutes transcribing this excerpt – and be sure to listen with your mouth!

Put your transcription aside.

Now, speak your excerpt out loud – *in your Donor's accent.* You've spent a good chunk of time with your Donor, listening with your mouth and getting super-specific about how you'd relay this phonetic information to someone else. As a result, you've soaked up a lot of data!

Speak your excerpt one more time, in your Donor's accent (which we'll rename "the Target"). Then, speak the words of your excerpt again, only this time in *your* accent (your Home). Alternate speaking the excerpt in Target and Home accents. What do you notice shifting in your Posture to make these Pronunciation changes possible? Which parts of your vocal tract move and in what ways as you alternate between Home and Target?

Just for fun, speak your excerpt in your Target accent, and then add some prosodic variety, like you did in Exercise 12.3. How consistent can you stay in Posture and Pronunciation as you add possibilities to Prosody?

Notice how it doesn't take much – just a *microtranscription* – to lead from narrow phonetics to an intuited sense of Posture. While you wouldn't want to base your accentwork on only three to five seconds of a sample, you're already picking up useful hints about Posture and even Prosody by listening carefully with your mouth for Pronunciation clues.

Exercise 12.8: Posture Coaching

Pick up your narrow transcription again and find a partner. Once again, one of you will be the Coach, and the other will be the Performer. We recommend that you each get ten minutes to act as Coach.

Coach, give your narrow transcription to your Performer and have them read it aloud. It may take a few tries to work through the narrowness of your phonetics, so help them understand any symbols or diacritics you've written down. There's just one rule: *you can't model any of the sounds for them.* If you'd like to edit your transcription, to communicate new or different information to your partner, do so now.

Your next goal is to get your Performer as close to the Donor's Pronunciation as possible *using only Posture coaching notes.* That is, you can tell them where or how to move their articulators, but don't include *any* information from People, Prosody, or your own modeling. These parameters mean you won't ever speak the words of your excerpt; only your Performer will speak the text while you coach their Posture. In the last two minutes of the session, you can model the excerpt or play the original audio. Again, notice how playing the sample impacts your Performer's experience.

When you've both had a chance to act as Coach, discuss your experiences. Besides the narrow transcription, what was it like to have only Posture as a coaching tool? Where did you run up against the limits of Posture-only coaching? How did coaching through Posture and narrow phonetics give hints about the other Ps? Take your observations to a class discussion.

As in Exercise 12.4, constraining your choices for coaching and feedback illuminates the strengths and limitations of Posture and narrow transcription. You may find that there's a lot of intuitive overlap with the other Four Ps, and that information about People and Prosody can also seep in organically of their own accord. Restricting our skill set is helpful for strengthening one part of our abilities; yet the relief we feel upon hearing the original speaker is indicative of the true potency that can only come from an integration of all our accent skills.

End of Part Two Skills Celebration

Wow! Congratulations! Woohoo!

You've explored the four perspectives on accent that we call People, Prosody, Posture, and Pronunciation. You've done some deep dives into distinct aspects of accentwork, built skills specific to each, engaged your entire self to put them into practice, and then opened up possibilities for connecting them to the art of performance.

May we reiterate: Wow! Congratulations! Woohoo!

Take stock of what you've gathered so far through your dedicated work on your Big Accent Project. Let's seize this opportunity to organize your declarative knowledge and remind you of your procedural wisdom. You'll also (hopefully) realize that you're well on your way to performing in your chosen accent – or perhaps even a few accents!

Prepare an Accent Mini-Celebration to share with your class. This Mini-Celebration does *not* have to be a finalized, set-in-stone, ready-to-publish presentation of the accent in question. We like to think of these Mini-Celebrations as being framed by the phrase, "Here's what I'm thinking right now about [this accent] . . ." Anything you've gathered so far is subject to change, and you are more than welcome to share unresolved questions, curiosities, and unknowns as part of your Mini-Celebration.

Include information from each of the Four Ps in your Mini-Celebration, and feel free to highlight their overlaps. Present them in any order that feels right. We do have one recommendation: when sharing your Mini-Celebration, *play a sample of one of your Donors first*. Not only does this welcome that person into the space, but it also helps your audience make sense of the information that follows. Your Mini-Celebration could include hand-outs, audio clips, visuals, movement, music, phonetic transcription, and group activities. Oh, and it might be fun to do some modeling of your accent – or maybe host the entire Mini-Celebration in that accent!

We'll be looking at options for your (Big) Accent (Project) Celebration in the next Module, but for now, revel in whatever way feels best for you. You deserve it!

PART III
PERFORMANCE AND PLAY

MODULE THIRTEEN
ACCENT CELEBRATIONS

Throughout this book, you've explored the interactions between procedural and declarative knowledge. You've developed accent skills, and you've also grown in your ability to describe what you know about accents in performance. It should come as no surprise, then, that you'll want to include both modes of thinking when it's time to organize what you've learned, either in preparation for performance or in order to share your findings with others. Even as you assemble the analytical information you need to summarize the essential features of an accent, you'll draw upon your embodied experience to expertly and fluently perform it.

This comprehensive gathering and refining of knowledge is what we call an **Accent Celebration**. At the end of Module Twelve, you created a miniature version of an Accent Celebration. In retrospect, that was more of an Accent Shindig, an informal gathering of facts that you can share with friends and back up with bite-sized examples. A full Accent Celebration is an even more thoughtful, specific, and thoroughly prepared enterprise.

A Celebration provides three big gifts:

- **A process**: Going through the steps of collecting, analyzing, and arranging your accent findings brings you insights, organizes your thoughts, and builds your skills in performance.

DOI: 10.4324/9781003314905-16   189

- **A resource**: We could call this gift a document, or a map, or an outline. It gives you a single location for collecting, crystallizing, and structuring what you know about the accent, procedurally and declaratively.
- **A presentation**: By crafting your understanding to share with others, you make it more accessible and coherent to yourself. When you prepare for your Celebration as you would for a performance, a lesson, or a TED Talk, you get a better handle on what's essential to communicate out of all your previous hard work.

Let's Get This Party Started

An important first step is to acknowledge that this is *your* Celebration. It's a collection of your observations and the product of your curiosity, starting from your "home base" and your ever-evolving understanding. What other people take from your Celebration will depend upon the unique biases of *their* accent experiences. We'll take you through a process and give you pointers based on our experience, but what follows isn't a strict style guide. It's a template for you to adapt in the ways that best suit your learning and performance needs.

Preparing for an Accent Celebration boils down to three basic steps.

Step One: Gather

As you would for any good party, your first step is to gather resources. Your main resources for accent investigation will be audio and video recordings. You can collect those by recording Donors directly or by finding samples online. You can research what linguists have to say about the accent you're celebrating, though you'll want to compare their observations to the primary sources you collect. You can also find or create visual elements that will come in handy for communicating what you've learned.

Step Two: Take Stock

Now it's time to unpack everything you've gathered and go over it in fine detail. As you did in Modules Four through Twelve, investigate your gathered samples from the perspective of each of the Four Ps. Listen with your vocal tract and test out your discoveries through performance.

Work through each P with an expectation that you'll be back for a second pass; with every sweep through your materials, you're likely to uncover more information that deepens your understanding of the complex whole.

When you discover a useful detail in an audio or video recording, edit it down to a small extract that showcases what you've found. We call these tailored samples **tokens**. They're especially helpful because they provide evidence of and modeling for the features your Celebration draws attention to.

For all your observations, whether audio tokens, written notes, web links, or imagery, it's a good idea to give your folders and files detailed and memorable names like "London_Thompson_KIT.mp3" or "Lima_Posture_Drawing_1.jpg" or "Nairobi_Weblinks.doc." This practice makes your resources easier to locate and access later.

Step Three: Lay It Out

Document and organize your discoveries in language you can share, detailed phonetic transcriptions, and visual representations. You're preparing the spread for your Celebration!

It could also be helpful to track which details of your analysis are salient for performance as they emerge. What leaps out most readily to help you embody the accent?

That's not to say that other features of the accent are less important or meaningful – accentwork lives in nuance! But you may find that certain centers of gravity in Posture or memorable patterns in Prosody or key phonemic targets in Pronunciation allow the rest of the accent to fall more easily into place. You'll want to highlight those in your Celebration, especially if you want (or need) to keep it succinct.

A Local Habitation and a Name

With each iteration of observation, testing, and editing, your Celebration will coalesce into a form that you can invite others to experience. This may be a written document, a memorized performance, a website, or another multimedia platform. The format of your Celebration is yours to invent. The goal is to bring together what you've learned in a way that's accessible.

Check It Out!

Web Resource 13.1 Celebration Venues

Since digital technology advances exponentially, we'll refer you to **Web Resource 13.1** for a list of potential "venues" for Accent Celebrations. We've put special emphasis on those that are most user-friendly and low/no-cost.

Regardless of which format you choose, be sure to convey the most helpful information for performance of your accent. The Four Ps were structured as a guide for this process, allowing you – and anyone enjoying your Celebration – to be confident that each of these vital perspectives is addressed.

Nevertheless, it's easy to fall so deeply into a single aspect that you run out of time to cover other important ideas and experiences. For example, it can be profoundly enjoyable to give an extended discourse on the cultural context of your Donors, whose history, art, culinary achievements, slang, and points of local pride you've come to admire. However, if you fully indulge your enthusiasm, you may look up from your notes and discover that you've only got five minutes left to summarize all of Prosody, Posture, and Pronunciation.

Find ways to present an even balance of the Four Ps, which also helps you resist making assumptions about where your readers – including future you – are coming from. Push yourself to gain experience and craft language around the aspects of accent with which you're less familiar or which you find difficult. Challenge yourself to condense pages of analysis in your favorite P to its most essential features so that it doesn't outweigh the rest of your observations.

How much information is enough? That's a question you'll only be able to answer through repeated practice. Your Accent Celebration should aim to find the sweet spot between "too little" and "too much," based on your preparation process and performance requirements. Decide what level of investment in your Celebration best serves your needs – and don't be afraid to create multiple versions! A lavish feast for a deep dive can be condensed to a sampler platter for quick reference without losing any of the richness in your preparation.

Think about how to make your Celebration easier to take in. If you share your Celebration aurally, leave space to listen and repeat, and consider elements of audio design that guide your listeners through the Four Ps. If you share your Celebration visually, use white space, font sizes, colors, and images to move your readers easily from one section to the next. You don't need to make each Celebration a masterpiece, but the more appealing your Celebrations are to the senses, the more access you'll give to the valuable research contained therein.

Consider these suggestions for each of the Four Ps as you design and structure your Celebration:

- **People**
  - *Introduce your Donors!* After spending time cutting up sound tokens, organizing lexical sets, and carefully extracting prosodic patterns, you'll undoubtedly be on a first-name basis with your Donors. Taking time to introduce them – with brief biographies and sociolinguistic context – allows your readers to more readily associate the sounds of the accent with a very real person and their cultural context.
  - *Always come back to accent.* Again, your work with People can open up some exciting opportunities for empathy-building, and you're more than welcome to pepper your Celebration with images and sounds of the landscapes, architecture, and cultural practices in which the accent is embedded. As beneficial and enriching as this cultural research is, make sure the information that makes it into your Celebration supports your conclusions about and embodiment of the accent. Additional trivia, while fun to include, can distract from the ultimate goals of the Celebration.
  - *A picture's worth a thousand words . . . maybe.* Imagery can connect us with cultural context, but be wary of any design elements in your Celebration – including photographs, soundscapes, music, art, and film – that reduce a group of people to easy stereotypes. The power of design is such that it evokes context in compelling ways, but aesthetic elements can also give the impression that they define all people in a region, society, or culture. Similar

risks lurk in comparing Prosody generally to a style of music or a Posture to a type of geography. Remember: correlation is not causation!

- **Prosody**

  - *Go for multi-modal.* The musicality of speech can be tricky to describe, and certain readers may struggle with it more than others. As much as possible, combine audio samples, written description, visual representation, and movement (just as we did in Modules Six and Seven). The more approaches you take to reaching your readers, the more opportunities they'll have to find an access point that works for them. If you find the description of Prosody challenging, going for a multi-modal approach can also expand your options for describing and embodying what you hear.

  - *Follow the salience.* Remember that while there's a lot you could say about Prosody, you're looking for those aspects that capture something about the accent that's productive (rather than exhaustive or reductive). Start with the question, "What is prosodically salient about this accent?" The features that leap out to you are probably those that you could easily reproduce and improvise with.

  - *Find a few functions.* As we explored in Module Six, when prosodic attributes combine, they can be used to communicate *functions* connected to linguistic meaning. By locating musical patterns that mark functions (like questions or exclamations) for your Donors, you can adopt those patterns into your own prosodic toolbox. You could also notice how your Donors highlight prosodic stress using pitch, length, loudness, and timbre. After finding a handful of these functions, you can deploy them in performance to give shape to the accent without needing to write out an over-detailed and inflexible score for every line of dialogue.

  - ***Satisfice!*** This word, coined by interdisciplinarian Herbert Simon, combines "satisfy" and "suffice," and it describes the process of settling on what's adequate rather than what's perfect.

Our Celebrations can't capture the wholeness of a single speaker's prosodic output, let alone that of an entire accent group. Use your audio samples, example sentences, and musical suggestions to hook your readers into careful listening and modeling, with enough basic patterns to get them started working on a script. From these launch points, real and organic expression can emerge through play.

- **Posture**

  - *Start from yourself.* There is no "universal basic posture," nor does any target accent's posture have a fixed, unchanging form. Instead, your descriptions of Posture are always in relation to whatever home base you start from. Try writing from the first person, judiciously scattering phrases like, "compared to my usual posture," or, "For me this feels . . ." If you're sharing this Celebration with someone else, ask them questions like, "When you listen to this sample with your mouth, do you want to open your jaw more, or close it?" If your readers come from different postural origins, learning about your process of discovery can help them negotiate their own way in, using your suggestions as a model.

  - *Leap at salience – and think through bias.* We're always balancing two powerful abilities: to make snap judgments, and to question those judgments. Often, you'll be most aware of the key shifts that define the Posture for you. Tracking features that are salient in your experience can quickly reassemble a Posture in your Celebration without overwhelming your readers with too much detail. If you find that there's one part of your vocal tract that you tend to omit in your description of Posture (like lip corners or tongue root), it might also be worth exploring in case your readers' experiences differ from yours.

  - *Include L1(s).* If you Celebrate an L2 accent of English, include a sample of the L1 for your readers. We mentioned in Module Nine that the L1 could be useful for your analysis of Posture, but it could be equally helpful for your readers as they do their own detective work. (You could also tease an L1 sample in People as a way of introducing another key element of cultural context.)

- **Pronunciation**

  - *Salience again – and bias again.* As we noted regarding Posture, Pronunciation can be efficiently packaged by focusing on salience. Which lexical sets are most important to you for capturing the essential markers of your target accent? Calling out the most salient sets will help your reader focus on which sounds need special attention and which sounds could just be left to flow from Posture. Again, however, salience and priorities are a reflection of your personal bias – and there's nothing wrong with that, as long as you're conscious of it! Tracking sounds that are less salient to you might provide access to different readers, though you may not need to include those details in every Celebration you create.

  - *Categories are key.* As we mentioned in Module Eleven, the lexical sets are an extremely helpful tool, but they have their limits and won't cover all the ground you want them to. Supplement the sets with pronunciation categories of your own, including consonants, unstressed vowels, and anomalies. Examples of categories worth tracking include various realizations of /L/, the realizations of /t/ between vowels, the unstressed vowels in words like *roses* and *Rosa's*, and what the heck happens with words like *on* and *dog*. As much as possible, see if you can find predictable patterns for your discoveries, and refer to other resources if some of those patterns have already been detected by other investigators.

  - *Free variation – call it out!* And sometimes the patterns just aren't there! So don't be afraid of ascribing certain pronunciations to free variation – or even a courageous, "I don't know!" As actors, we don't have the benefit of years of fieldwork, and sometimes the most we can offer about a pronunciation we've encountered is that it seems variable, at best. If you find convincing realizations that you can effectively embody, you don't need to categorize every sound you encounter. Just make sure "free variation" and "I don't know" don't become stand-ins for, "I don't care to find out."

These possibilities are meant to empower you to find the versions of your Celebrations that speak to your discovery process, your analysis, and your embodiment as a performer. For that reason, we encourage you to speak personally, acknowledge the biases of salience, and include the "just enough" amount of information that serves you in your acting. In sharing your Celebration with others, however, you'll likely discover that the benchmarks of salience shift. And that's great!

You can adjust an Accent Celebration for different audiences by empathetically running your analysis through *their* experience and noticing what might stick out to them. One recurring example is the previously mentioned case of **rhoticity** (see page 163). An Accent Celebration created in Missouri about an Ozark accent might not have a section on "R-Colored" vowels when shared in St. Louis. That same Celebration would probably need to reprioritize "R-Colouring" – rhoticity in sets like NURSE, NEAR, START, and lettER – when it's shared in London, Cape Town, or Auckland. As you shuffle between more and more accents – expanding your awareness of bias as you go – you can quickly and efficiently tailor your Celebrations by fine-tuning their priorities to accommodate potential readers.

Sample Celebrations

Of course, there's only so much you can learn from our advice thus far. In the end, you need to put it into practice and explore the results.

Web Resource 13.2 Sample Celebrations

In **Web Resource 13.2**, you'll find some sample Celebrations, created for a variety of teaching and coaching contexts and kindly donated by KTS teachers. Some of these online samples include our commentary on what we find especially effective. (Your instructor may also have some Celebrations to share!)

These samples are *NOT* authoritative. We're not offering them as "real," "correct," or "complete" analyses of the accents in question. Instead, we've chosen these Celebrations as representatives of particularly effective *processes*, the results of which are *right for* the time and place for which they were created. We want to call your attention to what works well in the crafting and presentation of these Celebrations, and we hope you find as much joy in exploring them – and stealing from them – as we have.

Note also that we've included the context for which these Celebrations were designed. The form is adaptable – different parameters for instructors, coaches, and learners produce different types of Celebrations. Placing these Celebrations online also allows them to evolve, which is another cornerstone of our approach using the Four Ps. No matter what form these Celebrations take or how they change, they still emerge from the same process of care, specificity, curiosity, play, and embodiment – a process you'll be stepping into soon!

Sharing Is Caring! And Scaring!

At the end of this Module, we ask you to create a full, glorious Accent Celebration based on everything we've explored so far. And then we'll ask you to share it, which can be valuable . . . and terrifying.

By the time you create an Accent Celebration, you'll have invested hours into your process of discovery and description. You'll spend a few more hours condensing your knowledge into a form that you and others can learn from. And then, maybe, comes something even *more* vulnerable: *feedback in front of others.*

We recommend a specific strategy for receiving public feedback on your Celebration: ask for the feedback you're ready to receive. Saying out loud what you're ready to hear can help you be present to hear it. Working with your classmates and your instructor, you can create a framework for consent as you enter into the sensitive exchange of feedback. For example, you could ask classmates if your descriptions of Posture resonated with them and helped them to reproduce that physicality; or you could ask your instructor for feedback on your use of phonetic transcription in Pronunciation. By asking for specific feedback, you frame the conversation not only around areas where you want to improve but also around areas in which you could actually receive what's offered.

Of course, when it comes time to *give* feedback in a similar setting, respect what you're asked for (instructors, this applies to you, too!).

Whether in a group setting or one on one, offer feedback only when asked and only toward those areas in which feedback is sought. This exhortation might seem like common-sense politeness, but it's an important point to remember as you grow more confident in your accentwork abilities and gain wisdom that less-experienced practitioners may lack. Extend the circle of courageous learning throughout the entire feedback process by providing support, respecting boundaries, and engaging with empathetic curiosity in everything you do.

Check-In

All right, it's time to create an Accent Celebration. Turn your BAP Accent Mini-Celebration from Module Twelve into a full-on Accent Gala. You've already done most of the investigative work required – and your Mini-Celebration gives you a basic outline that you can now fill in with more detail. You'll present this Celebration to your classmates, so take their expectations and experiences into account when designing the guide to your accent. Create a frame for the feedback you'd like to receive, and then celebrate your work!

Conclusion

Accent Celebrations are an essential element of accentwork. They provide the vital link between the declarative knowledge you absorb and the procedural knowledge you conjure up in performance. Celebrations are the place where you put your evidence on display, where you back up your performance with identifiable patterns, and where you put language around the physical sensations and intuited tendencies you detect in the accents of others.

In Modules Fourteen and Fifteen, we'll look at how you can weave your impressive accentwork into your acting process, with a focus on making accent an integrated part of your rehearsals and performances.

Let's do it.

MODULE FOURTEEN
EMBODIED PRACTICE

At this point in your accentwork, you've used the Four Ps to investigate the complexity of accent and integrate it into your lived experience, as an actor and a human being. You compiled your knowledge into an Accent Celebration and can demonstrate it through performance, both of which can be shared with others. We've laid out all the tools we have at our disposal, experimented with their creative and flexible applications, and pointed the way toward authentic and organic acting.

So how do you actually get there?

The answer to that question, as in most things, is *practice*.

"Time put in" is required for any type of skill-building, especially in the case of the fine motor dexterity needed for speech production. In order to move from knowing what to do (sometimes called "conscious competence") to just doing it ("unconscious competence"), we need to rehearse and re-rehearse the complex dance of impulses, intentions, and executions that make up our accentwork. By engaging in mindful practice, we build the strength, flexibility, and agility of our speech abilities.

Bear in mind there is no magical amount of "time put in." Some practice techniques may immediately awaken an intuitive aptitude you didn't know you had, and some may take a few days, weeks, or months of repetition to take hold. Practice as much as you're willing and able to practice, and remember that your end goal – acting in accent – is something that

DOI: 10.4324/9781003314905-17

you absolutely *can* achieve. Current research indicates that short, frequent bursts of actively engaged practice are far more effective than longer periods of passive repetition. Brief sessions that arouse your curiosity and interest, repeated often, do more for your long-term skills than overextended blocks of tedium and rote learning.

We've oriented this book around another strategy for building skills: zooming in and zooming out. An accent only exists as a whole, yet we've also learned a lot by examining the Four Ps one at a time, in great detail. Your understanding of one P ultimately enriches your understanding of all the others in combination, and an incremental approach gives you multiple analytic approaches – as well as methods for troubleshooting accent in performance.

The previous modules may have revealed that you're more comfortable with some aspects of accentwork than others. You may find that lexical sets appeal much more to you than doing sociolinguistic research. Or you may discover that certain accents defy your usual prosodic toolkit while others expose gaps in your postural awareness. Since our interest is in *building* skill, we want to offer some tactics for dealing with challenges in each of the Four Ps, while also strengthening your overall approach to acting in accent.

Building Accent Skills

The best way to practice your accent skills is to go through the Four Ps again. And again. And again! By creating a reliable process, your overall abilities in accentwork will increase with each successive application.

Comparative accentwork is also incredibly helpful. Having multiple accents in your repertoire tends to be self-reinforcing across all Four Ps; ease of access in the Prosody of one accent, for example, often leads to increased prosodic awareness in other accents. You can go back to older Accent Celebrations and refresh them with new knowledge, and familiar accents can gain in richness with an ever-expanding set of skills.

Learning an accent from scratch, however, takes time and care, especially when you're navigating your personal accent acquisition process for the first few times. In the lives of actors, whether in a professional or educational setting, time is a precious commodity. When the deadline for an audition or performance date is fast approaching, you may be most worried about the problems you're having with a particular P. Or you may want to strengthen your long-term abilities in Prosody, Posture, Pronunciation, or People, independent of a role for which you're preparing.

In the rest of this module, we'll explore options for practicing in the interests of efficiency and time management. The exercises we suggest are starting points. You may find variations and innovations that serve you better, or your instructor may have their own helpful strategies to contribute.

And you by no means have to try *all* the exercises that follow! Choose those that seem interesting to you, or that speak to the challenges you currently face in your accentwork. That might mean picking one exercise per P, or that may mean testing out each exercise in a P you find difficult. Consider performing or presenting one (or more) of these exercises in class; you can contribute to collective wisdom by working through your current challenges and sharing your current learning perspective.

Many of these exercises are also great for "freshening up" your accentwork. Any time your performance in accent begins to feel over-rehearsed or restrictive, revisit the exercises in this module. By asking you to find fluidity in each of the Four Ps, these exercises invite a sense of flow to emerge through the heightened demands of performance – while hopefully having fun!

Practicing People

Researching cultural context may seem like a *big* project, or it may feel somewhat distant from the dynamic parts of acting in accent. Yet the more you immerse yourself in the world of the accent you're creating, the more confidence you build in moving through that world and its circumstances. Test out some of these exercises to strengthen your fluency in cultural context.

Exercise 14.1: Rabbit Hole Reading

There are too many terms, themes, and topics about accent, speech, and language for us to cover in one book. If you've found anything we've mentioned thus far interesting, confusing, or too brief, do some research!

Use an online encyclopedia, articles, books, and videos to fall down a rabbit hole and see how it relates to our approach to accentwork. From the Great Vowel Shift to Yod Dropping, from labialization to lenition, from acoustics to the zygomaticus, follow your curiosity and see how much information you can connect back to your understanding of the Four Ps. Pursue all the tangents, click all the hyperlinks, and reference multiple languages and accents, not just the one(s) you're studying. What makes you curious? How far can you trace certain threads? Does any aspect of what you're looking up relate to your own speech? Or the speech of people you know?

After following your own interest, summarize your findings in a five-minute presentation. You can share this with your class, or just save it for yourself; either way, boil down your findings to *just* five minutes, complete with any materials you'd like to share.

Exercise 14.2: Compare and Contrast

For this exercise, think of two accents: one you really like, and one about which you have negative judgments. Those negative judgments may be totally involuntary – remember that our biases are shortcuts, and not usually ones that we've chosen.

Research the cultural contexts of both accents. Treat them the same in your research – in fact, consider constructing your research in the *exact same way*. For example, if you look up the linguistic influences on the accent you really like, look up the same facts about the accent you judge negatively. If you call out the sociolinguistic factors that play into one accent, identify the corresponding sociolinguistic influences on the other accent.

Notice where bias may kick in. Usually, it pops up when we stray from facts into opinion, or when we resort to binary verbiage. Whether it's calling the accent you like "funny" or "cute" or "good," or ascribing "ugly" or "harsh" or "rough" to the accent to which you're less inclined, notice how your bias may impact your research . . . or how your research may impact your bias.

Prepare a compare-and-contrast presentation on the cultural context of both accents. Your presentation *must* conceal your initial judgments: *your audience should not be able to tell which accent carries which of your biases.* Ask them to vote afterwards on which accent carried which initial bias, to keep you honest!

What did you learn about both accents through this process? What did you learn about your biases? How did you put the accents on equal footing in your presentation? Did any of your cultural context research influence your biases, in any direction?

Exercise 14.3: First-Person Show

Grab a Cultural Context Conversation from a previous Donor – or record a new one!

You're going to repeat part of Exercise 4.1 (page 51) by sharing your Donor's cultural context from the first person. Instead of giving a brief summary, though, you're going to recreate their words in an actual performance – we recommend a length of five minutes or more. Craft their Conversation responses into a solo piece that you can perform for your classmates, with a clear beginning, middle, and end. Theme the piece around their experience of language and accent, but feel free to include other information that you find illuminating.

You can perform this piece in their accent or not. If you've been working with this Donor for a while, why not put all Four Ps into play? If, however, your journey with this Donor is just beginning, then speak their words *in your own accent* – see what it is to take part of their story into your voice.

Your goal in this performance is to step into your Donor's words and stories as authentically and fully as possible. This isn't an "accent project" – this is a role! You are living in these words – and if you choose to do so in accent, you *must* live in that, too!

How did you approach your Donor's words as an actor? Which aspects of your Donor's circumstances did you need to call upon to perform "in character"? Were there any circumstances in their experience that you found harder to identify with? Were there any circumstances in their experience in which you found ease?

Practicing Prosody

Try some of the following exercises to further refine your production and perception abilities around the building blocks of musicality.

Exercise 14.4: Ear Matching

Web Resource 14.1 Ear Matching 1

Go to **Web Resource 14.1** and select one of our audio samples, or use one provided by your instructor. These audio samples are not in English; if you recognize the language being spoken, find one with which you're unfamiliar.

Mimic the musicality of the sample *exactly*, starting with just one **intonation phrase (IP)**, whatever you think that is for your speaker. You can hum the IP to begin with, but eventually, replicate the prosodic patterns using a phthong – but *no other sounds*! Your focus is solely on Prosody, not Pronunciation or Posture.

Your goal is to match the music in all its basic attributes – pitch, length, loudness, and vocal quality. If you find it difficult to mimic an IP, zoom in on one attribute at a time, then build out from there. Once you get one IP down, add a second IP, and then a third, and so on. How many IPs can you mimic with absolute fidelity? At what point do you need a reference – kinesthetic or visual – to help you along? Perform your longest memorized collection of IPs for your class.

Web Resource 14.2 Ear Matching 2

Repeat this experiment with an English-language audio sample, either pulled from **Web Resource 14.2**, drawn from your Donors, or provided by your instructor. Again, the goal is to produce an exact mimicry of the speaker's Prosody, in all its elements, building one IP at a time. You can even progress to mimicking the Prosody using English words, though try to maintain your own Posture and Pronunciation as you do so (it's hard! we know!).

How does your prosodic mimicry change based on your familiarity with the language? Did the non-English sample have any advantages or disadvantages in regard to your perception and production of Prosody? How about the English-language sample? Do any of the basic attributes of musicality provide more or less access to Prosody for you?

Exercise 14.5: Choreosody

Take one of the samples from Exercise 14.4, a selection from one of your Donors, or a sample from your instructor.

Choreograph a *full-body* dance along with your speaker's Prosody. That's right – not just your hands or feet, but your whole body. Get your spine into it! Get your hips into it! It should be abstract and expressionistic – don't pantomime what the speaker's describing.

It may help to build your "choreosody" (Greek *khoreia* "dance") one IP at a time; go slowly so you can listen carefully with your body. As you string IPs together, they should feel as connected (or not) as the speech sample itself. Rehearse until the movement is in your "muscle memory." After dancing your choreosody, try performing your Donor's IPs on a phthong *without* moving.

And then perform your choreosody for your class! Do it *without* audio first, then perform it again with your Donor playing in the background. If you feel up to it, conclude your performance with a phthonged version of your Donor's speech, without movement.

Does getting more of your body involved in Prosody help you perceive more detail? Which attributes of musicality are most salient in your movement? Which attributes are harder to capture? How does converting IPs into movement carry over to your ability to phthong them?

Exercise 14.6: Impossible Debates

This exercise comes from KTS Teacher Sonja Field, and it provides a playful way to engage with prosody as a communicative tool.

Find three IPs you can perform – from the samples in Exercise 14.4, from one of your Donors, or from your instructor. Use any strategy you find useful to memorize and perform all three IPs, using phthongs (no words) and matching their musicality exactly. Make sure they're distinct enough that you can tell them apart.

Find a partner. Engage in a debate using *only one* of your musical phrases – you take one side while your partner takes the other. Start by exchanging your points of view using only a phthong to express your IP – and then, as the debate continues, try taking your musicality into Somenish! Make sure you pick a topic for your debate that has no consequential or definitive outcome. Potential topics include:

- Which is better?
  - Dogs or cats
  - Chocolate or coffee

- Waffles or pancakes
- Fall or spring
- Salt or pepper

- Abolish one of the following forever:

  - Cheese or hummus
  - Ice cream or popcorn
  - Shoes or socks
  - Books or music
  - Shakespeare or musicals

Debates should move quickly; we recommend around one minute total. Hold additional debates, with new partners, using each of your IPs in turn. Then you can move on to . . .

Round Two! The next round of debates involves *two IPs* per partner. Argue for one side of an irresolvable conflict, and alternate between two of your IPs. You get to decide which IP to use based on what you receive from your partner. If time permits, proceed to a third round of debates, in which you use all three of your IPs in spontaneous response to your partner(s). No matter what happens, don't forget to win!

How does adding intention to IPs aid or challenge you? How do your IPs change in response to the circumstances of the debate? What aspects of your IPs stayed the same as you responded to your partner? Is there flexibility built into Prosody that allows it to adapt to the needs of communication?

Practicing Posture

The following exercises provide some additional exploration of Posture skills through the conscious practice of muscular specificity.

Exercise 14.7: Isolations Again!

Yeah, we'll say it one more time: practice your articulator isolations. They're worth repeating! And they build long-term physical skills. In addition to the isolations we introduced in Module Eight, you can find some other KTS favorites in *Speaking with Skill* and *Experiencing Speech.*

Exercise 14.8: Posture Characters

You'll want to have a good chunk of text memorized for this exercise, which is a modification of Exercise 9.1 (page 125).

Start with a feature of vocal tract posture that interests you. Examples include things like tongue root advancement, lip corner pinning, raising of the velum, channeling of the blade, etc. The feature you choose could be an old favorite, a recent discovery, or a part of your anatomy with which you're less familiar.

Imagine that you have an "engagement intensity dial" that you can set from 0 to 10. Set your chosen feature to 8. Let your vocal tract respond, so that your other articulators shape themselves around this exaggerated postural setting. You've now created a character, and one that might feel pretty close to a cartoon. Speak your text in this character, noticing how you can maintain this level 8 posture as you do so.

Shift your imaginary dial up to 10 (or go full *Spinal Tap* to 11) and do your best to communicate your text with authenticity at this level of articulatory engagement. Then play around with the dial, shifting the potential levels of muscular engagement in your devised character's posture. Spend some time in the middle, but also make sure to experiment with levels 1 and 2, which might feel closer to a **shimmering** version of your character's posture. Is it possible to find an equal amount of authenticity in both the maximum and minimum settings for this posture?

After you've had a chance to manage the dial, allow a partner to take control. They can call out levels of postural engagement from 0 to 10 or provide hand gestures for more gradual transitions. See if you can master abrupt changes as well as slow fades, all while communicating your text.

Were you able to find authentic communication at the highest level of postural engagement? What did you learn about the subtleties of the lower levels? Which was more challenging? How did you maintain a sense of Posture? Were other articulators besides your chosen feature particularly useful for maintaining your character's Posture?

Exercise 14.9: Posture Switching

For this exercise, you'll need two accents (in addition to your everyday accent) in which you feel comfortable. These can be old standbys or recent acquisitions – one could even be the subject of your BAP.

Warm yourself up in both accents by refamiliarizing yourself with their Postures. Feel free to consult audio sources as refreshers. As you settle into these Postures, find a **magic phrase** for each. A magic phrase is a short utterance that conjures up the Posture for an accent, in addition to salient sounds and prosodic features. For example, "I did hot yoga all afternoon," might emerge as a magic phrase for a London accent, or, "I washed the car by the piney creek," could serve as a magic phrase for an Appalachian accent.

Find a partner. First, exchange magic phrases from one of your accents – we'll call this Accent 1. Notice what it's like to listen in your Accent 1 Posture while someone else sends you sounds from a different Posture. After a few exchanges, both partners switch to their other accent (Accent 2) and exchange magic phrases.

Then, engage in a slightly more conversational adventure, changing between your phrases – *and accents!* – based on what your partner sends you. Each phrase is still associated with its accent and Posture, but you shift between them according to whichever phrase best suits the needs of the conversation. See what it's like to follow the impulse to communicate and let your posture switch in response.

What was challenging about this exercise? What was easy? Did anything surprise you? Did you learn anything more about the postures of your accents through "conversing" in them?

Exercise 14.10: Posture Switching Hot Seat

You can raise the stakes on Exercise 14.9 by putting one person in the Posture Switching Hot Seat. A volunteer (the Sitter) goes to the front of the class and faces their classmates – they're in the Hot Seat. (Actual sitting is optional.)

In Round One, the class spontaneously offers their Accent 1 magic phrases to the Sitter, one at a time. Every time the Sitter hears a phrase, they respond with their own Accent 1 magic phrase. These exchanges continue until the Sitter responds to everyone. (Round One could be extended with the addition of a Sitter-versus-class Impossible Debate, as in Exercise 14.6, using magic phrases from Accent 1).

In Round Two, the class again spontaneously offers their Accent 1 phrases to the Sitter, one at a time. Every time the Sitter hears a phrase, they *repeat the words of the phrase they just heard, in their own Accent 1.* The challenge is for the Sitter to remain in their Accent 1 – and its Posture – while repeating the words they hear in others' magic phrases.

Rounds One and Two are then repeated with Accent 2, first with an exchange of phrases and then with the Sitter repeating, in their Accent 2, the words they receive.

In Round Three, the Sitter *alternates* their responses between their Accent 1 phrase and Accent 2 phrase. Their classmates can offer up *either one* of their phrases, one at a time. The Sitter maintains a *regular switch* between their own Accent 1 and Accent 2 phrases, all while hearing an unpredictable mix of accents being offered by their classmates.

In Round Four, the Sitter alternates between Accent 1 and Accent 2, but now *repeats the words of the phrases they hear.* Some form of reminder gesture is helpful here – the Sitter would be greatly aided by holding up one finger for Accent 1 and two fingers for Accent 2 to track which Posture they're embodying. Obviously, this sort of posture switching involves a lot of complexity, so don't worry if things go awry when you take the Hot Seat – just notice what helps you find your Postures again and what it takes to keep them straight.

Whether you took the Hot Seat or not, what did you notice was difficult about this exercise? What seemed to be the most helpful strategy for maintaining a Posture? What parts of Posture were most resilient to changing words? What parts of Posture were toughest to hold onto?

Practicing Pronunciation

A particularly effective way to build skills is through play, and we offered a bunch of fun options for practicing Pronunciation skills through games in **Web Resource 10.3** (page 154). The two following exercises offer additional options for Pronunciation practice.

Exercise 14.11: Script Scavenger

Find a monologue, a scene, or, if you're feeling ambitious, an entire play or film. Conduct a scavenger hunt through the text (as you did on page 155) and find every word in a given lexical set. It might be most useful to search for the words from a less familiar set, so you get better at recognizing them in the wild. You can type or write the words in a list, highlight them in a certain color, or record yourself saying them in a voice memo.

You could comb through the dialogue of a single character – or every character! You could repeat this experiment for additional lexical sets, particularly those that give you trouble (oh, NORTH and FORCE . . .). Or you could go for the Ultimate Completionist Prize and identify every word by its standard set. Just take breaks when you need to, okay?

Use our resources to double-check your work, especially in cases when you're uncertain. And if you find words for which you (and the Internet) can't find a clear answer, write them down and bring them to your class. Your instructor or classmates might have some suggestions, or you may have found a word that defies categorization. Keep track of those outliers – next time, they won't catch you unawares!

Exercise 14.12: Sounds Abound

Take a sample of speech in a language you don't speak – use those from **Web Resource 14.1**, from one of your Donors, or one from your instructor. Pick a predetermined length to perform – we recommend thirty seconds or less.

Mimic the pronunciation of the speaker's phones as *exactly* as possible. Use all the tools you have at your disposal – narrow transcription, listening with your mouth, phonemic categories – but your end goal is to perform the phonetic pronunciation of the speaker *from (embodied) memory* – no notes! It may help to build this performance incrementally. Start with a small chunk of speech, only adding onto it once you can realize those phones with accuracy and consistency.

What are the challenges of learning to realize phones without phonemic meaning? How do you engage your pattern-seeking tendencies to get "off-book"? Do you feel like you gain any phonetic or phonemic insight from mimicking another speaker's sounds? Are there any aspects of your speaker's Posture or Prosody that seem to be unavoidable as you reproduce their speech sounds exactly?

 Check-In

Reflect on your experience thus far with the Four Ps. Do you feel like there are aspects of accentwork in which you are particularly strong? Are there areas in which you'd like to build more skills? What, for you, would be a reasonable path to acquiring those skills? What and how often would you want to practice in order to meet your goals?

Create a Skill-Building Plan for your BAP. Take note of the skills in which you're confident; seriously, make sure you write them down on your plan so you can take stock of what's already working. Highlight the skills you'd still like to develop so that you can add detail to your current understanding, better embody what you know, or find more nuance in your performance. Create a reasonable practice schedule, complete with exercises or activities you could regularly undertake to make progress toward your goals. Check in with yourself – weekly or monthly – to track not only if you're able to maintain your schedule but to celebrate your wins and take note of growth in your abilities.

Conclusion

From your first introduction to cultural context to your fully fledged Accent Celebration, you've been assembling a detailed map to reach a creative goal. Along the way, you've experimented with exercises, mini-performances, and plenty of physical engagement, preparing you for the culmination of your hard work: acting in accent.

Practice is the process of learning the route so thoroughly, step by step, that you no longer need the map. In fact, you can look up and enjoy the scenery, wander around, listen and breathe, and still end up exactly where you want to be. Practice embeds you in the terrain of the accents you study, and no matter how many times you tread the path, it always seems fresh beneath your feet.

If we leave behind yet another tired cartographic metaphor, however, we realize that this final stage of our work, the one we've been aiming for the whole time, is *play*. With enough practice, accent becomes part of the discovery, spontaneity, and organic response that emerges in truly dynamic acting. We've taken so much time, care, and effort to reach this point so that you can let it all go in the moment of performance and just *be in response* to your partners and the given circumstances. You're not "acting in accent." In the practiced state of readiness, acting *is* accent.

So settle in for the next and final module – it's going to be fun.

MODULE FIFTEEN
EXPERIENCING PLAY

You've made it. After hours of preparation and analysis and practice, it's time to let it all go and act. To find flow. To give yourself over to authentic performance.

But wait. What does that even mean?

Up to this point, we've assumed a familiarity with what acting in accent "should" feel like. We've previously used the words "authentic" (Greek *authentikos* = "original, genuine, principal"), "spontaneous" (Latin *(sua) sponte* = "of one's own accord, willingly"), and "fluid" (Latin *fluere* = "to flow") to describe what we mean. Thus, we might be able to say that we're looking for acting in accent that originates from the self, flows willingly and freely, and doesn't require forcing anything to happen. The addition of accent to your acting should in no way diminish the feeling of flow – otherwise, accent becomes an impediment, reducing the quality of every aspect of your work.

Finding flow is **complex**, in the sense mentioned all the way back on page 5. And that's a good thing! If we imagine accentwork as a confluence (Latin "flowing with") of simpler factors that are relatively easy to identify and explore, then all we have to do is throw them together and let the magic happen. Flow emerges when the components of your process interact and produce an effect whose sum is greater than its parts. The Four Ps allow you to identify and embody manageable aspects of

DOI: 10.4324/9781003314905-18

accentwork and practice them, so that they coalesce in the moment of fluid performance.

Viewed from another angle, however, we're playing. "Play" is a word whose meaning has remained remarkably consistent from its earliest traceable origins in Old English (as *plegan*, "to amuse oneself"). Play could be considered as giving over to imagined realities, a favorite pastime from childhood as well as the thing you do when you walk onstage or onto a set. Though it requires practice – as in music and sports – true play in acting tends to feel as consuming and unforced as a game of make-believe.

So how do you know when you're on the right track? What are the signs of flow and authenticity while acting in accent? How do you make sure your process – that thing you've been building up to now – is set up for your best work?

Unfortunately (and, perhaps, fortunately), the emergent nature of flow means that you're far more likely to notice when it's *not* happening than when it is. In fact, trying to turn play into a checklist is a surefire way to hold on too tight and ensure that you *don't* find flow, which usually results in a feeling of separation or being "outside" your performance. You've got to allow play to happen – and troubleshoot issues that arise by fixing them in your preparation, *before* they become interruptions in flow.

So let's trace these potential issues through a FAAQ – Frequently Asked Accent Questions – section. We'll explore suggestions for dealing with situations that come up fairly often when acting in accent, even after working through the Four Ps and engaging in regular practice. Then we'll wrap up with some exciting and skillful forms of play, which will challenge – and encourage – your mastery in accentwork.

All right. First question.

Q: My accent doesn't feel natural or organic or, well, "right." I feel like I'm faking it, all the time. What do I do?

A: First, *keep yourself in communication.* We can spend a lot of our time working on accents by ourselves, so rehearse in a way that allows your accent skills to emerge through communication. Every part of your investigation of an accent – listening with your mouth, mimicking, dancing along with prosody, listening to and executing phonetic realizations – can be rooted in a communicative context.

Communication involves two interwoven strands: giving and receiving. As you test out new Postures, Pronunciations, and Prosodies, send them *to* someone or something – a nearby photograph, houseplant, or an "imaginary other" you create especially for this purpose. Remain open to the possibility that you could also receive something back, even if it's just an awareness that your words and sounds have an impact on the world around you.

The earlier and more frequently you integrate your accentwork into communication, the more ready it will be as a vehicle for self-expression. Test out everything – a sound, a word, an IP, a magic phrase, entire monologues – by creating a relationship with listeners, even if they're imaginary or inanimate. Then, when you have the luxury of an acting partner and an audience, your accent will be baked into your communicative strategies rather than sitting awkwardly outside them.

It may also help to *think of accent as the manifestation of circumstances in your speech.* The accent you're practicing arises from where your character was born, where they've lived, who they grew up with, how they pursued their education, and how they wish to be perceived now. As you step into the life of a character, you may be aware of "how you sound" – as would the character! Make that awareness part of your circumstances, and notice how certain words, sounds, and melodies help you deal with the problems you need to face in the story. See what you discover by embracing the weirdness of accent as part of your character's speech history and how it might resonate in the story as a whole.

Finally, *maybe it's not right!* Your perception of not-rightness could be a valid piece of feedback that you're giving to yourself, indicating that there's more work to be done. You may be holding the accent at a distance, or dealing with some inner resistance to its unfamiliarity or uncertainty, which leads to the feeling of "faking it." Any time we try something new and less rehearsed, a very reasonable part of us doesn't feel safe letting the world perceive us in that way and holds back. Accept the gift of discomfort as a guide. Let it point you toward a solution, with patience and kindness for yourself as you further refine your process.

Q: Most of the time, the accent I'm using feels good, but certain words – or combinations of words – really trip me up. How do I deal with those?

A: *Slow down.* Whenever you want to build fine motor skills, start small and slow. Isolate the sounds or words that give you trouble, practicing at a slow tempo until you can reliably realize the details you're targeting. Gradually speed up, bit by bit, until you reach performance speed. Next, integrate the trouble spot into its larger spoken context at a slow tempo. Then speed the whole thing up until you can perform it fluently and accurately.

If this sounds like practicing a musical instrument or a sport, that's because it is! We're using the same process to form new neural and motor pathways. When stepping into a new accent, you need to *forge new memory connections*, between the concept you want to communicate and the fresh arrangement of sounds you'll use to communicate it. In other words, you need to give your mind an additional way of sending an idea to someone else. Try some of these strategies for building those connections:

- Get familiar with tricky word(s) in different contexts. Improvise new uses for those word(s) – generate new sentences with them, incorporate them into a spoken stream of consciousness, toss them as interjections into other dialogue.
- Build imaginative connections to words. When you speak them out loud, explore the inner life you associate with them. Delve into what the words mean to you in a wide variety of contexts, including the sensory information that arises as you imagine them. For example, the word "beautiful" could invite daydreams about sun-dappled daisies, a seaside cottage, or a sumptuous chocolate ganache cake. Explore them all!
- Create movement in the rest of your body to associate with new sounds. As we saw with Prosody, you can reinforce the intuition of your vocal tract by calling upon the support of movement.
- Use only the tricky words in your dialogue, or only the stressed syllables of those words. Can a syllable carry the full richness and intention of an entire line?
- Remind yourself what makes you say the word(s) in the context of the script. In doing so, you recontextualize them: they stop being "your problem," and they become the solution that's *right for* the circumstances.

- Actually try to mess the word(s) up. By embracing the challenge of them, you can release from the protective habits that tend to brace you against "failure." People make mistakes, including the people you play in performance. So encourage yourself to "make a mistake" and see what emerges on the other side.

Q: Even if I practice the words, I still feel like I "fall out" of the accent, no matter how much time I put in. What do I do then?

A: There's another way to frame this: it's likely you're *falling into* another accent. You may be falling out of one accent because you're being imaginatively drawn into another accent. This "falling in" often occurs when you perceive that accents share features, with an overlap in one of the Ps quickly cascading through the others.

Of course, an especially easy accent to fall into is *your own accent!* After all, it's the one you're most familiar with and has the readiest associations with most of the words you speak. At any moment when your target accent feels uncertain – either in preparation or performance – your home base accent is on standby to handle the complex demands of communicating your experience.

In cases of falling into another accent, *identify the* **handholds** that bring you back to your target. Again, the Four Ps give you specific features to grasp – physical markers of Posture, distinctive patterns in Prosody, characteristic sounds in Pronunciation. Start by identifying which P is most helpful for getting you back on track – it may also be the P that's the root cause of your uncertainty. **Magic phrases** (see page 209) are one of the most useful handholds you can create for yourself; repeat them throughout your text whenever you feel like you're falling away from your targets.

Q: Accents "put me in my head." I find myself thinking too much and not able to focus on my partner or my circumstances. How do I make sure accentwork doesn't interfere with my acting work?

A: The anatomical location of this feedback is telling. If you start to feel too "head-based" – or more cognitively oriented – *move accent back into your body*. Any time you begin working with accent, give yourself a full-body warm-up – even for a few minutes – and allow yourself to feel physically present in your environment. Wake up your senses, through sight, sound, touch, smell, and taste. Bring all of you to living in accent.

It may also help to *feel the vibration of your voice* as you speak. Use your accent as a chance to feel and resonate (literally) with the sounds of your voice. Just remembering that your entire body is available to assist in communication might help you move from "thinking about" accent to embodying accent.

If you notice that you feel constricted in your body while acting in accent, consider *adding movement.* Accents emerge from all sorts of human bodies, from bankers to ballerinas, so allow yourself to move in new, different, or unplanned ways as you practice speaking text – or improvising! – in accent.

You might also capture some of your inner thoughts and *put them into verbal form.* You may turn up such gems as, "You sound phony!" or, "Watch out! There's a tricky bit coming up!" Articulate these "intrusive" thoughts and improvise a dialogue to accept them into the flow of your experience. With a thought like, "You're going to make a mistake," you could respond with, "So what?" or, "Real people are *so* inconsistent." By welcoming each thought that wanders your way, you include *all* your experience in performance, bringing the life "inside your head" to the immediacy of the circumstances you're dealing with.

Q: I don't have time to prepare <u>every</u> accent in such detail. How do I do all this preparation if I'm working on a compressed schedule? Is that even possible?

A: Yes! It is!

Our first suggestion is perhaps the least helpful when facing a time crunch: *arrive prepared.* Build skills in anticipation of future challenges. When you have time, apply a generous and leisurely exploration of the Four Ps to the accents you want to have in your wheelhouse. Set aside specific chunks of time to research, analyze, and practice accents you want to have ready for the future. Don't wait for auditions to prompt your accentwork – get ahead by acquiring accents that boost your casting potential. That way, you'll have skills ready and resilient for those unavoidable moments when the pressure is on.

As you build your abilities through practice and repeat applications, *get familiar with your process.* What works best for you? What are your priorities in accentwork? How do *you* gather sources, mine them for clues, extract info on the Four Ps, and set up a practice routine? It may help to do a meta-reflection after acquiring a particular accent: how did your learning process take place? What worked? What didn't? And don't be afraid to change things based on the demands of the project at hand!

When time is of the essence, *stick to the script.* Improvising is an advanced skill. Don't worry about taking that ability into a last-minute audition. Focus on what the script asks you to do, and build fluency and authenticity in the words on the page. You just need to . . .

Satisfice. The Four Ps give you specific areas to focus on, troubleshoot, and practice in. Sometimes, you just need to get enough of each P to make it through the script. It's important to put forth your best effort, but if the clock is ticking, get done what needs to get done. And take comfort in the fact that even your most hurried efforts will be more thorough, more careful, and more based in real evidence than almost anything else your auditioners see. You won't be perfect, perhaps, but you will be *satisficient.*

Q: How do I know when I've done enough? You said it yourselves, this work is complex and deep and could go on <u>forever.</u> When can I just go perform?

A: As we implied in the previous response, you've done enough *when the needs of the project are met.* When you're able to embody the circumstances, relationships, and stylistic demands of the collaborative effort in which you're engaged, you've done enough. You may not be able to convince a real-world native speaker that you're a local, but your goal is to serve the story, not mix in unnoticed as a spy.

As an artist, however, you may find that answer unsatisfying, particularly if you're inhabiting an accent for your own enrichment, with no due date in sight. In those cases, you've done "enough" when your work allows you to act with *freedom, imagination,* and *impulse.* When you can play in the accent, you've most likely reached some degree of unconscious competence and are more than ready to list that accent on your résumé. Of course, you can always stay curious and add more nuance. From the secure foundation of playful embodiment, learning more won't feel belittling – it will only augment your possibilities.

Q: But what if I don't sound "right"? For that matter, how do I ever know if I sound right? What if my perception of the target accent is "off"? Or if my production of the accent is off, and I don't even know it?!

A: The simplest way to check, using your own perception, is to *record yourself*. It may be a little uncomfortable to listen to a recording of yourself – approach it with the same balance of empathy and analytical rigor that you bring to your Donors. This is a chance to check in with your work and make sure your interior perceptions match what's being received on the outside.

Listen through the perspective of each of the Four Ps. Your ability to detect your own tendencies will increase with each accent you analyze. This same process will also encourage you to build trust in yourself. Trust needs to be earned; the more often you engage in the process of accent acquisition and reaffirm that your skills are growing, the more confidence you'll build in your accentwork and the accuracy of your perceptions.

You could also, of course, *consult a coach or instructor*. One big advantage of doing your own accent preparation is that you can work much, *much* more quickly with a trusted outside ear. You can specify what type of feedback you'd like to receive and zoom in with more certainty on performance problems that bother you. (If you'd like to know where to find a coach, we recommend starting with ktspeechwork.org/teachers.)

One final suggestion for detecting the consistency of an accent is to *feel for posture shifts*. If, while rehearsing or performing, you sense your posture shifting from practiced centers of gravity, that's usually a reliable indication that something is wandering off-target. Small shifts in posture can snowball and quickly impact the other Ps, so stay physically curious if you sense you might be missing a mark or two.

Q: I know directors/producers/casting directors sometimes ask for a "heavier" accent. It's possible they may even be looking for a stereotype or a caricature because they think it's funny or they're playing into biases I find offensive. Is there any way to change my accent without violating my values – or to stand up for my values without losing my job?!

A: Woof. This is a tough question – and we're so glad you asked it!

First, remember that your collaborators, in any capacity, want the project to be good. They want it to be well-received, to impress their audiences, and to earn everyone involved a decent paycheck. You're engaged in the same effort, though you may be coming in with a better understanding of what that means in terms of accent.

Always attempt to *translate the notes*. See if you can take what they're perceiving and adapt it to the descriptive framework of your acting-in-accent process. For example, if they ask for a "heavier" accent, that most likely means that they want something more marked *compared to their expectations* (see page 66). You have strategies for adjusting Posture, Prosody, or Pronunciation on sliding scales, so crank up those shifts and see how that changes the feedback from your collaborators. Of course, sometimes this process of translation means saying "yes" to a note while using your advanced accent expertise to make a completely different adjustment that achieves the same outcome. No need to publicize your brilliance – do your job, do it well, and enjoy the satisfaction that comes from bringing integrity to your process.

In those instances, however, where translation does not suffice, *hold boundaries where possible*. Often, we actors are not in a position where we can stand up for what's right without risking our livelihood or professional connections. Our hope, in Knight-Thompson Speechwork, is that we can gradually change the culture of accentwork through conscientious, courageous, and passionate artists like yourself. The more of us that advocate and stand up for the equitable and mindful embodiment of accentwork, the more leverage we have to make our world a more connected and compassionate place.

Q: Can you just record my lines for me in accent, and I'll copy those?

A: No.

And in Performance Bind Them

Throughout this book, we've returned again and again to the idea that the Four Ps are a framework for reaching our ultimate (alliterative) goal: *Performance*. The Four Ps are synthesized through your artistry to become the embodied experience of an accent, living within the given circumstances of a story.

What we'd like to offer next is a challenging, skillful, and deliberately silly exploration of performance, in all its multi-layered glory. Aware of the skills you've gained and the practice you've put in, we're inviting you to step into a new kind of fluidity and spontaneity. At the same time, the exercises that follow may, at times, cause a bit of overwhelm – which we actively encourage! From that state of intentional chaos, new possibilities may emerge and new understandings may spring to life. By encouraging you to play, we hope to makfchaose the prospect of not-knowing just as exciting as the skills to which you can so deservedly lay claim.

It's time to play with rigor, to trust in the unknown, and to be utterly serious in your profound ability to have fun. In other words, you're ready for . . . the Accent Olympics.

Accent Olympics

You've done the hard work. You've prepared an accent, faced challenges, and vanquished them with new ways of thinking. You truly have the mind, heart, and vocal tract of a champion.

Fail Forward!

As a Championship Accentworker, you are by now very well trained in failing forward. That is, you've repeatedly thrown yourself into new experiences with your accent skills, come up against the limits of unfamiliarity or inability, and watched your progress seem to crash and burn around you. Yet you arose like a phoenix (phone-ix?) from the ashes and *learned from your mistakes* – which turned them into *lessons* instead. We want to turn a spotlight on this skill you've been exercising, of learning courageously from error and misfire, because even as you reach new levels of intuitive play, you might still find yourself in moments of uncertainty, doubt, and seeming failure. These are all opportunities for growth and future victory, Champion, and you're only getting richer and more resilient with each attempt at glory. Onward!

For the Accent Olympics, you'll need to prepare *at least* two (2) accents in which you can play (other than your own) and a piece of off-book text. Write the names of your accents on separate notecards, which you'll use in the games ahead.

Exercise 15.1: Accent Olympics Training

Work with a partner for this opening round. One person starts as Speaker, while the other is Listener.

Speaker, communicate your text to your Listener. While you do so, *switch between accents* at will, using your notecards to indicate in which accent you're performing. Since you get to control the switch, see what it's like to follow the natural transitions in your text as well as attempting to surprise yourself mid-sentence. If you begin to lose the accent in play, make use of magic phrases, **thinking sounds** (page 119), or other **hand-holds** (page 217) to get back on track. The more accents you bring to this round of the Olympics, the more frequently you should plan on switching.

After the first Speaker has shared their text, switch roles and repeat the exercise.

Notice what you experience when switching between accents. How do you maintain the flow of communication? Do you notice anything interrupting your focus and flow? Where are there opportunities for more ease? If you find this task easy, look for opportunities to reduce effortfulness and still achieve your goals.

Exercise 15.2: Accent Olympics Qualifiers

The next round of the Olympics adds a little bit of social charge. You and your partner will volunteer to demonstrate your accent-switching abilities in front of the class. Make sure both partners get a chance to share in public. The use of handholds is not only allowed but encouraged.

How does sharing in front of an audience change your experience of play? What strategies help you stay in flow during this round of communication?

Exercise 15.3: Accent Olympics Quarterfinals

Go back to having privacy with your partner. Decide who will be Speaker first.

Speaker, once again, you'll communicate your text with your Listener. This time, however, *your Listener* will control the shifts between accents, using your notecards to signal you. Continue to use handholds as needed or wanted. Your Listener should aim to surprise you while you share your text – and notice what happens! Then switch roles.

What is it like to give control of accent switching to your partner? How do you maintain communication and fluidity in your play?

Discuss with your partner where you ran into challenges during performance. How could you practice to "tune up" the rough spots? Which skills and strategies from previous modules might help you transition between accents *during* performance?

Exercise 15.4: Accent Olympics Semifinals

Volunteer with your partner to demonstrate Exercise 15.3 in front of the class. As always, use handholds to guide yourself through the switches your partner conducts, and fail forward – you can learn as much from where things break down as you can from where they hum along!

What is it like to share this version of accent switching in public? How do you maintain communication in public performance?

Exercise 15.5: Accent Olympics Finals

Volunteer with your partner to perform in front of the class – no practice round this time!

As Speaker, your Listener will once again control your accent switching, except this time, they'll signal *gradual shifts in accent*. While you're communicating, they'll indicate slow glides from one accent to the other using your notecards as visual cues. This version of sharing will result in unpredictable and unrehearsed *blended accents* – see if you can hang out in the middle zone between accents and still communicate your text!

This round will more than likely cause the whole process of acting in accent to break down. Excellent! Fail forward with curiosity to see what happens when you throw your play into a bit of chaos.

As a reward for making it through your performance in the Accent Olympics, give yourself a chance to perform the entirety of your text in one accent. After so much courage and experimentation, you deserve a lived experience of your text from top to bottom. And, of course, once you've demonstrated your superior accent ability, act as Listener for your partner.

What was it like to enter new territory and encounter potential uncertainty with familiar accents? Were you able to communicate while between two accents? What do you gain from this exploration? How does it apply to your understanding of accents – both the ones you've prepared and in your accentwork overall?

Make sure to honor all Accent Olympians with thunderous rounds of applause, ample praise for their courage and fortitude, and, as appropriate, a rousing Omnian anthem of acclaim. No matter how bizarre the results, your Olympian accent experience deserves recognition and celebration for all that you've dared to learn and achieve.

Advanced Play Practice

The Accent Olympics are designed to push your accent skills to their limits and invite the type of discovery that arises from the unknown. We want you to explore the outermost range of your abilities so that you can not only recognize how far you've come, but also build resilience in your ability to not-know, even at your most knowledgeable.

Here are a few additional exercises that encourage an advanced level of play.

Exercise 15.6: Identity Out of a Hat

Get two hats (or boxes or bags). In one, on scraps of paper, put descriptions of posture features – see page 130 for a list of possibilities. In the other, put paralinguistic prosodic modifiers (pitch, pace, mood, relationship). See **Web Resource 15.1** for possible suggestions.

Web Resource 15.1 Possible Paralinguistic Features

Draw clues from the first hat to build a posture. Run some Omnish through that posture to discover its variant of Somenish. Shift from Somenish into your Acting Language, which will have an accent determined by the posture. Perform a memorized text in that accent. Then, draw paralinguistic modifications from the second hat, one at a time, to create variant *vocal identities* within the frame of this improvised accent. Notice what it does to the text and to your understanding of the accent you've generated.

You could also replace the clues in the first hat with actual accents that you know, so that you're working from known Posture, Prosody, and Pronunciation patterns. How do paralinguistic "notes" influence your play in accents you already know? Do any of the suggestions from the second hat seem to fundamentally alter your accents?

Exercise 15.7: Oscillating Accents

Perform a scripted scene with a partner. During your performance, alternate between accents that you know. You can alternate with each line or, for even more fun, within lines. You could preassign accent switches or let them emerge spontaneously and see what happens.

Notice that the most masterful skill of this exercise – and, indeed, of several exercises in this module – comes from the *subtlety* of your shifts during performance. As opposed to signaling to audiences that you're switching between accents, see how easily and effortlessly you can make transitions happen. Work this ease into your rehearsal with your partner, so that your accent shifts are a secret you share and which your audience only gets to recognize after the fact.

Exercise 15.8: Part in a Blender

Summon a blended accent from Exercise 15.5 and perform a piece of text – or a scene with a partner! What sort of practice does it take to find and maintain a blended accent of your own devising?

 Check-In

Look back at your experiences to this point and write down your responses to the following questions: What are the questions you have about acting in accent right now? What areas of uncertainty remain? How could you experiment through performance to address those questions? How would you outline or describe your preferred process for approaching an accent now? How would you prioritize the steps of your process to support you in learning *any* new accent?

Conclusion

Pause for a moment.

Look around you right now. Take in your environment. Orient to the light, the air, the temperature, the sounds, and the people around you.

This, right now, is what it feels like to arrive at the end.

Of course, it's never really the end. It can't be. You'll continue to observe and experience. You'll continue to perform and give feedback. You'll continue to learn, from yourself and from others. The process you've gone through in this book will shift and adapt and change within you with every breath taken, every sound uttered, and every thought communicated.

We hope you feel joy in having propelled yourself on this journey through accent. We hope you feel justifiable pride in your dedication to the expansion of your abilities and the cultivation of your curiosity. We hope you feel exuberance, solemnity, gratitude, and passionate vibrancy for the accents you've immersed in and inhabited. We hope you had *fun* – and experienced a little magic while you were at it.

Now go play – and thrive.

GLOSSARY

accent – the aspect of language variation that's experienced in physical embodiment; while connected to how we think about and structure language, it only manifests in the action or performance of communication.

Accent Celebration – a KTS "term of art" for the process of collecting, analyzing, and presenting information about an accent.

acoustic – (linguistics) refers to those aspects of speech sounds that are physical and measurable, as opposed to those perceived by a listener.

Acting Language – a language you know well enough for acting, whether your first language or an additional one; a KTS "term of art."

allophone – one of many different realizations of a single phoneme.

articulatory – describes those features of human speech that are physically produced through the movement of the articulators (the muscles, tissues, and structures of the vocal tract).

auditory – (linguistics) refers to the features of human speech that are interpreted through hearing and related neurological processes, as opposed to the actual physical properties of speech sounds.

center of gravity – (Posture) the point or points in the vocal tract around which the movements of articulation cluster; a KTS "term of art."

complex – a property inherent in many phenomena, in which seemingly simple elements interact with each other to produce incredibly varied, intricate, and unpredictable results.

confirmation bias – a psychological tendency to evaluate incoming information as supportive of preexisting beliefs; this bias can also lead to searching for and recognizing only information that confirms what is already believed.

connectivity – (Prosody) the sense in which speech feels smoothly linked (*legato*) or disjointed and separate (*staccato*).

covert prestige – a secondary valuation based on some other aspect of social capital; examples include a sense of coolness, friendliness, piety, or some other valued quality.

descriptivism – (linguistics) a school of thought which seeks to understand and describe what is, rather than prescribing "correct" pronunciation or usage.

228

dialect – a variety of language in which a particular set of patterns is shared by a group in the way they communicate; potentially includes grammar, vocabulary, and morphology.

distribution – (linguistics) a rule-governed process that allows for prediction of where things occur; for example, in which environments the different allophones of a phoneme will be used.

duration – (Prosody) as an **acoustic** property, the measurable time in which a sound occurs.

dynamics – a term from music referring to levels and movements in subjective **loudness**.

emic – /ˈimɪk/, derived from "phonemic"; describes a point of view towards an observed culture that seeks to understand it in its own context. Emic investigations involve empathy as a tool of understanding.

etic – /ˈɛtɪk/, derived from "phonetic"; describes viewing a culture from an outsider's point of view. Etic observations tend to apply a single conceptual framework as a reference point to observe and compare cultures.

focus – (linguistics) where a speaker directs their listeners' attention in speech; tends to use the prosodic attributes of pitch, length, loudness, and vocal quality to that effect.

formality – (linguistics) the degree to which a speaker molds their speech, consciously or unconsciously, to meet the expectations of a standard.

frequency – (Prosody) measures the number of sound wave oscillations per second in hertz (Hz); 1 Hz = 1 cycle per second.

fundamental frequency – the lowest of the layered frequencies of the voice (F_0), which represents the vibration speed of the vocal folds.

"General American" – refers to an accent of English spoken in the United States without specific reference to any region or locality; the quotation marks are an indication that it should be viewed with some skepticism.

handholds – the salient aspects of Prosody, Posture, or Pronunciation that make it easier for an actor to quickly grasp and "handle" an accent; a KTS "term of art."

harmonic frequencies – frequencies layered on top of the fundamental frequencies, also called "overtones"; the arrangement of harmonic bands of sound energy is perceived as speech sounds.

identity – a pattern of belonging, often defined by what or who is like the pattern in question; in simpler terms, someone or something being what it is; from Latin *idem* "the same."

idiolect – the unique language variety particular to an individual.

interocept – refers to feeling one's internal state; from Latin *intero-* "inside" + *capire* "to take, grasp."

intervals – (Prosody) the difference between two pitches, often with recognizable qualities; in music theory, these are given names such as *minor third* or *major fifth*.

intonation phrase (IP) – a measure of linguistic musicality, whose boundaries help communicate meaning; in English, an IP is a division of speech musicality with a single prosodically stressed item (*nucleus*); also called a "prosodic unit."

inventory – the items in a system; for example, the allophones used in a language constitute the inventory of all available sounds (compare with **distribution**).

isochrony – (Prosody) refers to the way languages measure out syllables over time; from Greek *isos* "equal" + *chronos* "time"; a now disputed idea that may still provide a helpful starting point for analyzing prosody.

L1 – /ɛl wʌn/, for any given speaker, a language acquired in early childhood, in which they feel totally fluent, which arises from intuitive understanding, and with whose community of speakers they identify.

L2 – /ɛl tu/, for any given speaker, a language with less fluency, less intuitive recourse, and/or less identification with a linguistic community than occurs with an L1.

language – as a specific (not general) noun, a *way of communicating* shared by a group of people; a specific variety of encoding and transmission, like English, Farsi, Tagalog, Xhosa, or Te Reo Māori.

length – (Prosody) the perceived relative temporal dimension of sound segments; **auditory** counterpart to **duration**.

lexical stress – the inclusion of some degree of stress within polysyllabic English words; typically, one syllable has *primary stress*, while others have secondary stresses or remain unstressed.

linguistics – the academic study of language.

loudness – (Prosody) the perceived volume of a sound; **auditory** counterpart to **sound pressure level**.

magic phrase – a short utterance that conjures up the Posture for an accent, in addition to salient sounds and prosodic features; a KTS "term of art."

magnet sounds – the **centers of gravity** of a Posture expressed as particular speech sounds; provide links between Posture and Pronunciation.

markedness – (linguistics) a pronunciation or accent that stands out as notable to a listener, relative to their linguistic context.

merger – (Pronunciation) occurs when two lexical sets are realized in an accent in so similar a way that the two sounds are perceived as identical by the speaker.

minimal pair – also called a "contrastive pair"; a set of words in a language which are distinguished by a difference in a single speech sound; for example, in English, "pit" and "bit" – the difference in voicing in the initial consonant marks the presence of two distinct phonemes and enables the recognition of two different words.

modal voice – the quality of phonation characterized by maximum vibration along the full length of the vocal folds; also referred to as *chest register*.

mora – (Prosody) a unit of speech in some languages (Japanese and Ancient Greek, for example) that can sometimes be smaller than a syllable.

obstruent – in linguistics, obstruents (such as fricatives, affricates, and stops) are contrasted with sonorants (approximants and vowels); KTS has adopted this term to describe any sound formed by obstruction of the vocal tract, contrasting with **phthongs**.

Omnish – an improvisatory exploration tool, derived from the Latin *omnes* "all"; Omnish is a vehicle for communication that includes *all* consonant and vowel sounds that could exist in real, human languages; this tool is explored more fully in *Speaking with Skill* and *Experiencing Speech*; the verb form is **to omnate**.

clinical Omnish – a mode of Omnish in which methodical attention to the covering the full range of human speech sounds takes precedence over expression.

orthography – written text or its spelling.

paralinguistic – that which communicates information beyond the meaning of words conveyed; includes many aspects of prosody, as well as facial expressions and gestures; from Latin *para-* "alongside, beyond."

perception – (linguistics) the process by which signals from the outside world are received, interpreted, and converted into mental constructs available to a listener; contrasts with **production**.

perceptual filter – a KTS "term of art" for one method of highlighting specific information in a complex data set; the five filters explored in Module Two are Acting, Communication, Belonging, Evolution, and Patterns.

phone – a specific speech sound produced by a speaker; transcribed in brackets [].

phoneme – a collection of phones that share an identity in a language user's mind; transcribed in slashes //.

phonemic interference/inference – occurs when existing mental constructs, based on an expected phoneme, interfere with the ability to grasp incoming phonetic information; an unconscious kind of inference, rapidly but not always accurately guessing the sounds that come next.

phonology – the systematic, linguistic organization of the sounds of a language or accent, and the study of it.

phthong – as a noun, a speech sound made through shaping of the vocal tract to produce distinctive resonance patterns without resorting to obstruction; as a verb, **to phthong** is to shape voiced flow; a KTS "term of art" contrasting with **obstruent**.

pitch – (Prosody) the **auditory** quality of sound that relates to **frequency**; higher frequencies are perceived as higher in pitch, lower frequencies as lower in pitch.

Posture Zero – the starting point of a person's vocal tract posture, from which assessment of other postures is made; the collection of physical habits and tendencies accumulated through the process of learning spoken language.

prescriptivism – (linguistics) a school of thought focused on locating, analyzing, and teaching the prescribed or "correct" pronunciation of words; now discredited.

prestige – (linguistics) the valuation of a particular language variety, used as a signal for the assessment of an individual's power and position in a social hierarchy.

overt prestige – the primary and original definition of prestige, referring to those in a dominant position in society.

probabilistic – predicting an outcome based on a judgment of what is likely or probable, not what is certain.

production – (linguistics) the process by which mental constructs are converted into the physical gestures and acoustic output of speech; contrasts with **perception**.

prosodic stress – the means of highlighting information through musical attributes within an intonation phrase; also called *suprasegmental stress, sentence stress*, and *emphasis*; falls on the lexically stressed syllable of the most important word in the phrase.

realization – the specific way in which speech sounds are articulated; e.g., phonemes are realized as phones

Received Pronunciation (RP) – a term which originally described the pronunciation of English in the nineteenth century considered to be generally accepted or *received* as "correct"; came to be applied to an ever-changing accent used by English elites.

reduction – (linguistics) the tendency of sounds in unstressed syllables to change in quality relative to their stressed forms; also called *weakening*; reduced English vowels tend to become shorter, quieter, and more centralized (closer to /ə/); reduced consonants may be devoiced, weakly articulated, or eliminated entirely.

rhotic – refers to the phoneme /r/ (Greek *rho*); in English dialectology, rhoticity refers specifically to the realization or omission of this phoneme after a vowel in the same syllable; in *non-rhotic* accents, the words "father" and "farther" would be pronounced in essentially the same way ['fɑːðə]; in *rhotic* accents, they would be distinguished as ['fɑːðɚ] and ['fɑɹðɚ].

rhythm – (Prosody) the interplay of lengths of silence and sound to produce a sense of semi-predictable timing.

robust – able to resist the destabilizing impact of perturbations to the system; healthy, resilient, adaptable.

salient – leaping out as noticeable in perception.

satisfice – term introduced by Herbert Simon to describe the process of settling on what's adequate rather than what's perfect; combines "satisfy" and "suffice."

shimmer – (Posture) a term coined by Dudley Knight to refer to small exploratory movements of the vocal tract.

silence – (Prosody) a prosodic attribute arising from the absence of sound; an essential component of the rhythmic aspects of prosody.

sociolinguistics – the study of linguistics as it interacts with the social dimension of human experience.

Somenish – an improvised "language" employing some, but not all, of the sounds of human speech; the verb form is **to Somenate**.

sound pressure level – (Prosody) measures the displacement of the medium through which a sound wave travels (typically air for speech); measured in decibels (dB).

split – (Pronunciation) occurs when a speaker has differing pronunciations, which are predictable and rule-based, within a single standard lexical set, leading to the formation of two new sets.

stigma – the marking of specific behaviors, beliefs, or practices as inferior, distasteful, or shameful; stigmatization is one means by which overt prestige maintains influence within a social hierarchy.

stress – (Prosody) the creation of prosodic contrast to draw attention to a particular cluster of sound(s), usually a syllable.

syllable – a unit of speech smaller than a word; connected speech is composed of these units, distinguishable as pulses of vocal energy.

tempo – (Prosody) an overall measure of the *speed* of communication, measured most often in syllables per second.

thinking sound – vocalizations used to make pauses in speech; also called a *hesitation sound*.

token – small, edited examples demonstrating accent features; used in Accent Celebrations.

tonal language – a language that uses pitch to distinguish meaning between otherwise phonetically identical words.

vocal quality – (Prosody) a prosodic attribute that can be influenced by numerous factors, primarily those of resonance and phonation.

INDEX

accent: accent acquisition i, 201, 220; and "being in your head" 217; blended accents 224; and coaching 220; contrast with dialect 8, 10–12, 14, 140; doing "enough" 219; donor 57, 59, 60–61, 74–75, 89, 99, 104, 119, 130–132, 136, 155, 160–161, 163, 168, 172–173, 176, 179–180, 183–184, 186, 190, 192–193, 204–206, 211, 220; and embarrassment 54; and "failure" 217; and faking it 214; falling out *vs.* falling in 217; and handholds 217, 223–224; Home and Target 184, 217; and improvisation 194, 216, 218–219, 225; invented accents 27; living in accent 66–67, 218, 226; as patterns 35, 43, 49; in performance 16–17, 49, 51, 60–61, 66, 200; as phonological difference 148–150, *150*; and primary source collection 57–59, 67–69, 161, 190, 219; on résumé 219; in the self 5, 16–17, 60, 200; and sounding "right" 219; and sound substitution 139–140, 173; strong/heavy *vs.* weak/light *see* markedness; as survival skill 18, 23, 54, 116; working descriptions of 5, 7–8,

10, 15, 33; in the world 16–17, 49, 51, 60–61, 64–68, 73, 129, 140, 163–164, 173, 219

Accent Celebration 45, 200–201, 212; and different versions of 192, 196–197; and feedback 198–199; format of 191–198; Mini-Celebration 185, 199; as presentation 190, 198–199; as process 189–192, 198; as resource 190–197; samples of 197–198; and visuals 190–191, 193–194

accent identity: and Posture 124, 129, 137; and Prosody 77–78, 90, 99–100, 104

Accent Olympics 222–225

accent samples 57–58, 155, 176, 179, 183–184, 211; audio 22, 36, 59, 67–68, 74, 82–88, 91–92, 94, 99–100, 104, 117–118, 160, 162, 167–168, 180–181, 185–186, 190–191, 205–206, 209; as tokens 191, 193; video 67, 129, 190–191

Accents of English (1982) 152, 169

accent switching 223–226; and gradual change 224–225; *see also* posture switching; posture switching

233